SORT OF
A CRICKET PERSON

Other books by
the same author include

SORT OF
A CRICKET PERSON

E. W. Swanton

FONTANA/COLLINS

First published by Wm. Collins 1972
Second impression 1973
First issued in Fontana 1974

Copyright © E.W. Swanton 1972

Made and printed in Great Britain by
William Collins Sons & Co Ltd, Glasgow

TO MY WIFE, ANN

ACKNOWLEDGEMENTS

Permission to use copyright photographs is acknowledged as follows: Central Press Photos, nos 4, 5 &
8; Willie Alleyne, 2; Mrs E. W. Swanton, 1; the
British Broadcasting Corporation, 3; *The Sun*, Melbourne, 14; Ken Kelly, 17.

CONTENTS

PREFACE TO THIS EDITION

It is quite an exciting thing, even for a hardened old hand like me, to be writing a Preface for a paperback edition. For any author 'going into paperback' must conjure up happy visions of a new and bigger public. Apart from all else it touches the vanity.

This Fontana version of the book first published in October 1972 contains nearly all the meat of the original: everything in fact save my excursions into two other games near to my heart, Rugby football and golf. It has been necessary to compress the original edition just to the extent of the three chapters devoted thereto. The other fourteen remain intact, revised only in respect of a few slips which, however carefully one combs and checks the proofs, it seems impossible to avoid.

In the nature of things this paperback will catch the eye of a wider readership and, one hopes, a younger one. Up to a point it will be dealing with what for them is unknown territory: a journey into the past. Cricket has changed a great deal in some outward respects since I came first to know it in the 'twenties. At the higher levels it is perhaps all a bit fiercer. It is the focus of more universal attention, by reason of radio and television. The instant stuff has brought to some extent a different audience, and the cost of the greater popularity may have been a lessening appreciation of the finer points. Yet its skills are essentially subtle, and for those who are once firmly attracted the charms of cricket have an unending appeal. Likewise its heros, whose names will be found in profusion throughout these pages. To the new generation who are about to meet them all, from Hobbs and Bradman right through to Sobers and Cowdrey I can only wish the happiness from the game that I have enjoyed for upwards of half a century.

April 1974

INTRODUCTION

Once upon a time two small girls were looking at the television when my face appeared on the screen. One of them, after recovering from the initial shock, I dare say, showed some interest, whereupon the other asked who it was. 'Oh,' came the reply, 'he's sort of a cricket person – and a friend of daddy's.'

I'm grateful to my old companion of the links and cricket field, Eric Pemberton, for this little story, and to his daughter, Juliet, now by the way full-grown, for putting the matter so neatly.

The question that immediately arises is whether the sort of cricket person that I have been justifies me in writing a sort of a cricket book. That you are shortly to discover, one way or the other. Meanwhile, perhaps I should try to account for my temerity and simultaneously indicate the guide-lines I have set myself.

This is a sort of an autobiography. In writing it I have tried to keep before myself the thought that what people will be chiefly interested in are the events I have seen and recorded, and the people I have met. I have tried to make this an objective rather than a subjective exercise. By great good luck I've seen much of the best cricket that has been played for all but half a century. I've known nearly all the more distinguished cricketers, and even played with quite a few of them. Throw in a long association with the BBC and a highly unglamorous but not uneventful war, and, broadly speaking, you have the scope of the narrative.

Having said as much I should already have relieved the reader of any fears of being inflicted with a lot of nostalgic stuff about childhood which, in any event, was thoroughly normal and unremarkable. There are those who profess an interest in juvenile memories. I can only say that, as a reader, I have usually either skipped or skimmed impatiently through the early years even of great men. The middle teens, surely, are time enough to start the story.

I was born on 11 February 1907 at Forest Hill on the southern outskirts of London – in my youth a leafy, quiet, comfortable suburb. Seven at the outbreak of the First World

War, I recall hearing the distant roar of the Silvertown Explosion as I was being hustled up to bed, and seeing the placards announcing, in type of funereal purple, 'Death of Kitchener'. My first picture of Forest Hill Cricket Club, of which my father was for many years Treasurer, is vaguely of the cricket but rather more clearly of the pavilion sparkling with hundreds of coloured lights cheering the scene at the alfresco concerts which used to enliven the summer. My father's eyesight never gave him the chance of being a good cricketer, but I inherit from him the love of games that he had until he died in 1966 at the age of eighty-seven, having apparently been, for some years, 'the father of the Stock Exchange', from the genial society of which he could not be persuaded to retire until a few months before his death.

My two sisters married, respectively, painting and the Church. Ruth's husband, Edmund Nelson, has been particularly appreciated at Cambridge where his portrait of G. M. Trevelyan hangs in the hall of Trinity; that of E. M. Forster at King's. More recently he has painted Michael McCrum for Tonbridge School, where he was headmaster before going on to Eton. Tina's husband, W. A. M. Langdon, is Vicar of Charminster in Dorset, and a canon of Salisbury. The arts run strongly there, too, for my nephew, David Langdon, is Director of Music at Summer Fields, the famous Oxford preparatory school.

While echoing wholeheartedly Dr Johnson's maxim that, 'no one but a blockhead wrote save for money', this book has afforded me a good deal of pleasure mixed inevitably with a measure of pain, the proportions being roughly divided between what it has been agreeable to write about and what the reverse. Though most of it has been a pleasure, the bad times cannot be ignored, and where these involve the criticisms of individuals one sometimes found oneself up against the difficulty that the truth, as one saw it, might reflect none too well upon either a friend or someone who is dead. As to friends, the reader must be left to draw his own conclusions from reticences at certain points. As to those no longer alive I have used my discretion as regards accepting the convention of 'De mortuis . . .'. Occasionally, one has had to strike a balance between justice to others and respect for the feelings of relatives. In an infinitely more lofty context Cardinal Heenan, writing of his earlier years, has chosen the title, *Not the Whole Truth*. I suppose most memoirs might be so called. But the book that sought to whitewash everyone and everything would be too insipid for words.

Talking of friends (as, of course, this book is constantly doing), one of the decisions one had to make concerned the use of Christian names. Not many years ago it would have been unthinkable to use them, and I am old-fashioned enough to resent being called by my Christian name (or rather, my nickname) by someone I scarcely know. But I have fallen to some extent into the modern fashion, for to use only the surname when writing of someone whom one has known well seemed rather stilted. So I have dotted Christian names about but only used them alone when I have been on those terms with the person concerned.

Much of the fun and interest I have had from my job has come from the opportunities it has afforded to meet people of every kind and every degree of distinction. What well-known people do and say usually interests people more than the comments and deeds of those whose names mean little or nothing. So I've tried to find something worth recalling about many of the personalities I've run up against, and if anyone wants to call that 'name-dropping' I cheerfully plead guilty to the charge.

I must gratefully acknowledge the permission of the Editor of the *Daily Telegraph* to quote from my own work, and from other writings in the paper; that of the Editor of *The Times* for leave to quote from an obituary notice of Bernard Darwin; of Mr Esmond Warner to print a letter written by his father, Sir Pelham; and of Sir Edward Beetham to print a letter from him to me. And I must record thanks to various helpers, headed by my assistant, Mr Irving Rosenwater, whose single-minded devotion to cricket I have never seen equalled; also, for secretarial services, to Mrs S. B. Gambrill, to Miss Mary Johnson of Barbados, and Miss Julia Reeves; and not least to Mr John Woodcock and Mr Charles Impey for suggestions after kindly reading much of the manuscript.

The appropriate attributions are made under all photographs where the source is known; only in a few cases has this defied investigation.

Lastly, I doff my hat to the successive editors of *Wisden*, into the last fifty-odd issues of which I have been diving these many months, trying to ensure that however often the reader may find him- or herself in disagreement as regards opinions expressed, he may not be in a position to contradict on matters of fact.

Sandwich   *April, 1972*

I

The Universal Thread

The day that Germany invaded Poland, Ian Peebles and I concluded a last hilarious lunch at the old International Sportsman's Club at Grosvenor House, and prepared to set off for Uxbridge where 999 Battery, Royal Artillery, were poised for action. When we had presented ourselves to a territorial recruiting officer in a dingy office in Victoria a week or two earlier this was the unit to which we had been assigned. It was, incidentally, only RA by courtesy since it manipulated not guns but vast metal 'ears' mounted on platforms, by means of which one listened for the sound of aircraft.

The car wheels were almost turning when on a sudden instinct I slipped back into the club and sent a brief wire, which simply said that we two were on our way to Battery 999, RA, and that although it was probably now far too late the address was such-and-such if Lt-Colonel S. W. Harris of the Cavalry Club had any use for us.

Transition to the military life in the days following left little time for vague speculation, and I had scarcely given the random wire another thought when a week or so later a rather testy major sent for me, and what did I know of a Colonel Harris of the Bedfordshire Yeomanry, RA, and why had two gunners of his battery applied for transfers and commissions in this irregular fashion. So it was that Peebles and I were allowed to proceed from Uxbridge to Dunstable, there to join Stanley Harris's young (sic) officers of 148 Field Regiment, RA (like nearly all Yeomanry the BY had become field gunners). Ian's *métier*, as it subsequently turned out, led him ultimately to a hush-hush job at the War Office. I on the other hand stayed with the regiment, and so found myself in due course at Singapore, and finally as a POW on the Burma-Siam railway.

The moral of this story might simply be that the Devil looks after his own, or it could be said to reinforce the old army axiom, 'never volunteer'. I tell it merely to underline how, though as a Christian one must believe 'there's a Divinity that shapes our ends', the universal thread that directs the pattern of all our lives seems to be just common-or-garden luck.

In the spring of 1939, as I was returning from South Africa with MCC on the *Athlone Castle*, Stanley Harris had said to me, 'When the war starts in September you and Ian must join my regiment'; but he had added that we (who shared a flat in the Temple) should first do a spell in the ranks as Territorials, in the HAC or elsewhere. This, somehow, we had not got around to. Ian had just taken over the captaincy of Middlesex from Walter Robins; I was pushing my way keenly up the broadcasting ladder, commentating on the Test series against the West Indies, in company with Howard Marshall and Michael Standing.

The summer had been all but over before, in sudden panic, we scrambled into 'something', fearful that, as so many others seemed also to be thinking, the army was a sort of club that might declare itself at any moment full up, with ourselves excluded. I had all but completely forgotten about the casual offer on the *Athlone*, and it was the merest chance afterthought that impelled me to send that wire.

I expect it may have been a more or less casual conversation that had landed me in the purlieus of Fleet Street some fifteen years earlier. Once it was tacitly agreed between my father and me that I should not follow him into the Stock Exchange – a decision never to be regretted on either side – the question remained: what to do with the boy? A friend with whom my father used to travel to the City was a director of the Amalgamated Press, a limb of the Harmsworth empire that published everything from encyclopaedias to *Comic Cuts*. Coming one morning into London Bridge I suppose Tod Anderson, a large and genial man, will have said, 'Better send him to see me.' And so it came to pass. For better or for worse, my course was charted.

Quite why the *Evening Standard* took me on to their sports staff three years later in September 1927, I cannot guess, but it was probably because, apart from a weekly article by W. J. A. Davies, the greatest of stand-off halves, recently retired from playing, they had no regular writers on rugger. It was typical of the less intense newspaper attitude to games in those days that the Internationals were reported by a very able all-round journalist, Norman Hillson by name, whose chief qualification for this particular assignment, I seem to remember, was that he had been at school at Rugby. If there was a big League of Nations story at Geneva, the star reporter could hardly be at

Cardiff or Murrayfield. Thus by the time I was twenty-one (having also been to a good rugger school, Cranleigh, where I showed no skill whatever as a footballer), I found myself on the long train journey down to Camborne with the Rugby Union party, prepared to report the first of the England Trials and to pass critical comment on those aspiring to win their caps or retain their places.

There I was hob-nobbing at a precocious age with magnificos like Wavell Wakefield and Cove-Smith, improperly qualified for the job and no doubt a size too large for my boots. Supposedly, one listened and learned, and grew somewhat in competence. But my own experience, writing rugger from the outside in the sense that I had been nothing of a player, has always made me sceptical of games correspondents who have never learned at first-hand. I know what I missed myself. Writing cricket was for me an altogether different proposition. Having played all my life I at least wrote from within.

But to return to the theme of luck. One midsummer day in 1932 I was at the old Leyton ground, then the Essex head-quarters, watching the famous partnership of Holmes and Sutcliffe piling up their mighty first-wicket stand. Eventually the magic 555 ticked up on the board, and that ancient record of two other famous Yorkshiremen, Brown and Tunnicliffe (554 v. Derbyshire at Chesterfield in 1898) was outstripped. Now there was but one telephone, and that a public one on the ground in those days. The Press Association and the three London 'evenings' all had their stories to get across, and the *Standard* was, I suppose, on this occasion last in the queue. At any rate their man committed the unforgivable crime. The luck having run against him, he missed the edition.

This is the sort of thing that happens to all of us sooner or later, but for me it was at a particularly unfortunate time. In May I had been told by my sports editor that I should be going out to Australia in the winter to cover the MCC tour. I had been given lots of space, had reported the only Test of that season, the first ever between England and India, and was, of course, on top of the world. As the summer advanced, the office grew evasive about Australia. Finally, at the last minute, it was announced that the tour would be covered by S. Bruce Harris, who was despatched hot-foot to the Scarborough Festival to pick up all he could about the game. Humiliation indeed – Sam Harris was the lawn tennis correspondent! At the time I was told that Harris's greater news experience had determined the decision, but some years later I heard that the choice had been switched because of the episode at Leyton. 'If he can't get us the story from the East End, what will he do at Melbourne and Sydney?' So ran the reasoning.

Now at twenty-five I may have been young to become the first journalist ever to have been sent on an overseas tour by an individual newspaper, as Bruce Harris was, but if that was so I was a good deal better qualified than a very decent, conscientious fellow who knew nothing about cricket at all. Soon he was in the thick of the Bodyline tour, the most explosive of all sporting stories, one of only three men on the spot writing for the British press: Jack Hobbs and Warwick Armstrong being the other two. The essence of the Bodyline row between England and Australia in that winter of 1932/3 was the moral question: Were these English tactics, as developed by Douglas Jardine, the captain, and exploited with deadly effect by Harold Larwood, fair or unfair? It was Englishmen who had brought cricket to the colony of New South Wales, just as they had introduced it wherever the Union Jack was flown. Now it was English sportsmanship that was in dispute: as Australian crowds reacted violently, their batsmen were pummelled black and blue, and accusing cables flew from Adelaide to London.

Play in Australia ends at breakfast-time in England, and the evening papers are therefore first with the story. The morning press accordingly used Reuter's report, which in the tradition of agency service was factual and impersonal. To the 'evenings' everyone perforce turned. The *Evening News* had Warwick Armstrong, that famous and formidable Australian captain who had humiliated English cricket just after the war and, with his hostile, uncompromising manner, had made few friends in the process. Armstrong's cables were critical of Jardine's methods, though not violently so. Read today, his cuttings seem logical and restrained. However, his were Australian views. Clearly, it was thought, Armstrong would take the line he did.

What of Jack Hobbs in the *Star*? He had written against the growing vogue of short fast bowling on the body the preceding August, having had a dose of it, which he openly resented, playing for Surrey against Yorkshire at the Oval. (The offending bowler was Bill Bowes, who with Bill Voce was also employing Bodyline in Australia.) I have recently re-read the Hobbs cables and confirmed my memory that so long as the tour was in progress, though regretting the outcry, he refrained from condemning the cause. As an old England cricketer of the utmost esteem, the most famous of living players, Jack Hobbs was in an unenviable position. Could he, with quarter of a century of Anglo-Australian cricket just behind him, turn against his playing colleagues in the heat of the battle – against Jardine, his own county captain? He did not – until he arrived home in April, when he said unequivocally that he thought Bodyline was unfair and should be stopped.

From the Australian Armstrong there came criticism, from Hobbs as from Reuter's Gilbert Mant (his work unsigned) just factual description. What about the *Evening Standard*'s Bruce Harris? His was the only other voice. In Harris Jardine was shrewd enough to see a valuable ally. Harris, a stranger to cricket, looked for someone to help him; and who better than the captain? Jardine saw in Harris the ideal man to speak in his defence. Each in fact needed the other. So from the outset Harris supported the English tactics, giving the general public at home just the stuff they wanted. Soon he was being widely syndicated to the provincial evening papers, and after the tour it naturally followed that he was soon out with a book entitled *Jardine Justified* – with a warm foreword by Jardine. Circumstances, therefore, gave Harris's writing an importance out of all proportion to the intrinsic worth of his opinions.

Naturally, as the story gradually unfolded, to reach its climax in the Australian Board of Control's exchange of cables with MCC, I envied Harris his opportunity, and wondered how I should have tackled the job had I not been deprived of the chance. At the end of the season at Bournemouth I had seen Bill Bowes flirting with the short fast stuff to a modified leg-side field, and had instinctively disliked it. Gubby Allen was already a friend, and he, it was known, from the start of the tour had refused to have any part in the tactics. He played in all the Tests, bowling fast to an orthodox field. 'Plum' Warner, the MCC manager, who had shown me kindness, and of whom I stood in some awe, had been strongly critical of Bowes's bowling in Surrey v. Yorkshire, writing as cricket correspondent of the *Morning Post*, even if on the spot, like Hobbs, he now maintained a diplomatic silence.

Though this was not known at home until they returned, the majority of the side, while maintaining a united front in public, also deplored Bodyline in private. In addition to Warner and Allen, Bob Wyatt, the vice-captain, also opposed it. So did Walter Hammond and Les Ames, for instance, among the professionals, and the remaining amateurs, Freddie Brown and the Nawab of Pataudi, with both of whom I had played myself.

In short, I cannot think that, if I had gone to Australia, I would not have come down on the anti-Jardine side in the *Evening Standard*; and if I had done so, this must have made for a rather different climate of opinion in England.

Gradually, in the years that followed, the truth about the whole sorry business filtered through, and the umpire was empowered to stop Bodyline by a change in the laws. But it was a slow process, and even within the Committee of MCC the divisions were such that, as I will show in due course, a break in the sequence of Australian visits was only avoided by a narrow voting margin. The Australian team to England of 1934 very nearly never came at all.

Looked at thus, my ill-luck with the telephone at Leyton had considerable consequences.

Soon, however, the pendulum of fortune was swinging towards me once more. I was lucky enough in 1934 to persuade the Empire Service (as it was then) of the BBC to take a weekly sporting talk. Then, through a chance remark when playing cricket at Sir Julien Cahn's house, I found myself invited by that egregious sporting millionaire to join his team on a tour of Canada, USA and Bermuda, which greatly quickened my appetite for cricket travel. Whether or not it was this eager, thrusting background that impressed the editor of the *Illustrated Sporting and Dramatic News* I do not know, but the next thing was that James Wentworth Day was commissioning a series of articles on the sporting histories of the public schools that finally took in more than eighty schools, ran for about three years and involved something like a quarter of a million words.

Needless to say I met a great many new people, especially sporting schoolmasters, saw a good deal of England, and picked up six guineas a thousand – plus expenses! If that doesn't sound an awful lot in the 'seventies, it was more than chicken-feed to a thirty-year-old before the war. Fifteen hundred a year went quite a long way.

One thing leads to another, and the luck of being invited to make that tour to Bermuda had an unexpected sequel when in due course the ADC to the governor, Lord Carew, wrote asking me to bring an English side to the island in the summer of 1935. The plans went forward to the point when it became apparent that the Bermudians were not able to find the money for our passages, as had been arranged. (It turned out that they had used the considerable profit from Cahn's tour to take themselves to Canada instead.) So I had a team, but nowhere to go. Why not the Channel Islands, which MCC and the Incogniti, among others, used to visit? So we went to Jersey, and everyone enjoyed themselves a lot, and Raymond Robertson-Glasgow, on being asked to name us, promptly said, 'The Arabs', and that was that. Thus we came to life and are still going strong thirty-seven years later, though the Founder, who never misses a match except by dire necessity, no longer encumbers the field, confining himself to advice – when asked for, of course – and exhortation from the pavilion. We flew from Heston on that late summer morning of 1935 in a machine of incredible fragility, and when, having fortified ourselves freely on the journey, we skirted the cliff-top and landed on Jersey beach we had made a small item of cricket history by becoming the first cricket side to travel by air.

Friendships must contain a considerable element of luck, at least in the original accident of contact. I got to know Harry Altham at Eastbourne where I used to take my summer holiday playing at the Saffrons, that delectable ground, against the club touring sides that proceeded along the south coast in August. Harry brought the Harlequins, the most distinguished of them. We also met at the end of every April at Oxford, where I took part in the Cryptics' tour, while he spent the last ten days or so of the school holidays before returning to Winchester helping successive university captains to sort out the talent, and with advice and coaching generally. I naturally went to him for help with the Winchester article in my *Sporting and Dramatic* series.

Like everyone else who knew Harry, I had the greatest admiration for him, and was both flattered and surprised when early in 1938 he wrote asking me if I would collaborate with him in a second edition of *A History of Cricket* which had been published twelve years earlier. Harry was a great inspiration to and encourager of youth, and it was characteristic of him to have offered the opportunity to someone of my generation when he could easily have recruited a man of greater maturity and reputation. Thus I found my name coupled with his in the standard work on the history of the game, and coming in for some of the reflected glory. George Lyttelton, who used to delight everyone with his reports of the Eton and Harrow match in *The Times*, wrote kindly about the book in *The Observer*, while J. B. Firth, the distinguished literary editor of the *Daily Telegraph*, reviewed the new edition in the main leader-page article: a good, solid chunk, every bit of fifteen hundred words.

Whatever the stars foretold for me in 1938, here comes another bit of luck with happy consequences. I determined, if I could, to go as a free-lance with MCC that winter to South Africa, and, the *Evening Standard* being uninterested, the best bet seemed to be the BBC. Would they take some running commentary and summaries of the five Test matches, and furthermore recommend me to the South African Broadcasting Corporation? S. J. de Lotbinière, head of Outside Broadcasts and one of the great BBC figures of his day, was cautiously encouraging, but since I had not then done any running commentary – only talks, and mostly for the then Empire Service – he very reasonably called for a trial run. I was allotted Surrey v. Lancashire at the Oval, sharing half an hour before lunch and half an hour in the evening with P. G. H. Fender who was reporting Sussex v. Yorkshire at Hove.

Now on the second afternoon of the game it chanced that Henry Longhurst, an old friend who had also for a time shared the comforts of King's Bench Walk and Mrs Smallbone's cooking, was getting married and I was to be an usher. It seems now a foolhardy risk, but I left the game for the wedding, returned in time to be 'filled in' on the score and details, and settled, full of bonhomie, into the tiny room beside the scorers' box to hear Fender perform for the first fifteen minutes from Hove. Or, rather, just in time to hear him say that it had been raining there, the score was such-and-such, there was no play at the moment, and he would hand over without further delay to me at the Oval.

This was something the raw recruit hadn't bargained for. I wasn't worried at the prospect of talking for half-an-hour. Far from it. But nine Surrey wickets were down, and nothing was less likely than that Ted Brooks and Alf Gover would last that time. I had no idea whether between innings one should return listeners to the studio or keep going. In the event there was some mild fun to be had with the last-wicket stand – always good commentary material – before, inevitably, one of them got out and the field emptied. Ten minutes on the microphone can be a long time, especially with no Webber or Frindall to cough up 'records' and figure details. I'm not sure that we had scorers even in Test matches before the war,

18

certainly I had none that day. What I talked about goodness knows, but out it came – 'associative material', as I came to learn, it is known in the OB department. I ended by giving an over or two of the Lancashire second innings, and by the time I came off the air at six o'clock 'Lobby' had got through to the engineer with a message of appreciation. Apparently my coping with the situation had gone down well, and a contract for coverage in South Africa followed! The best time to drink champagne is surely in the morning, but, on this occasion anyway, it served me well in the afternoon.

There is, of course, no time when the individual is so hapless in the hands of fate, or chance, as in war. In the POW camps in the Far East, survival depended on the luck of avoiding really acute attacks of the common plagues : dysentery, malaria and beri-beri. I escaped tolerably lightly in this respect – I suppose the loss of five stone can be so called. But my real bit of luck happened before captivity, during the brief, disastrous battle of Singapore.

On Saturday, 14 February 1942, I was establishing a new observation post as the ragged line fell back towards the perimeter of the city. Lone Jap snipers who had infiltrated during darkness were said to be becoming a menace, and as I surveyed my new zone while my signaller went back for the telephone wire, I spotted something glinting in the sun towards the top of a tree left front. In their jungle green shirts and trousers, the Japs were hard to pick out, but I reckoned I'd seen the glint of spectacles, and as the signaller had left his rifle with me, aimed a few shots into the foliage. No movement, no falling body.

When after some time my signaller had still not returned I decided to go back down the hill and give him a hand. Foolishly I left his rifle at the OP, and more foolishly still I had forgotten about the glint in the trees. Suddenly, a sub-machine gun started up and I felt a heavy blow on the right elbow – which hastened my retreat to cover very considerably. At a range of about a hundred yards I must have been the next best thing to a sitting target; but I was hit just the once, and that by a bullet that made only a flesh wound, missing the point of the elbow by half an inch. So I was twice infernally lucky; first that the Jap was not only short-sighted but obviously cross-eyed, secondly that he had so narrowly missed shattering the joint. In the first weeks, after the capitulation that followed next day, a lack of food and drugs caused the deaths of many from wounds almost as superficial as mine.

A final thought on this first and last close encounter with the Jap in battle is that the enemy that cannot be beaten is utter weariness. I like to think I would have shown rather more common sense if I had not been tired beyond imagining. When my battery-commander, Bill Merry, who succeeded me at the OP, was killed next morning he was said to have been 'out on his feet'. We never had a chance to get our second wind.

When the war ended and I returned to pick up the threads again, the only post I could lay claim to was Cricket Correspondent of *The Field*. The editor, Brian Vesey-Fitzgerald, had appointed me in August 1939 in place of Neville Cardus, and though he hadn't known for a long time what had become of me he had been kind enough to keep the place open until I got back to England in October 1945. Also I supposed I might continue more or less where I had left off with the BBC. The *Evening Standard*, however, had more or less dispensed with my services shortly before the war – a certain incompatibility grew up between the sports editor and a brash young man who had too many irons in the fire for his liking. The *Illustrated Sporting and Dramatic News* had become *Sport and Country* but with all the emphasis on pigs and cows. Moreover, Jimmy Wentworth Day had long since moved on. So, of course, I began to look around for a staff appointment.

Once again the luck was with me, for although all the cricket jobs were occupied, the chances were that one of them might be free in the foreseeable future. When Leonard Crawley went to see the late Lord Camrose directly the European War was over, he had been offered the choice of writing for the *Daily Telegraph* on cricket or golf, being, of course, well qualified to tackle either. Fortunately for me, he settled for golf, whereupon Lord Camrose appointed as cricket correspondent a most unlikely person, Sir Guy Campbell, who was sixty-one and primarily a golfer. He had given John Astor (the late Viscount Astor of Hever, proprietor of *The Times*) his cricket colours at Eton in 1904, and had long been identified with *The Times* as one of the subsidiary golf writers to Bernard Darwin. He also dabbled in golf architecture, and was a highly engaging little man with whom I used to watch and report the

Canterbury Week, his one regular cricket engagement of the year.

Guy, it was said, needed a car to meet him at Paddington and a messenger to convey his words of wisdom to the office from Lord's, which was the scene of the first post-war Test against India. He reported that, but the arrangement was then terminated, I imagine by mutual consent, and everyone was left wondering how his lordship, the very shrewdest of judges, had come to pick him.

In mid-season the *Telegraph* now lacked a cricket correspondent, and I was soon making my way to the fifth floor to see Seymour Berry, now Lord Camrose. The result was engagement, at first on a monthly basis, and before long I was up at Manchester reporting my first Test for the paper (as well as broadcasting about it). In my time there had been quite a string of *Daily Telegraph* cricket correspondents, first Colonel Philip Trevor, then Howard Marshall, then, briefly, P. F. Warner, followed by Douglas Jardine and, briefest of all, Campbell. The luck for me lay in my having good friends with an ear to the ground, and in my being available when the chance offered of one of the plum sporting jobs in Fleet Street.

Let me relate one more item of luck, and for me very much the most important in my life, before I end this introductory chapter. In December 1957 'Critch', otherwise Brigadier-General A. C. Critchley, CMG, CBE, DSO, and his wife Diana asked me to the Golf Foundation Ball at Grosvenor House. 'Critch', who had lost his sight with tragic suddenness as a result of an infection several years before, was still chairman of the Foundation, and the chairman's party was mostly a young one, composed of friends of their son and daughter, 'Jeeps' and Glenna. However, two older friends were asked, I to escort Diana and Ann Carbutt to keep 'Critch' company. Ann, who had been recently widowed, was fond of him and was one of many friends, as I was also, who used to try and make life more bearable by calling in on him at Wentworth.

She had just about heard of me from people who knew us both, and I equally vaguely remembered photographs of an attractive girl golfer called Ann de Montmorency, who was portrayed in the press dashingly (for the thirties) arrayed in waterproof trousers. I might well have met her famous father, 'Monty', a redoubtable all-round games player – golf, cricket and rackets – and Eton housemaster; but he died just before the war, and I never did.

The point is that I very nearly never met his daughter, for she was weak from a bout of 'flu, and only decided at the very last moment to make the effort to come. It was a fateful decision for her and for me, since in two months to the day we were married.

2

Early Nets

On Saturday afternoon, 14 June 1919, Surrey collapsed 'inexplicably', as they say, in their second innings at the Oval, whereupon those redoubtable characters, Philip Mead and George Brown, knocked off the runs for Hampshire and gave them an unexpected victory by six wickets.

The sight of the players trooping in, in the evening sunshine, following the winning hit, is my first clear cricket memory. *Wisden* tells me that the day was a Saturday, and since I was a weekly boarder at my preparatory school, Brightlands, at Dulwich Common, now the boarding house of Dulwich College Preparatory School, I no doubt made a circuitous journey home, taking in Kennington *en route*. From *Wisden* it is also apparent that this was only the fifth first-class game played at the Oval in this first summer of peace – so I hadn't wasted much time! At the age of twelve plus the bug had already bitten.

Those school holidays I again found my way to the Oval, and this time saw a performance more to my taste, for Donald Knight, resplendent in Harlequin cap, going in first with Jack Hobbs, actually took a hundred off Yorkshire in each innings – and in two days at that. The first cricket figures to impress themselves on my young mind from first-hand were his 114 and 101.

All county cricket was conducted over two days in 1919, because it was thought, when, directly after the Armistice, arrangements were hurriedly made for a resumption of operations, that three leisurely days in the lively post-war world would be more than people had the time or inclination to spend. Half a century and more later we are still wondering about the ideal duration of a county match, and with more urgent reason. In those days the two-day experiment was universally condemned and abandoned after this one season. History tells us that no one liked the long playing hours, or the preponderance of drawn games. (A shade over half the matches were finished in 1919 – a proportion that is scarcely attained today.)

I recall nothing of my first sight of Yorkshire except Hobbs and Knight batting together, and putting on a lot of runs – it was something between 50 and 100 in each innings. Alas, then, George Hirst in his last full season made no more impact than had W. G. Grace whom I am supposed to have watched from my perambulator on the Forest Hill ground around 1910. But of most of the *dramatis personae* of those early Oval visits I was, of course, to see much more: Holmes and Sutcliffe, who had begun their long and prolific first-wicket partnership only the month before, Wilfred Rhodes, Emmott Robinson, Abe Waddington, Andy Sandham, Bill Hitch, Alan Peach, Herbert Strudwick, Phil Mead, Lionel Tennyson, and several more.

Little though I can have dreamt it I was due actually to play one day with some of these great men, and to know them as friends. In charity games in the thirties I took the field with Jack Hobbs himself. At Beckenham long afterwards I was often in the same side as the then captain of Surrey, C. T. A. Wilkinson, who, extraordinary to say, was a still active and effective cricketer almost to the age of seventy. Lionel Tennyson, to his indignant disbelief, I bowled at Lord's for a duck.

J. N. Crawford I have heard much of from H. S. Altham, who received his Repton colours from him in 1905 and who always maintained – with a good deal of emphasis if necessary – that he was the best schoolboy cricketer ever. I did once play against Jack Crawford in a weirdly assorted side containing K. S. Duleepsinhji, Peter Eckersley, two or three New Zealand Test players, and several septuagenarians (or thereabouts). But his powers had waned, and it is tiresome that his 92 in an hour and a half against the Yorkshiremen in that far-off match of 1919 made no impression on me. Nor was I present at the Oval a week later when Hobbs and Crawford, with less than three-quarters of an hour to make 95 to beat Kent, actually got them in 32 minutes. This, though it rates as one of the classic fast-scoring feats, would not have been at all to my taste, for though the Oval was within reach and such places as Canterbury, Maidstone and Tonbridge were not, my heart had already been lost to Kent.

Who else of these post-first war Oval cricketers came later into my life? Rockley Wilson, of course, who has been more affectionately quoted and caricatured than almost anyone in cricket history – of which, incidentally, he was an authority only with his fellow don at Winchester and life-long Altham. Did Rockley at the Oval flick the ball in underarm from the boundary as he did when he went out with MCC to Australia the following year, thus earning from those uninhibited crowds the mocking nickname of 'Miss Wilson'? I cannot say, but the book records that his supremely accurate and seemingly guileless slow bowling took six top Surrey wickets.

Yorkshire's captain, Cecil Burton (DCF) was coaching the Oratory boys – and with marvellous success – when, almost twenty years later, I spent some hospitable weeks at the school writing my junior part of the second edition of *A History of Cricket* at the invitation of Harry Altham aforesaid.

As to Donald Knight, he put me up in due course for membership of MCC, and together we played a good deal of club cricket, wherein I had the privilege of observing his flowing, graceful, wristy batting from the other end. Donald became a warm and faithful friend. He was in the handsome tradition of Malvern batsmanship which was founded by the multiple brotherhood of Foster (seven altogether) and perpetuated after the Days (S. H. and A. P.) and Donald by such men as Errol Holmes and Geoffrey Legge.

I declare an interest, for early heroes are ever the most glamorous; but I must say that I never saw so elegant a stylist as Donald Knight. Maybe, looking back, one might call it a slightly mannered style. Where there was no running to be done he was apt to linger a second or two on completion of the stroke as though to assure himself that all was exactly as it should be. It was essentially the fulfilment of the best in the Public School style of his day, seen in an age when a backlift was worth calling a backlift, and before the utilitarian five-day Test method had impressed itself on all and sundry by aid of the telly.

A cat may look at a king and vice-versa, and occasionally Donald had to look at me. Once he had to for rather a long time, and I hope it may be thought permissible to drag the little story in here. The great Knight came one Sunday in the thirties to Beckenham as captain of a powerful Musketeer side which had been got up by a genial old buffer long retired. Beautiful day, beautiful wicket. He won the toss, but the ancient manager had a strong theory about it being better in one-day cricket to send the others in.

Donald, with much misgiving, acquiesced in this and did as he was advised. Our captain Ronnie Bryan, ex- of Kent and one of the famous brothers, said 'I don't know why, but we've got a terrible side. The only hope is if you and I go in together and stay there.' Well, we did, and we both got hundreds, and put on over 200 for the first wicket, which enabled our side to get about 270 and win the match. D.J.K. not many!

The story has a moral, or, rather, two. Firstly, in good conditions it is almost always best, if you win the toss, to bat first, and get the runs on the board. Also, old buffers who have long given up should not presume to air their opinions, least of all to a distinguished player and student of the game who may even be (as in this case) an England cricketer. *Don't interfere!* Spending, as I now do, several days each summer hovering around a club with which I have a fairly close honorary connection, I am constantly reminding myself of this. Constantly but, I fear, not invariably with success.

In 1921, the year I went to Cranleigh, my father made me a junior member of Surrey, and so, as it turned out, directed my steps more definitely towards a life-long connection with cricket. Now I could practise and be coached in the schoolboy nets at the Oval in the Easter holidays. I also had the run of the pavilion, and so could peruse the great ones at close quarters.

We boys were looked after by the Second XI and ground staff, the whole being under the command of the head coach, Herbert Thompson. We had an innings in the morning, another in the afternoon, and after gobbling our sandwiches a third, unsupervised, in the lunch break. My own special coach and favourite was Harry Baldwin, small, dark, and a brilliant out-fielder whose skill was always much applauded when he came out as twelfth man. That was generally as far as he did get, for, avidly though I looked for his name in the papers, and while he always seemed to be written about as a hopeful prospect almost until he retired, he just never quite made the powerful Surrey batting side of the twenties. An innings of 63 not out against Gloucestershire was the best he achieved – I've looked it up out of cautious habit, and it's true, but I really didn't need to. It's just one of the early figures that time hasn't erased. Incidentally, in case the name still carries a familiar ring, H. G. Baldwin became one of the best of umpires, served for many years on the first-class list, and stood in Test matches.

We were privileged youngsters, naturally, to be a humble playing part of the Oval scene, and to be able at the same time to watch the county side, at practice as well as in the middle. The summers of one's youth seem always to have been warm and sunny – though I do remember, one April, being driven out of the nets by a snow-storm. The wickets of memory accordingly are generally hard and true, and so far as the Oval is concerned 'Bosser' Martin's were of surpassing excellence.

Only this fact, probably, stood between Surrey and the championship. They were always there or thereabouts, but they never quite made it because the bowlers had such an uphill job. They worked away, Hitch of the stuttering run, P. G. H. Fender, 'Surrey's Peach', a round-faced, smiling, square-shouldered figure, who bowled medium-fast and hit thundering hard and straight, Tom Rushby, and the rest. The guileful captaincy of Fender sometimes worked miracles, but it was just a little too hard going. Peach was a cheerful soul, the very picture of the best sort of county pro of the period.

Rushby regarded life with a graver eye, a tall, erect, moustachioed medium-pacer, who was perhaps feeling his forty years (though cricketers went on playing longer then than now) at the time I remember him. At all events there was, I've since heard, a convention surrounding him which was apparently understood and tacitly accepted by all concerned. Every now and then at the prospect of more donkey-work on another hot, hard day, Rushby staged a stay-at-home. There would arrive at the secretary's office from one of the nearer suburbs a laconic telegram of the briefest possible kind. It simply stated RUSHBY ILL – RUSHBY. For the next engagement back he would be refreshed and fit for further toil. No solicitous enquiries would be made as to his health. The malaise was not referred to.

The presiding genius in those days was, of course, Jack Hobbs, but much of the glamour surrounded P. G. H. Fender, who took over the Surrey captaincy in 1920 and held it for twelve strenuous years, during most of which he was as good an all-rounder as anyone in England.

He was hero-material for any boy, a fine, wristy hitter, dangerous leg-spin and googly bowler, and, not least, a remarkably slick picker-up of slip catches with the spectacular trick of throwing the ball nonchalantly away over his shoulder almost as soon as his fingers had grasped it. 'Good old Percy' to the crowd, Percy George to the generality of cricketers, and 'Bill' to his closer friends, Fender was very much one of the sporting personalities of the day.

On his form and reputation as a tactician Fender might well have been appointed captain of England at home, or of a touring team abroad, but it was said that he was not in special favour 'at Lord's', and other claimants with good credentials were preferred when J. W. H. T. Douglas's reign ended. First (in 1921) came Lionel Tennyson, then, within the next five years, Frank Mann, Arthur Gilligan, A. W. Carr, and finally Percy Chapman.

'Lord's' in those days and in this sort of context meant George Robert Canning, the fourth Baron Harris, of Seringapatam and Mysore, and of Belmont, the last of the autocrats of cricket history. Lord Harris died in 1932, aged 81, and he was never more to me, of course, than a distant figure pointed out in some awe by older friends in the Long Room. He held the reins as Treasurer of MCC from 1896 to the day of his death, and what he said, at Lord's as in Kent, was law. Fender's prospect of leading England can scarcely have been helped by the fact of his having written on the MCC Australian tour of 1920–21 while a member of the team. He was engaged by the old *Daily News*, Rockley Wilson by the *Daily Express*, and as to the latter I have seen, thanks to his nephew, David, a wire from his editor suggesting that his stuff, in vulgar parlance, might be pepped up a bit. Both, and especially Wilson, had certain critical things to say about some of the umpiring in the series, but it was not felt that such judgments came best from members of the team and a resolution was accordingly passed at the 1921 MCC Annual General Meeting deprecating the reporting of matches by players concerned in them.

This reminds me of one of the best-known Rockley Wilson stories to which his writing from Australia obviously provides the background. The scene is the Long Room, with Rockley conversing in a group, lifting his heels and swaying up and down as was his habit, tugging nervously at his tie, and repeating each jerky, often pungent phrase.

Rockley espies Lord Harris approaching, saying to his companions: 'Excuse me, excuse me, here comes Lord Harris, here comes Lord Harris.'

'Good morning, m'lord.'

His lordship, scarcely pausing, offers one finger, and moves on, but scarcely quickly enough to avoid hearing the swift follow up. 'Lucky to get a touch really, lucky to get a touch!'

One can't help taking Lord Harris's side in the matter, even if Rockley does not seem to have written anything which by modern standards would be thought much out of place. The point is, though, that he really shouldn't have been saying anything at all. The home country is still today, as, naturally, it always has been, sensitive to the reactions and behaviour of its visitors, and it needs little stretch of the imagination to picture the extra 'chippiness' of the average Australian of half a century ago.

As it happens, thanks to Irving Rosenwater, who can generally be relied on to put his hand on most things, I've been able to look through an assorted cuttings-book of the 1920–21 MCC tour. There's nothing therein under the name of Fender to which reasonable exception could be taken, but Wilson had a tilt at the crowd during the Fifth Test at Sydney with the following result as reported by Reuter's Special Correspondent:

The Fifth Test match was resumed today in pleasant weather before a moderate attendance. The wicket was reported perfect. Mailey and Gregory opened the bowling to the English not outs, Rhodes (10) and Wilson (5).

Wilson was booed on emerging from the pavilion, the demonstration being in connection with the Yorkshire amateur's cables to England, extracts from which have been cabled out here showing that Wilson accused the crowd of jeering Hobbs on account of his slow movements, which were due to his leg injury.

Wilson was soon out stumped, but during the few minutes he was at the wicket his batting was frequently derided.

As Wilson was retiring he was hooted, and cries were raised of 'Get home, you squeaker.'

In the members' reserved enclosure Wilson stopped to speak to someone while the hooting was in progress, but M. A. Noble, the old Test player, came up to him, linked his arm in Wilson's, and advised him not to argue.

Hobbs succeeded Wilson at the wicket, and he was the recipient of a wonderful ovation . . .

I have a feeling that Rockley was too rare a bird for the taste of the Australians of his generation, and there is another earlier Wilson story, less generally circulated, which at least suggests so. We go back to an Officers' Mess in the Middle East, with Rockley finding somewhat tedious the recital by an Aussie brigadier of the exploits and recent dispositions of his troops. They had been situated apparently around the Sea of Galilee.

Rockley, *sotto voce* and with the usual tie-pulling paraphernalia: 'Ha, ha! Ha, ha! I bet the shepherds watched their flocks *that* night.'

Does this seem amusing to those who never met and savoured the man? I scarcely know, but it still brings a laugh from me, and it may perhaps to any who, in one war or the other, had cause to respect the Aussies' reputation as the best scroungers bar none. In a class of their own! There will be a good deal, by the way, in this book about Australia and

Australians, and by the end of it I hope that more serious reasons will shine through to account for my admiration and affection for them.

Meanwhile I seem to have strayed quite a bit from the cricket of 1921 as seen through the eyes of the fourteen-year-old Surrey member, and we'd better get back to the Oval because it was in that summer that I attended my first Test match. The Ashes had been already retained by Warwick Armstrong's team; the rubber was lost. But England, after eight – yes, eight – successive humiliations, had put up a better showing in the Fourth Test at Old Trafford, and they certainly did so at the Oval, even if the weather and lack of time prevented them driving their advantage home.

I remember the hubbub in front of the pavilion (I was safely inside) on the first afternoon when after rain there was one of those irritating delays before anything happened. Tennyson and Armstrong at last descended the steps to inspect, the crowd cheering our man who palpably wanted to play (England were batting) and booing Armstrong who even more obviously didn't. I remember the heartache when Frank Woolley was brilliantly thrown out by Bardsley from down by the score-board on the tram side. The ball hit the stumps, but even to my immature eye the great man, trotting in his somewhat stiff-legged way, could have spurted and made his ground if he had seen the danger just a fraction earlier.

Twenty-three he had made, and according to *Wisden* 'had batted beautifully'. I admit no flaw in Frank's cricket, save that, as subsequent experience showed often enough, he was not the greatest runner between wickets. Woolley and Knight were now, I am quite confident as regards my memory, on twin heroic pinnacles. Though I ses it as shouldn't, I wasn't a bad picker – in those days anyway.

Monday was fine, and I can see the bare paths up to the wicket made by Gregory and McDonald as they bowled endlessly to Philip Mead. When the latter was joined by his captain, Armstrong bowled slow-medium outside his pads, a sort of negative leg-theory with several fieldsmen round the corner. After the first three balls had passed harmlessly by without a stroke played Lionel Tennyson walked up the wicket and said something to Mead, who thereupon swung hard at the last three balls, and cracked them all for four. Armstrong promptly took his sweater while the crowd crowed. Mead (182 not out) and Tennyson (51) added 121 in 100

30

minutes, so the book says, and all in all it was a good day for England.

I don't think I can have been there on the Tuesday, for I must have remembered Armstrong having his final revenge on the crowd, stretching his huge frame on the grass at the fall of a wicket, and reading a newspaper that had been caught by the wind. Arthur Mailey, that great Anglophile and dear man, was fond of telling how when after the game he asked Armstrong (for whom he had no great admiration) why he had done it, the answer came, 'I wanted to see who we were plying.'

I dare say that it might almost have been said of Armstrong in 1921 as it was written of 'the Demon' Spofforth by Cardus that he let in with him the coldest blast of antagonism that ever blew over a June field. When invited down to the Committee Room at Lord's so that friendly agreement might be reached regarding hours of play and such-like matters, the story goes that he declined to enter, stood at the door in his flannels, cap on head, and took an utterly recalcitrant attitude in respect of every detail in dispute. Not an endearing man in his playing days, by all account, though a tremendous cricketer.

But I can conclude this small sketch on a warmer note. When I spent an evening in Armstrong's company up at Brisbane during the Test of '46 he reminisced nostalgically about 'the old country' and I swear his eyes were moist with affection. Whether this change of sentiment just reflected the mellowness that so often comes to warriors with age, or whether it owed something to the Buchanan's whisky whereof he held the Australian agency, and which made him a fair-sized fortune, I would not be sure. Perhaps it was a case of a bit of both. At all events it is a memory one recalls with pleasure. Though philosophically speaking he may have broadened, physically, Armstrong – who had to stoke the ship on the way over to England in 1921 to keep his weight within twenty stone – had very perceptibly shrunk. As I saw him at Brisbane he would have nowhere near filled the vast flannel shirt that still hangs as a peculiar memorial to him among other assorted cricketana in a glass case in the Melbourne pavilion. In company he was benign, though in print still prepared to fire off some pretty sharp critical salvoes at the other outstanding Australian cricket figure of the last half-century, Don Bradman. These, too, proved to be a final burst, for 1946–47 was his very last Australian summer.

A final memory of cricket in 1921 is of my first visit to

Lord's, and I am sorry the impact it made is so shadowy. Why it should be I don't know, since the game in question was that in which Middlesex retained the championship title they had won so dramatically, also against Surrey, a year previously. That had been 'Plum's' last match, with all the attendant sentiment, to say nothing of the exciting circumstances of the victory.

But this was a battle of high drama, too, wherein Middlesex ended the first innings 137 runs behind (132 in reply to 269), bowled Surrey out a second time for 184, and thanks to R. H. Twining and Jack Hearne, who made 277 together in just over four hours for the second wicket, won the game shortly after six on the third evening by six wickets. (The paid gate, by the way, was 47,919: total with members something like 60,000.) I would dearly like to say to my old friend, Dick Twining, that I saw the innings of his life, but I cannot honestly declare I did, and suppose I watched one of the earlier days.

What I do most vividly recall was a brief encounter – indubitably my first – with an MCC member. At the Oval Test I had borrowed my father's binoculars, and left them on my seat at an interval, to find them gone on my return. Having somehow got hold of another pair I was bold enough to ask my neighbour if he would keep an eye on them for me. The reply was flattening. Whatever might have happened to my property in the Oval pavilion would not befall it here. The very suggestion was apparently quite insulting. Collapse of small boy. If he hadn't realized hitherto what a solid gulf existed between Lord's and the Oval he knew it now.

The earlier memories are generally the most easily recollected, and at a remove of a full fifty years the sights and scents of Cranleigh group themselves with a surprising clarity as one casts the mind back to my first term in the summer of 1921. The life of a completely unremarkable boy of that period at one of the then less famous public schools is of scant interest, obviously. But not so, necessarily, the place itself, its ambitions, standards, and attitudes which I expect were general enough among institutions of a similar kind.

Cranleigh was one of the many foundations of the first half of Victoria's reign built on the principles of Arnold's Rugby to give boarding schooling to a rapidly expanding middle-class. In our case the idea was to cater for the youth of Surrey. It was a bearded and literally Venerable Archdeacon of Surrey, Sapte by name, who agitated other worthy citizens to found a school in that quiet pastoral setting below the North Downs, and we only narrowly avoided being labelled the Surrey County School. It was no accident that the foundation coincided almost exactly with the opening of the single-track railway which wound its unhurried way from one village to another roughly north and south across the Surrey-Sussex border between Guildford and Horsham.

I write in the past tense, for this particular branch was a pre-Beeching axeing. But it had played its part in bringing this lovely rural pocket within access of London : within range but not too easy a range. Above all, its one-trackedness meant (presumably) that it was not worth electrifying. And so Cranleigh and its neighbourhood have largely escaped the dormitory development that has taken so much of the character from the over-populated southern countryside since I was a boy.

My visits, in connection with the *Sporting and Dramatic* articles, to many public schools in the 'thirties, from the greatest to the 'illustrious obscure', enabled me, I think, to see my own in fair perspective. Academically I dare say we were a bit sub-standard, possibly because the endowment on the scholarship side was so slender. In point of general *esprit de corps*, especially as expressed in games, we made up, I should have thought, all that may have been lost on the books, and if there had to be a balance one way or the other I suppose that this was the way that our headmaster would have chosen. He was the Reverend H. A. Rhodes, a shortish man but with the largest, bluest, most protuberant eyes I have ever seen. They seemed to penetrate the secret hiding-places of a boy's heart and mind : in short an enviable item of professional equipment. His look was dominating. The eyes had it. Rhodes personified surely as well as most of the schoolmasters of his day the *mens sana in corpore sano* of the Arnold ideal. An Oriel exhibitioner in the heyday of that college, he was also the university soccer captain.

If really hard work was for those who liked it, Rhodes expected a reasonably steady diligence, and any abrupt decline involved quite simply a headmaster's beating. I imagine the essential difference between 1921 and 1971 as regards work was the absence then of pressure. I was forward enough to pass School Certificate in my second year – distinctions in English and Latin – then was allowed to free-wheel pleasantly with only the mild challenge of the London Matriculation intervening. However I was not for the university, and was allowed to pass a restful year in the Upper Sixth reading and writing. For the combination of those early distinctions and my father's friendship with the director of the Amalgamated Press had been enough to suggest an eventual essay into journalism. To stimulate my literary proclivities I was specially provided with *John O'London's Weekly*, and set to read a book of pen-sketches by A. G. Gardiner called *Prophets, Priests, and Kings*.

J. S. Purvis was a notable figure in the inter-war Cranleigh scene, a tall, good-looking man with a peculiar form of dry banter and – both in and out of chapel – a bass voice of impressive quality. His was the best house, whence came three of the seven rugger internationals produced by the school in the years 1923–39. He took holy orders some years after my time, returned to his native North Riding, became Canon and a distinguished Archivist of York, and on his recent death aged eighty-five rated a half-column obituary in *The Times*. I find it a faintly depressing thought still that here was a scholar who might have done much for a more eager, receptive mind than mine.

Religion at Cranleigh conformed to the general public school pattern of the day: centre of the road stuff with much more about Duty and Behaviour than about God and His Church. The ecclesiastical guard – of Rhodes, of the Reverend R. H. C. Mertens, of the Reverend T. W. Thomas (afterwards a much-loved Master of Llandovery) – was middle, a little inclined to leg. If my impression at this distance is to be trusted Evangelicalism was respectable, Anglo-Catholicism not. So far as I know only the schools of the Woodard foundation departed from the norm. Lancing's religion might be as high as their soaring chapel – but no whiff or tinkle of 'smells and bells' for us!

As to the staff there was something to note and to admire about all of those whose personalities have endured the passage of time: Frank Winsloe, who looked after the cricket, and with his brother ran the Bursary, OCs both who gave a lifetime of service to the school, two other brothers, the Hopewells, 'Monty' Aldridge, 'Dick' Harris, whose efforts to teach me music, alas, met no answering chord; Cecil Crowhurst, another late taker of holy orders; Max Machin, a scholar in the Purvis mould; old E. A. Clare, who really did care about my cricket – for the meagre and much-belated reward in his old age of a few reminiscent days in the sun in the Players' Enclosure at Hastings; and a figure of formal dress and awesome dignity, G. L. N. Antrobus.

34

He it was who taught me English and Latin, who banged home the basic rules of syntax, who induced in me an appreciation of the derivation of the one language from the other, who persuaded me when in doubt to go back to the Latin root, and who impressed in my lazy head the proper construction of an English sentence. He took trouble over my essays, trivial though they no doubt were, and gave me a respect for good English and some sort of a critical standard. When I stumble over a method of expression I sometimes today think back on Antrobus's form-room in the Merriman block, and wonder how he would have advised my tackling it.

As Antrobus influenced me I have no doubt the reader may recall some schoolmaster who equally helped him : and I dare say he may regret, as I do, that, whether from shyness or lack of thought or a combination of both, one never expressed one's appreciation. Maybe the schoolmaster reckons that if only one in ten returns to give thanks the other nine are not necessarily ungrateful. I like and admire most schoolmasters, and have often envied their lives. And, by the way, I would always strongly recommend to anyone with any ambition to write to stick to his Latin.

There were, of course, the inevitable figures of fun : the bearded Herbert who sang with such exuberant gusto in the choir, and Clinton who conveyed the mysteries of book-keeping to those scheduled to receive them. If I had been one it would certainly have proved a useful investment. I might also have participated in a scene that must have been richly comical. Mr Clinton was always in difficulty getting his forms started because boys straggled in with one impertinent excuse after another. One day for a long time no boys came at all, and when they all cascaded in together, each with an excessive number of books, and plumped themselves down at their long desks, these all forthwith collapsed, so that boys and books and benches, ink, pens and the whole paraphernalia of learning subsided in an unholy tangle on the floor.

Above the chaos bleating cries arose. 'Sir' came in for a multitude of injured complaints. It was a bit thick, Sir, someone must have taken all the screws out of the desks. A joke's a joke, Sir, but this was a bit much. The clear implication was that the whole affair was Sir's own fault. No doubt at the height of the hubbub Sir's long-suffering colleague teaching next door looked in to discover what the uproar was about, and hurriedly departed, a witness to his shame, and to a story that would lose nothing in its telling in the Common Room.

How many perpetrators were there, I wonder, of this particular rag? How many screwdrivers did the job? Did anyone 'own up'? Who did the repairs? Perhaps the missing screws were 'discovered' by someone, planted in the wretched fellow's own desk. That would have been a subtle touch.

One thing is sure. If a schoolmaster has allowed things to get as much out of hand as this there is only one answer so far as he is concerned, and that is to move on somewhere else pretty quick. To another school or, preferably, another job. There is a blessed knack in keeping boys in order which is given to some and denied to others. It can come easily to the meek and yet elude the strong. It was said of one tough hero of the famous England packs of the 'twenties that he had to give up schoolmastering because he simply could not maintain any sort of discipline. Clinton was another of the same kidney.

Herbert by contrast was not raggable, it was just that the sight of him 'rendering' a particular chapel solo was somehow inexpressibly funny. His lines told us how at the last day the eyes of the blind shall be opened, and the ears of the deaf shall be unstopped, and the mouths of the dumb shall sing. Little Herbert managed to convey that he himself had been suddenly released from all these dire handicaps, and that he was making the very most of the three faculties having been restored. The wide eyes and the fully opened mouth, to say nothing of the quivering beard, let themselves go in such an ecstasy of feeling that by the time he reached the next bit about the lame man leaping as an hart the congregation was reduced to helpless, silent mirth. In the end the anthem had to be tactfully dropped from the chapel calendar.

Happy days they seem, retrospectively at least, and were I believe in fact. On the whole we liked our masters, and the general atmosphere was one of easy tolerance. There was however one startling exception to this generalization, and it concerned the football code of our recent adoption. Which brings me to the maker of the Cranleigh rugger which was our pride (if not always our unalloyed joy).

Charles Gower was a Welshman brought up in South Africa – which gave him, in combination, an impeccable rugger background. He had no great credentials as a player – a knee, so legend said, had spoiled his chances of a Cambridge blue before the First War, and he never played after being invalided out of the army, and coming to Cranleigh in 1916. But as a coach he was superb, with a dedication to perfection and an enthusiasm that were irresistibly infectious. It is perhaps questionable if the boys of the 'seventies would have 'taken' his robust style. At all events in his own day he had a national reputation, and I cannot think that anyone would have made so much of the talent at his disposal.

At a distance of fifty years one sees clearly the afternoon scene on St Andrew's Field in the Michaelmas term; the cries of Gower in all his moods as he spent himself in admonishing, cajoling, and (occasionally) praising the participants in First Scratch; the long blast on the whistle denoting half-time; and then the brief descent to Fourth, Third, and finally Second Clubs, where Swanton buried his head a bit deeper in the scrum, praying to avoid notice. As Gower approached each game it spurted to a fever of activity, relapsing perceptibly on his departure as the master-in-charge resumed a less exacting control.

On First XV match-days the whole school watched. The enthusiasm was considerable, the standard remarkably high. The Gower creed was 'the simple thing done well – and at speed': the perfect giving and taking of passes, incessant backing-up, relentless pressure. The arts of the game, the swerve, the dummy and 'the scissors' were adornments to the basic foundation.

The schools we played in term-time, Mill Hill, Christ's Hospital, The Leys, and the rest were not nearly strong enough, and the more exciting games were those against the clubs, Blackheath, the Harlequins, and London Scottish. The Scottish first 'A' was beaten, I think, seven years running. Once Gower scared the Fifteen by pointing to a good result for The Leys against Bedford, then with Uppingham about the best school side in the country, exclusive, we thought, of ourselves. The Leys were beaten 55–nil, and it was said that throughout the game not a Cranleigh pass was dropped.

I remember being taken by my father at the end of term to Queen's Club, and the shock of Downside beating us 15–5. A few days later, though, we beat Ampleforth 18–nil. There were fierce holiday games, too, against Blundell's including the one when after a narrow victory it was pointed out that Cranleigh had played sixteen men. Someone was late, and Gower and the captain had each nominated a different replacement. The papers made much of this story which was less strange than it appears because in those days Cranleigh invariably played seven forwards and eight backs. But, of course, the 'victory' could not be counted.

The school heroes were, inevitably, the football heroes, and there was a great thrill when H. P. Jacob went up to Oxford in the bye-term, played at once for England throughout their Championship season of 1924, and later that year gained his blue, by so doing displacing one member of the famous Oxford-Scots threequarter line of I. S. Smith, G. P. S. Macpherson, G. G. Aitken, and A. C. Wallace. Jacob in full flight was a wonderful sight, but as a boy he rated second to L. S. F. Leroy, who on leaving school emigrated forthwith to Canada, and had subsequently to be content with the modest distinction of representing his adopted country against Japan. There are impartial people who say that there has never been a better schoolboy player. The footballers of the early post-war period formed the new Old Cranleighan RFC which made its mark in the rugger world some ten years later.

The best-known subsequently of these, though he was not outstanding as a boy, was M. A. McCanlis, who followed Jacob in bringing the name of the school to the forefront at Oxford in a day when university games-players loomed much larger on the sporting and social scene than they do today. Maurice became house-captain of East, I his deputy. His career as a footballer illustrated for me an early lesson in the all-important part played by temperament in the development of a sportsman. Natural ability will take one so far, but not very – unless it is matched by application and hard resolve, and these are qualities that can be nurtured and built up.

Maurice at Cranleigh was a distinctly variable threequarter for whom things had to go right. Sometimes he'd tackle, sometimes he wouldn't somehow be there, and Gower would explode with Welsh indignation. If he didn't go so far in this case as to say 'You're funking, boy – funking' the implication was present. I can write this now surely because by the time he got his blue on the wing Maurice was an immaculate defender. As a full-back in his last year at Oxford he got as far as the final England trial, whereafter, becoming a master at Cheltenham, he matured his game with Gloucester in the tough West-country school. By 1930/31, when he played in the centre for England, he had become a magnificent tackler. There was no more courageous footballer in the International Championship.

There was cricket in the blood, for Maurice was the grandson of that Captain W. McCanlis who in the 'nineties had laid the foundation of Kent's great pre-war teams by founding the Tonbridge nursery: a splendid bearded figure reputedly still a good player at the age of seventy-five. At school Maurice was a better all-round cricketer than footballer and in his year of captaincy, 1924, we actually had, thanks to him, quite a tolerable side. He had a natural out-swinger, and when I managed to escape from the Amalgamated Press on a Monday morning of July 1926 to see something of my first University Match, the score-card told me that Cambridge had lost three wickets cheaply, those of E. W. Dawson, K. S. Duleepsinhji, and F. J. Seabrook. All had been caught Legge, bowled McCanlis: caught at second slip. That out-swinger afterwards grew somewhat elusive. But he played three years at Lord's, being captain in his last, and is still Cranleigh's only double-blue, for two major games anyway. Within a couple of years Jacob had led Oxford at Twickenham, McCanlis at Lord's, both afterwards giving their lives to teaching.

This provokes a thought. Since Maurice took a History Exhibition at St Edmund Hall he would no doubt have been strong enough academically to have made the university anyway. But 'Jake' (he is the only close friend whose Christian name I simply never knew) was accepted by Christ Church before passing Responsions, and I seem to recall quite a press commotion, since he was already an International, when he did get through and so made himself available for a blue. I deduce from this that the Oxford of today would not have looked at him twice, nor even perhaps would a 'red-brick'. So no degree, no school-mastering, and Cranleigh would have been infinitely the poorer. As house-master, Second Master, and in an interregnum Acting Headmaster, no one had a stronger or a better influence upon many generations of boys. With university selection nowadays based purely on the merit of written work, the schools must get along without the Jacobs, men of character and dedication who used to be their backbone. So much the worse for them!

And, of course, so much the worse for the Universities, both the ancient blue ones and the modern red. I imagine that Peregrine Worsthorne voiced the thoughts of many when he wrote recently in the *Sunday Telegraph*: 'The ill-advised expansion of University education has spawned a mass of rootless, semi-educated intellectuals in puerile revolt against the values of the past.' It's a sentence that bears reading and re-reading. The context of Worsthorne's remarks was the sickeningly-prejudiced, left-orientated series on the British Empire presented by BBC television; but how much of the evil in modern society, the contempt for old moral values must be laid at the door of these 'rootless, semi-educated . . .'!

I said at the start of this chapter that my personal impact on Cranleigh could be of only negligible interest, and I merely add therefore that I was an ineffective rugger player who got nowhere – too spindly and too slow – and though I played once for the XI (and made 33 against the masters) that, for all my keenness and the Oval coaching, was the modest limit of my cricket success. My Valete notice on leaving at the end of the 1924 Summer Term was not spectacular. Yet my years had been happy ones, and interest in things sporting had survived the lack of personal success.

3

Sporting Fleet Street

From school to Fleet Street – or, to be exact, to Fleetway House, the headquarters of the Amalgamated Press, which lay a couple of hundred yards north of Ludgate Circus, in Farringdon Street. There I spent just three years, making tea, sub-editing, acting as general dogsbody, and soon striving to augment a starting wage of twenty-five shillings a week by contributing to any newspaper whose sports editor showed the faintest inclination to accept my wares.

The first thing one discovered was that entry to the sporting world of Fleet Street in the 'twenties lay through a number of doors marked Saloon Bar: also up the stairs, flanked by innumerable Spy cartoons, of the Press Club off Salisbury Square. Then there was Anderton's Hotel – and, a little later, the Temple Bar Restaurant where the clientele was to me of dazzling distinction.

If you wanted to make the acquaintance of the great men who wrote those very long, precise, well-informed, supremely dignified, unsigned columns in *The Times*, the place to find them was The Baynard Castle in Queen Victoria Street, a few yards up from Printing House Square. There I would drop my heavy 800 words on Old Merchant Taylors *v.* Cambridge, or London Scottish *v.* Bristol, or whatever it might be, and Bob Lyle, the sporting editor, would give it to somebody to run an eye over, stick a heading on, and, in due course when he turned his reluctant steps to the office, deliver to the printer. Much of the subbing, such as it was, was done in the pub over a tankard of beer. In due course Captain R. C. Lyle (who, by the way, was the first BBC racing commentator) would go back and make up the page, or depute someone else to, R. B. Vincent perhaps, the inimitable 'Beau', or another who was officially referred to by his war-time military rank, Captain J. A. Board.

In those days, on *The Times* at any rate, inside and outside staff were one. People turned their hand to what was required, and most of those concerned were very versatile. They wrote a lot, and drank a good deal, and resignedly accepted the subbing as a necessary chore. 'Beau' Vincent and Jack Board and also little Sir Guy Campbell were primarily golfers, who when the Halford-Hewitt Tournament came along each April at Deal lined up under the colours of Haileybury, Wellington, and Eton respectively. They were understudies to the Golf Correspondent, Bernard Darwin, but they wrote also about lots of other games and notably cricket.

The most versatile of this galaxy, and a person of boundless charm and a whimsical humour, was F. B. Wilson. As a cricketer Freddy had captained Harrow and Cambridge. He was adept at all the court games, and as a young man his eye was so keen that it was said he could beat all-comers at ping-pong using a table-knife. He had originally been brought on by Northcliffe with whose encouragement he developed a racy, abbreviated style of reporting soon after the tabloid *Daily Mirror* burst upon Edwardian England. After the war Freddy wrote for *The Times* (then controlled by Northcliffe), but he was never a staff man, worked on a space basis, and it was said that at one time or another he covered some twenty different games or sports for *The Times* – and that he never earned £1,000 a year from them. His son, Peter, the famous sporting columnist, who now perpetuates his father's name on the *Mirror* – and, I suspect, picks up about as much in a month as his father earned in a year – confirms my recollection.

I can think of a dozen or more sporting journalists of that generation or thereabouts who were uniformly courteous and kind and helpful to me as a young man, but the memory of Freddy, so amusing, so gentle and generous in his writing and in his talk, has a place of special affection.

I can recall only one little story about him, and that at second-hand. He was playing once for a side of W.G.'s against sixteen of somewhere or other – games against odds were a quite common occurrence in those days – and after the experts had made a pile of runs they duly went out to field. In the first over Freddy picked one up low down at slip and threw it back to the bowler. At the end of the over W.G. said it looked a fair catch to him. Had he caught it? When Freddy said well, yes, he had but after all the poor chap wasn't off the mark, W.G. tugged his beard.

'Be careful, young man,' he said, 'there are another fourteen of them waiting, you know.' A slight tale, as I say, but it seems to fit both their characters perfectly.

Another *Times* man (of much versatility) was O. L. Owen, who was simultaneously their chief correspondent for Rugby football, athletics, and boxing. Think of the output in days when reports of quite ordinary moment ran the length of the column. It was nothing for Owen to motor out in the morning to the provinces for a game of rugger, return to the office, write his report, then make his way to the Albert Hall or the White City, cover a boxing match, and hand in his final copy at Printing House Square around midnight. I believe his remuneration for his triple activity was, like Freddy Wilson's, measured in hundreds rather than thousands.

Owen – thus called both by acquaintances and close friends since his names were Owen Llewelyn Owen – had a fund of colourful reminiscence guaranteed to while away the longest journey. He had seen and covered all the Olympic Games at least since 1908, and had not missed a rugger international since goodness knows when. He had been on the spot at Cardiff when Teddy Morgan scored the disputed try against the 1905 All Blacks, had been at Epsom in Persimmon's year, and reported prize fights practically since the dawn of time. But he had participated too. Between the soup and the fish he might have put Dicky Owen over for the winning try at Swansea, knocked in a goal or two at Ipswich (or was it Norwich?), and not least frequently, on being given the clue by one of his regular audience, gone a few rounds as sparring partner to Gene Tunney. There was a time, too, I rather think, when he and W.G. had put on a few runs together, but the detail escapes me.

War and gore came a good deal into his talk, and not merely the Great War. Whether he'd literally been in on the relief of Ladysmith or witnessed the peace signing at Vereeniging I couldn't positively say, but he could give gripping first-hand accounts of the Boxer Rising. There was a scene, I remember, wherein Owen wreaked horrible carnage on a station platform dripping with blood.

Let me not suggest the picture of a bombastic babbler. Owen was always started off, and kept going, by judicious questioning or the letting drop of a name or place that revived a well-worn story. The railway carriage group might contain Howard Marshall of the *Telegraph*, little Freddy Dartnell of the *News Chronicle*, Leo Munro of the *Express*, J. P. Jordan of the *Mail*, Owen and young Swanton, and as Owen talked on knowing glances would be exchanged.

Wait a minute, he couldn't have been in Canton in October 1912 – didn't we hear last week how he saw Jack Johnson lie down for the count and lose the heavyweight title to Jesse

Willard? If his memory for detail was ever timidly doubted, Owen turned his wide blue eyes full on the questioner and disposed of the matter with bland, unruffled confidence. I never heard him contradicted. He was a master. Moreover, after all allowance was made for a vivid Celtic imagination, his experience was prodigious.

A temperate man in contrast to most of his sporting contemporaries he lasted correspondingly longer. Indeed when I became the first chairman of the Rugby Football Writers' Club in 1960, he was still going to matches though nominally retired, and was our natural choice as president. He was a firm friend to me over a span of forty years. Founder and editor of the Rugby Football Annual, and later author of the original official history of the Rugby Union, now superseded by U. A. Titley and Ross McWhirter's magnificent work marking the Centenary, the game owes him a vast debt.

Indeed British sport generally is much beholden to these games writers of the 'twenties and thereabouts, whom I got to know and admire as a young man. They knew their subjects, very often from first-hand, and they had a strong sense of the traditions behind the games concerned. These were the early days of signed and specialist games-writing – signed apart from *The Times*, that is to say – and the foundations they laid were generally sound ones. They concentrated more perhaps on the narrative than on critical analysis, which for its part was informed and generous.

I don't know when I first heard Bernard Darwin's well-known axiom that a man might miss a yard putt for a championship and yet be a good Christian husband and father, but, apart from one or two scallywags on the sporting columnist side, that roughly expressed the professional philosophy of the men whose names are sprinkled throughout this chapter. They wrote with insight and charity, *as* sportsmen *to* sportsmen.

As to 'Bernardo', as Bernard Darwin was known among his friends, he was without any doubt the unquestioned leader in the field of games-writing, the uncrowned king of the whole fraternity.

With what others did I rub shoulders, and to whom else did I listen as a precocious tyro? Well, let us cast an eye over the cricket press-box. To Sydney Pardon, the famous editor of *Wisden* (1891 to 1925) I was merely briefly introduced by my father outside the Oval press-box. He died in harness, preparing the 1926 edition.

There were three others in the Cricket Reporting Agency all of whom became in turn editors of *Wisden*, Charles Stewart Caine, Sydney Southerton, and Hubert Preston. Stewart Caine fathered me when I first became a member of the Press Club. He succeeded Sydney Pardon and edited eight issues, the last when the Bodyline furore was at its height, he having the taxing job of making some authoritative comment before the true facts of the matter had filtered home. He had spent a lifetime in what was commonly known as 'Pardon's', and I had this to say of his work and of his relationship with the brotherhood in *The World of Cricket*:

> The Pardon brothers reported games with a conscientious integrity, a good taste, and a reticence, which was a particularly important factor in the development of cricket – still an emerging game when Caine first took up his pen. In no one were these principles more firmly implanted than in him, and in consequence, perhaps no sporting journalist has ever been held in greater respect and affection. He was, as may be supposed, very much of the 'old school', to whose memory it is a privilege, however belatedly, to pay tribute.

If Stewart Caine was steeped in cricket, even more so was Sydney Southerton, who was the son of James, who played for England in the first of all Test Matches, at Melbourne in 1876/7. This Sydney was a warm-hearted fellow, and something of a rough diamond, in contrast to Preston, a sober chap of formal dress and rigid principles who struggled to combat acute deafness with an expanding ear-trumpet. Making conversation one morning in the office lift, Preston remarked that he had a hedgehog at the bottom of his garden. Southerton, perhaps nursing a bit of a hangover, suggested gruffly and coarsely where he might dispose of it. But 'Deafy' Preston can hardly have heard him because he added a postscript to his nature note: 'Yes, it's been there for a fortnight.' The joke had a long run, and ages afterwards Raymond Robertson-Glasgow might come up to one and remark in confidential tones, 'there's a hedgehog at the bottom of my garden . . .'

Of 'Crusoe' more anon. His cricket-writing did not begin in earnest until he abandoned schoolmastering, to be exact in 1933. In the mid-'twenties the regular writers included, beyond those already mentioned, H. J. Henley of the *Mail*, H. A. H. Carson of the *Evening News*, J. A. H. Catton of the *Evening Standard*, Colonel Philip Trevor of the *Telegraph*, and of course Neville Cardus of the *Manchester Guardian*.

'Berty' Henley, despite 'a leg' which had plagued his life ever since he had spent an appalling number of hours wounded and helpless in No Man's Land around 1915, covered the theatre as well as cricket and rugger, a dear full-sized Cockney character with a stick, a healthy thirst and a unique preference for the Oval, which he loved, over Lord's, which he said he hated. Perhaps the Oval bitter was more to his taste. He was unique also for me in that he was the only man who invariably called me 'Jimmy'. His nagging disability meant that he some-times saw rather less of the game than he should have done, but he had a rare knack of picking up the flavour of a day's play, or of a personality, without apparently paying close attention.

Harry Carson was a tall, grave man of much charm and impeccable manners who made a comical contrast with his professional evening paper rival, Jimmy Catton, who was so small that if his chair was a low one he could barely see out of the press-box window. I knew little Catton in a manner of speaking before he knew me, because at the Amalgamated Press I graduated to a paper called *All Sports* to which he was a regular and voluminous contributor. Catton came from Manchester where he had edited the then well-known *Athletic News*, and he belonged to the school which held that one word should never be used if two would serve. Since for *All Sports* he got the standard rate of a guinea a thousand (I used to have to mark up the issues for contributors' payments), this no doubt was only common sense.

When Hobbs was batting at the Oval he would soon have the crimson rambler speeding to the confines, while a few para-graphs later the Surrey crack would be despatching the leather spheroid to the ropes. Colourful stuff! But it offended the priggish eyes of the young sub-editor into whose head Antrobus had inserted the principles of good English. So he used to sub Catton's copy, at first judiciously but, as he grew bolder, in the most wholesale way, re-writing great chunks of it. I was always expecting a complaint which would have been amply justified, but at length it became obvious from his silence that Catton never read a word of his stuff. So long as the cheques came in he was happy.

I did not know Neville Cardus until I aspired to the dignity of writing about Test Matches (in 1930), but Philip Trevor soon befriended me, and I used to watch a lot of cricket and rugger in his company and that of his faithful daughter. The latter became indispensable, for the old fellow's eyes grew very poor, and a misty afternoon, say, at Richmond Athletic Ground (he was the *Telegraph* rugger man as well as cricket) had him groping much more than the rest of us. It was lucky that the lady knew quite a bit about both games, as indeed did her father. He had managed the MCC side to Australia in 1907/8 (this was the first of Hobbs's five visits), and played a deal of good club and Army cricket.

Though he could be caustic about slow play – like at least one of his *Telegraph* successors – Trevor, in the tradition of his generation of games-writers, found a kind word for everyone when he could. This extended, as I remember, in sometimes saying flatly 'Good too was so-and-so', without specifying further. The *Telegraph* by-line used to give not only his rank but his CBE, which somehow seemed to add weight to his judgments.

The *Daily Telegraph* sports editor of the day was Frank Coles, a journalist of the old easy-going, highly sociable school who nevertheless held on, about the last survivor of his type, until he gave way to the present sports editor, Kingsley Wright, at the beginning of 1961. The contrast between the methods of these two reflects the vastly greater pace and urgency of sporting journalism today. The much wider range of games to be covered, the popularity of sport under floodlights, and (for a variety of technical reasons) the earlier press-times all combine to make the modern job a highly complicated exercise in time and motion.

Everyone must write exactly to length (though there has to be a little latitude in case anything really remarkable blows up), and, just as important, the copy has to be telephoned in instalments to a close time schedule. Otherwise, with an average of 22 columns of sport a day and in the height of the summer as many as 29, the stories could not possibly be sub-edited, set, and corrected in time to catch the various editions. I suppose that Kingsley Wright, in terms of the amount of space for which he is responsible, has one of the busiest jobs in Fleet Street. Yet despite all the hustle, and the hands through which it passes, a month can go by without an error in one's copy – which is a high tribute to the Sports Editor, to his Deputy, Ted Radford Barrett, to his Assistant, Roy Standring, and everyone else concerned.

One evening at Lord's not long before he died, I ran into Plum Warner around ten minutes to seven after the day's play in a Test Match, and he said : 'Well, Jim, just off to write your piece?' He was astonished when I told him it was all written, and my secretary should have finished the telephoning in a few minutes. He said, 'You know, the Editor of the *Morning*

47

Post, Gwynne, used to drop me at the Conservative Club after a day's cricket and say, "Now, Plum, treat yourself to a glass of port after dinner, settle down and give us your thoughts, and I'll send a messenger for them at half past ten." '

Perhaps half past ten would have been a little late for Coles, but the story illustrates well enough the difference between the old sporting journalism and the new. But back now to the old.

The provinces had their stalwarts in the games-writing line no less than London. One particularly comes back to me, A. W. Pullin by name, a thick, bearded fellow who for forty years wrote about cricket and rugby football for the *Yorkshire Post* and the *Yorkshire Evening Post*. It was said of him that he ripped off two columns a day in the summer and a mere column in the winter. He was very close to Lord Hawke, whose captaincy of Yorkshire coincided with the first half of Old Ebor's sporting life – that was his sobriquet – and I suppose that the tradition of friendship and co-operation between the Yorkshire cricket writers and their successive county captains dates back to the 'nineties when they first became associated. Two stories emerge through the mists about Old Ebor.

Once upon a time, in the heyday of Holmes and Sutcliffe, he betrayed his principles by arriving late to notice that Yorkshire were batting, and the score was going nicely with no wickets down. Promptly he got to work, regaling his evening paper readers with some good colourful stuff about yet another fruitful association by the old firm, who following their recent fine form were once more despatching the leather, etcetera, etcetera. Whether his running story, sent in those days by wire via post office messenger, had got as far as another 'three-figure collaboration' – or words to that effect – history does not record. At all events he was pulled up very sharp by a wire from his editor saying the agency score gave Holmes's partner as Leyland, and what about it.

It was true. A strain or some other cause had kept Herbert Sutcliffe out of action and so the *left-handed* Leyland had been sent in instead. Poor Pullin hadn't noticed, and as he was built on somewhat pontifical lines I'll bet the rest of the press-box enjoyed the joke. Was he reduced, I wonder, to the conventional cover-up : *it subsequently transpired that* owing to a strain – and so on. But Maurice was a left-hander. Oh, dear !

The other press-box story, I fear, ends with Old Ebor being thwarted too. When early patrons arrived at Lord's on the Monday of the 1926 Lord's Test against Australia they found a great disturbance going on in the middle because there was a large wet patch on the wicket. It was not sabotage, as it turned out, but either a leaky hose-pipe or a careless groundsman or both. Anyway the game was delayed a bit, and here was quite an evening paper story.

Pullin, as was his habit, arrived very early this time, ascertained the facts, wrote his piece, despatched it via the post office messenger, and sat back complacently to enjoy his scoop while his rivals arriving one by one hurried to try and catch their editions. His composure was interrupted at length by a messenger with a wire in his hand calling his name. ' 'Ere,' said the lad, 'the postmistress says you must have this back. She can't read a word of it.'

Well, well. But Old Ebor was a faithful old war-horse, and his *Talks with Old English Cricketers* will keep a place on my shelves when much modern stuff has to give way. It was his revelations about the straits of poverty to which some of these heroes of the past were reduced that first roused the conscience of the public and the county committees, Yorkshire's not least.

All copy, of course, in those days was handwritten, and the old fellows would have looked very askance indeed at a typewriter. Indeed I remember that they took it extremely amiss when P. G. H. Fender arrived armed with one at a Test at Old Trafford in the 'thirties. I think his was the first typewriter to appear in a cricket press-box – and he was promptly relegated to the Annexe!

I am reminded by this that I myself introduced one at Twickenham around the same time – perhaps I got the idea from P.G.H. Anyway the University Match with its early kick-off on a Tuesday in December was in the 'thirties considered right for large coverage, and I had *carte blanche*. I therefore took to the Twickenham box a colleague with a noiseless machine and simply dictated *sotto voce* from start to finish. A boy was kept running to and from the telephone putting over the copy, and the result was not a column or even two but one whole *Evening Standard* page : I suppose well over two thousand words, all dictated and delivered within a minute or two of the final whistle. Looking back it strikes me as rather a good effort. Such, by the way, was the space given to amateur sport in those leisured days, such the public interest built up in heroes like Cliff Jones, Wilfred Wooller, Peter Cranmer and other famous blues, both dark and light.

The games-writer of my early days saw a good deal less of the players than their counterparts today, and there was a well-respected convention that forbade the invasion of dressing-rooms. If they were independent of the players they had a strong sense of fellowship among themselves. They had, too, an evident affection for the games they wrote about. And they were uniformly helpful to someone more than ten years younger than the most junior of them.

If these men influenced my formative years, so in a broader way did that remarkable coterie which used to forgather around J. C. Squire, the poet and literary critic, at the Temple Bar Restaurant, opposite the Law Courts and next door to the offices of the *London Mercury*, of which he was the eccentric and benevolent editor. The *Mercury* made no money and took up much of Jack's time, and it was said that he kept it on chiefly out of charity towards the various young writers for whose work it provided an outlet.

Jack Squire was an endearing person, untidy to a degree, unpunctual, intensely gregarious, with a brilliant mind which a permanently harassed secretary did her best to bring to bear on the urgent matters of the moment: the weekly *Observer* article, for instance, the regular book review in the *Illustrated London News*, which he contributed almost until his death; articles and verses that editors were clamouring for. Jack once described himself as 'a social centipede with a foot in a hundred worlds'. One of these worlds revolved around Temple Bar, and Jack was good enough to admit me, not of course out of interest in my modest sporting journalism but because he was devoted to cricket and rugger, and giving a welcome to the young, especially if they were interested in games, was second nature to him. His cricket club, The Invalids, has been immortalized by A. G. Macdonell in his cricket match chapter in *England, Their England*, and I am glad to have helped a little in perpetuating that extraordinary company by getting Alec Waugh (Macdonell's Bobby Southcott, who played such an eccentric innings) to contribute a reminiscent essay on the club to *The World of Cricket*. I was a member, and never, if I could help it, missed one of *The Cheshire Cheese* suppers, though I don't remember possessing the tie of orange and hospital blue. And though I had to work on Saturdays, and never to my eternal regret had the experience of playing under the captaincy of 'Mr Hodge', I did represent The Invalids, of all unlikely things, at soccer.

This was a more modest follow-up on New Year's Day 1930 of the cricket match promoted by Jack on New Year's Day 1929, on Broadhalfpenny Down. The sun had shone, many pictures had been taken, and all had gone too unbelievably well for a repeat to be risked. In our football match we had Squire, himself, so short-sighted without his spectacles that he had much difficulty in locating the ball, and two of his sons, and Archie Macdonell, and Alec Waugh, and A. D. Peters, the literary agent, and two really high-class footballers, Kenneth Lindsay, a Corinthian and an Oxford blue (and later a member of Attlee's first Labour Government), and J. B. Priestley. On the way from the station in the taxi the captain told Priestley: 'Jack, you'd better play left back.' When the great man surprisingly demurred and said on the contrary he would play right back it turned out that in his youth Burnley had angled for his services – apparently in vain. At the age of thirty-five Priestley showed glimpses of the old skill, but Swanton in goal was all too fallible, and thanks to him Jack's village won a narrow victory.

That was a notable day, but what would I have given to undergo Jack's cricket captaincy at first-hand. Like many highly intelligent people with a love of cricket he had little understanding of the game: which, of course, did not prevent him theorizing about it. Waugh illustrates this beyond argument:

Once against a good side, on a good wicket, in a half-day game, he opened his attack with his second and third change bowlers. At tea, with the score 165 for two, he explained his plan: 'I thought I'd get two or three quick wickets, then loose my good bowlers, when they were fresh, against the tail.' It was contended sometimes that the strategy of his captaincy consisted in the creation of situations when he would be justified in putting himself on to bowl. But I think that he believed in his own bowling. And he did, indeed, quite often get a good batsman out, caught off a careless mishit after three sixes in a row or yorked on the second bounce. But he did not take himself off when he had broken a partnership.

My last memory of Jack is of him hollering away on the touch-line for Blundell's at one of the annual Cranleigh-Blundell's matches in London at the start of the Christmas holidays. It must have been early in the 'fifties and he had by now been knighted 'for services to literature'. Heavily bearded, and even more dishevelled than of yore, he looked a highly improbable recipient of the accolade. Some of those many worlds of his had clearly seen the last of him. But the same warmth was there, and the recollection of old friends. One of these, by the way, has escaped mention so far, namely

J. B. Morton, who was, indeed still is, Beachcomber of the *Express*. After lunching at the Temple Bar Johnny Morton's habit was to buy a big stock of newspapers and magazines from the stall at the top of Middle Temple Lane, walk down to his office, and dash off several of the daily columns at one go. Thus apparently he culled his ideas. So derived the immortal exploits of Captain Foulenough and those unusual Doctors, Strabismus and Smart-Alick. One afternoon following a lively session I bowled some sort of improvised ball at Johnny, who was guarding with a walking-stick the lamp-post at the junction of Fleet Street and Chancery Lane. When the policeman on point duty strode solemnly over to move us on Johnny said: 'What's the matter, officer, isn't my bat straight?'

The paper that seemed most receptive to my efforts was the *Evening Standard*, whose sports editor I persuaded to take regular columns on public school games and club cricket. A well-known character, A. Podmore, then had a monopoly of school news, which, as I remember, used to be collected by post and telephone by an ancient underling while 'Poddy', his complexion matching the cerise of the Old Haileyburian tie that he habitually wore, presided at the bar of Anderton's Hotel. I had the presumption to move in on the preserves of this, to me, rather formidable figure. Diary paragraphs were another regular source of revenue. When my *Standard* free-lance earnings reached somewhere around a tenner a week I wrote to them intimating with the brashness of youth that for a mere £13 they could command my valuable services full-time.

In a letter I still possess, Stanley Tiquet, a delightful man who aspired to absolutely no knowledge of sport, welcomed the proposal, though regretting the maximum remuneration I could expect was £11. So I bade a regretful farewell to all the pretty girls at the Amalgamated Press who ran the women's papers that were now prospering so hugely, and on 1 September 1927, took up my new job in Shoe Lane.

Five hundred and seventy-two pounds a year, by the way, was a fair salary for a young man living at home forty-odd years ago. I accordingly wasted no time in buying my first car for £120, a rather dashing royal blue AC. Before my twenty-first birthday then I was in a modest way 'launched', doing what I wanted to do, and with quite as much in my pocket as was good for me.

4

Enter the Don

The middle 'twenties was one of the less eventful periods of modern cricket history. In England the glamour of the Golden Age was just a nostalgic memory behind the present reality of Australian dominance. County cricket flourished quietly, and the traditional Lord's fixtures pursued their way almost unaffected by Test distractions. Between 1921 and 1926 the only visitors of Test status were the 1924 South Africans, and the only MCC tour to make anything of a stir was that to Australia in the winter of 1924/5. The uninterrupted annual cycle of Test visits to England did not begin until the West Indies tried their hands for the first time against our full strength in 1928. From that year to this, war-time excepted, no English summer has gone by without its quota of Test Matches. The middle 'twenties was the lull before the storm – and I forbear here to venture a view as to what was being gained by the flight from domesticity and what lost.

In June 1924, Arthur Gilligan and Maurice Tate bowled out South Africa at Birmingham for 30, the former taking six for 7. As captain-presumptive in Australia the following winter Gilligan had started with a bang, and all seemed agreed that at this time he was truly, authentically fast. In addition he was a dangerous tail-end hitter and a magnificent fielder at mid-off. His leadership of Sussex had everyone enthused, and in short he seemed the ideal man to restore England's fallen fortune. But in the Oval version of Gents *v.* Players some weeks later Arthur took such a severe blow over the heart that he was advised never to try to bowl fast again.

Needless to say he did try, but nature would not respond, and he was never the same bowler, or indeed the same cricketer. I recall this all-but-forgotten item as an illustration of how a chance accident can alter the shape of history. England under his leadership did win a Test Match against Australia that winter, and lost another only by 11 runs, but the Ashes stayed where they were. If Gilligan, in his early 1924 form, could have given due support to the magnificent

Tate, the tables might well have been turned.

An odd scrap of mild scandal comes back to me from that Birmingham Test of 1924. In their second innings South Africa, though beaten by an innings, made 390, and on the following Sunday Cecil Parkin, that rumbustious Lancastrian, wrote in the *Weekly Dispatch* that as they were piling up the runs he spent his time running about the outfield wondering how on earth he had got to the top of the English bowling averages. The score-book shows that Parkin's second innings analysis was nought for 38 in 16 overs, Tate and Gilligan again sharing the wickets. But the point is that here was another Test player making critical comment about a match in which he had been engaged. The MCC resolution of 1921 had not yet apparently been translated into a rule. But it may not be without significance that this was the last of Parkin's ten appearances for England.

My own first-hand memory of big cricket between 1921 and 1926 is an utter blank, but, praise be, I did sneak away from the Amalgamated Press to see snatches of the great Oval Test wherein the Ashes returned at last. On the third afternoon I arrived soon after lunch with the great drama on the bad wicket already enacted. The game, as it turned out, had been lost and won by the masterful batting of Hobbs and Sutcliffe on that Tuesday morning, and I only got there in time to see Gregory just tickle Hobbs's off-bail, the hero, then at the pinnacle of his fame, returning in triumph with the board reading 172–1–100.

Sutcliffe however was only mid-way through his marathon, and one sees him there in his finest hour, dark hair smooth and gleaming, crossing his legs and leaning on his bat when at the bowler's end with that air of imperturbable confidence that was peculiarly his own : immaculate, tireless and serene. The pitch had shed its worst, but Mailey, with his humming spin, was turning a lot. When he beat the bat on the forward-stroke, which was not infrequently, Herbert somehow managed to convey that this was an immaterial incident, due to a lingering spite in the pitch. He calmly inspected and prodded before taking guard once more. In the very last over a perfectly-pitched googly at last hit the stumps, and he was out for 161. By that time England were 375 for six, 353 runs on, and the top was off the wicket. Australia's situation was utterly hopeless, yet such was the awe in which they were held that we wondered still whether those runs were enough.

What a bastion was Sutcliffe for England – and how infuriating an opponent, utterly blind and deaf to any hint of personal fallibility. Peter Eckersley used to tell a story of him which has the merits of being both authentic and completely in character.

Once in a Roses' match Herbert was struggling hard and after a long time was still not off the mark. At last, playing the ball to cover's left hand, he called for a single. But either his judgment had slipped for once or he hadn't noticed that cover-point was a left-handed thrower, Eddie Paynter no less. The latter was in like a flash, hurling at the bowler's stumps and missing by an inch or two with the great man still yards from home.

The ball went for four overthrows, and while it was being retrieved Peter relieved his feelings.

'Herbert, you have the luck of the devil.'

No answer.

'You old so-and-so – you ought to have been out by ten yards.'

No answer.

Peter, determined to be heard, ejaculates something scathing a third time, whereat Herbert deigns to acknowledge his presence.

'I'm very sorry, Mr Eckersley, but I haven't the least idea what you're talking about.'

That's perfect Sutcliffe. The whole trifling incident was dismissed from his mind. His score was now 5, and the only thing that mattered was the next ball. And note the respect – as if to say gently 'You keep your side of the fence, and I'll keep mine.' In the language of his less refined fellow-Yorkshiremen, 'Get on with tha laiking.'

Again next day I rushed down to Kennington, just in time for the final scenes, the Australian collapse, the happy Test exit of Wilfred Rhodes, coming up to his 49th birthday, and the last joyful gathering round the pavilion as the youthful Chapman led his team in. One spectator at least made the most of it – which was just as well since twenty-seven years were to pass before he saw the Ashes similarly regained and the picture repeated.

A noble company it was that did the job: in batting order, J. B. Hobbs, H. Sutcliffe, F. E. Woolley, E. Hendren, A. P. F. Chapman, G. T. S. Stevens, W. Rhodes, G. Geary, M. W. Tate, H. Larwood, H. Strudwick. No second-classers in that lot!

I began reporting cricket for the *Standard* in 1928, as second string to J. A. H. Catton, and it may surprise younger readers to know that the one match I clearly recall in that year is the Eton and Harrow. Lord's in those days almost burst at the seams for this game that was so unlike any other. *Wisden* gives the paying gate for the two days in this particular year, for instance, at over 34,000. With members the company would have been around forty thousand. And for the ambulatory portion thereof, which went partly to see friends and be seen by them, and therefore paraded the perimeter, calling at the tents and arbours that covered the practice ground, or the coaches that lined the Tavern boundary, or the boxes above, the number must have seemed rather greater. Despite ropes and Keep Left signs it could take the best part of half-an-hour to circumnavigate the main ground. The throng on the field itself at the intervals, like a gently-stirring sea of confetti, was a sight to remember. Practically every man and boy was in morning dress, every woman and girl in the height of fashion. To the stranger looking in from outside, as it were, the atmosphere was that of a mammoth family party.

There was, and still is, however, one popular misconception about the Eton and Harrow Match – which is that no one either knows or cares about what is happening in the middle. If that is true of some, the majority mind very much indeed. No game in the calendar in fact aroused deeper, fiercer emotions – or, among a more restricted company, still does.

For the cricketers, naturally, it was a setting to inspire or to quell according to temperament. In 1928 there was one young man it brought the very best out of, Ian Akers-Douglas, who made 158 of the finest and most attractive runs surely ever seen from a schoolboy's bat. Ian's style was based on the eye and wrist of the rackets player, and though he afterwards made quite a few runs for Kent he never schooled himself to the right degree of restraint for consistent success against first-class bowling. But the brilliance of his play for Eton that sunny day in the whole gay pulsating context is fresh in the mind still.

It is time, though, to leave the glamour of Lord's on the occasion of its oldest fixture for sterner fields. I have called this chapter 'Enter the Don' because the arrival of Bradman was the most significant cricket event of my early days as a journalist, and indeed his first tour of England coincided with my promotion to the ranks of Test reporters. In the winter of 1928/9 Bradman made his bow for Australia in the first Test against England at Brisbane. Though his beginning was no more propitious than that of his side (and he was actually dropped for one match), by the end of the series he was established in company with Archie Jackson as a white hope of Australian cricket.

Of these two, Jackson, the stylist, was the hot tip; but it did not take Don Bradman long to change the rating. By the end of the first week of the tour I had seen him tot up 421 runs for once out: 236 at Worcester, followed by 185 not out on the old Aylestone Road ground at Leicester. Rather ill-luck he had at Leicester, for rain cut short the prospect of another double hundred when it was there for the taking.

Twice more at least in that month of May rain interrupted the Don's progress when his hungry eye was on the chase, the first in circumstances which give a revealing glimpse of his mentality as a young man. Percy Fender had been covering the MCC tour of Australia a couple of winters before, and was now combining the captaincy of Surrey with a good deal of cricket-writing in the *Evening News*. When it came to assessing the Australian prospects, that shrewdest of critics published his view that D.G.B. might be too unorthodox in his method to be a great success on English wickets: what served in his home conditions would not necessarily do here.

Unfortunately for Surrey this dictum had not escaped the little man's attention. He was about as quick in detecting a critical press comment of this kind as he was in spotting the googly – and just about as ruthless in dealing with it. So the Australians came to the Oval, and Don advanced to the wicket with a special glint in his eye. By 6.25 on the first day the score was 379 for five, and he was still enjoying himself with 252 against his name. He had been batting for just under five hours and Fender's analysis read – 21–1–75–2. It was at this point that the rain came, to his great chagrin for, as he says, 'Percy George was just getting his length and I was just getting my eye in.' He would assuredly have taken fresh guard on the Monday, but, alas, there was no further play in the match.

I mention the other rainy occasion in May 1930 because it had a sequel. Don was batting against Hampshire at Southampton on the 31st of the month, and in search of the 'Thousand in May' (or, to be quite accurate, by the end of May, for some of them have had innings in April), which to this day has been reached by only six men. When it began to rain as he approached the target, Lionel Tennyson good-naturedly kept his side in the field, so that he and they all got a wetting, until it was reached.

Years after, Bradman being now captain, Lionel during a Lord's Test Match went up to the Australian dressing-room and sent in his name. The reply came back that Mr Bradman was engaged and was sorry he could not see Lord Tennyson for the moment. There the matter would have ended, with Don probably making a later effort to seek out his caller, had not an Australian columnist heard of the incident and cabled back to Sydney a story of how Bradman had insulted an old England captain. Note it was an Australian journalist, and not a cricket-writer. The thing was promptly cabled back to London, and so made quite a stir in both countries. The matter of the generous gesture at Southampton was recalled. On the face of it Don had been impolite, or at best heedless to an older man of distinction to whom he owed some obligation.

The truth behind the facts, not hitherto told, is this. Lionel, having lunched far too well, went first to the England room and spent some time there. Don knew this, was apprised of his state of health, and decided he did not want his team to meet the great man in these particular circumstances. With one eye on the field and one ear cocked towards another visitor who was present, he sent his message.

Can one blame him? This was a Test Match, with all its attendant tensions, and there has always been a strict code (besides notices and doorkeepers) protecting the privacy of the dressing-room, which, normally, Lionel Tennyson would have respected as well as anyone else. But, of course, Bradman was very widely blamed on the facts as they were printed, and the really galling thing from his point of view was that, when interviewed, he could not give the valid explanation.

There is an ethical aspect to the affair. It is beyond question that the journalist in question did Bradman an injury. But did he write his story knowing the full facts or only the bare details within the dressing-room? As a member of his profession I prefer to believe he did not know all.

One might analyse the story a little further. Bradman does not expand readily, and since his first headlong rush to fame has been generally wary of the press, until individual writers gain his confidence, when they find him extremely helpful and considerate. Apart from his own performance on the field, he has accordingly suffered, from time to time, criticism to which a more extrovert nature might not have been subject – for instance Lionel Tennyson, hail-fellow-well-met with everyone and a universally popular cricketer. He was, incidentally, as Bradman is, a good friend to me, and I am sure that none of those who knew him will think the worse of him for my having told this story whole and in perspective. He is not the first old Test captain to have fallen victim to the hospitality of his friends on a cricket occasion, nor will he be the last.

This story has been included both out of belated justice to Sir Donald Bradman and also as an illustration of what mischief can be done by the publication of a certain sort of story. It is often loosely said of some paper, by the sort of person who aims for a cheap laugh by denigrating 'the press', that it is only interested in scandal and dressing-room gossip. Generally a close examination will show this to be a half-truth at best, and when such stuff if given prominence it is hardly ever the work of the cricket-writer.

Those who cover big cricket, and especially the cricket correspondents travelling with teams abroad, see and know about plenty of incidents that might be blown up into lively off-field stories. But they very rarely write them, recognizing that so long as he does not commit a public scandal the player is entitled to some private life, even on an international tour. Cricket's repute has certainly suffered since the war from lurid off-the-field disclosures, but this seamy type of journalism has been rather pathetic 'ghosted' stuff, appearing under the names of a few famous players who have been tempted by four-figure sums to reveal all.

Back now to the Don's triumphal progress in 1930. I was subbing in the office when the first Test was played at Trent Bridge – it is the first and last time I have missed a Test Match through being at the office end. Anyway his share of a fine game won by England was 8 and 131. The Lord's Test I did see and report in a secondary manner: the first Test I ever wrote about and in several respects the best.

There was a press annexe in those days at ground level among the public seats under the Grand Stand balcony, and from this angle (between cover-point and extra) I watched and enthused, suffered and hoped, as Australia crushed the English bowling, but not the spirit of the English batsmen whose second innings effort came near to saving this wonderful game. I can readily summon the sights and scenes of those four days in the sun: the peerless stroke past cover-point with which Woolley despatched his first ball for four; Tim Wall's catch right down on his boots, standing nominally in the gully but actually half-way to third man, that brought Frank's marvellous 41 to an unlucky close; 'Duleep' cutting and glancing on that first day; the little old King, with grey bowler, big button-hole, and high walking-stick, shaking hands with the players in front of the pavilion; Hammond pouching a slip catch off the very

59

first ball afterwards; the Don's unhurried entry into the sunlight; his swift advance down the wicket to hit the next one, from White, full pitch up to the Nursery Clock-tower; the board at close of play showing Australia 404 for two, last man (Woodfull) 155, number 3 155 not out; Bradman's further relentless plunder on the Monday; the wry joke of an improvised '7' having to be found for the Tavern scoreboard before the declaration at 729 for six; Hobbs being bowled out of the rough round his legs by Grimmett; Woolley smacking him for four, only to find that he had brushed the stumps with the back of his pad; Chapman apparently 'farming' Grimmett during his partnership with Allen and carting him lustily every so often into the Mound Stand; the excitement when Robins's spin on the dusty fourth afternoon for about half-an-hour raised feverish expectations; the splendour of the Maharajah Jam Sahib of Nawanagar, otherwise 'Ranji', in full Eastern dress, jewels flashing from his tunic and turban, holding a sort of levée behind the pavilion.

This, by the way, was the reputed occasion that prompted the immortal Maurice Tate to mutter, hand over mouth in his own unique, confidential way: ''Cor, see Ranji – looks a veritable 'Indoo, don't 'e?' An incontrovertible comment if ever there was one.

I must beware, by the way, of becoming enmeshed in detail of past matches or this book will run to an unconscionable length. If a reader wants to know more, the assumption must be that he has *Wisden* within reach. So, though with regret, let us leave Lord's for Leeds and that phenomenal first day. Or rather, for the eve thereof. Scene: the crowded Queen's Hotel lounge. From the other side of it, M. Tate espies me, signals, and those vast feet bring him clumping over. The young reporter is flattered at such recognition. Thinks: 'scoop perhaps?' Maurice puts hand to mouth while many watch and unburdens himself of the following confidence: 'We must beat these beggars this time.' I suppose I nod knowingly, feeling I am now really in on the tactics of the game. There was never a readier conversationalist than Maurice.

Twenty-four hours later, this time in the foyer, I come in in the company of Vic Richardson and young Stan McCabe. We have shared a taxi back from the ground, and on the way they have been saying, 'Well, we ought to be good for a drink from the little fellow tonight!' But now here is the Don saying to the girl behind the desk: 'I'm going up to my room. Will you please send me a pot of tea?'

Meaning glances pass between the other Australians, as 'the little fellow', heedless of any atmosphere, makes for the lift. In 1930 he was withdrawn, shy of the vast publicity that followed him, teetotal. Besides, by the Third Test Don and an Australian journalist were already composing his life-story – and that could be done only in the evenings. He was a man pursuing a goal with single-minded dedication. The idea of a relaxed drink with some of the team would, in 1930, hardly have occurred to him.

Did Don dictate another chapter of his book that evening at Leeds? I would not put it outside the scope of his energy – but consider how he had spent the day. He came in to bat in the second over of the morning and by lunch he had made 105. In the afternoon he added a further 115, and at close of play, against an English attack consisting of Tate, Larwood, Geary, Tyldesley (R), Hammond and Leyland, he returned, unbeaten still and seemingly as fresh as he had started, his share 309 of Australia's 458 for three. So toppled the Anglo-Australian record of 'Tip' Foster made at Sydney in 1903/4. His brilliant 287 had been scored in seven hours, that is to say at a rate of 40 an hour. Yet here was Bradman making upwards of 50 an hour off his own bat, for hour after hour, all along the ground, with scarcely a hint of risk and no more false strokes than could be counted on the fingers of one hand. (In fact, in contrast with his 254 at Lord's, which was chanceless, he here offered three very difficult catches, the first when he had made 141.) After a further hour next morning he was out for 334.

When the Headingley field is close-cropped and shiny, runs come there more quickly than in most places, for the Test pitch seems to be the highest point of a very shallow upturned bowl. The ball flows off the bat from whatever angle just slightly downhill. I can see fat Dick Tyldesley now at mid-off, narrowly failing to cut off a firm defensive stroke, turning and chasing the ball which rolls tantalizingly a few yards ahead of him, neither gaining on the other until the ball hits the rope a second or so in front.

It was after his Headingley experience that someone made bold to ask this sturdy son of the Lancashire soil his opinion of Bradman. He took the matter personally and is said to have tersely replied 'he's no damned good to me.'

Don was not much good to any English bowler in that triumphal summer of 1930, though it was in Lancashire that I did see him twice toppled cheaply, once by an expatriate

Australian, once by a Scot. At Aigburth early in the tour Ted McDonald, sinuous and sinister, knocked his stumps all awry. The next occasion was of much greater moment, the Fourth Test at Old Trafford, England having been saved by rain in the Third.

To the England team at Old Trafford came Ian Peebles, aged 22, an Oxford undergraduate who had made a highly unusual entry into big cricket, having been drafted into the 1927/8 MCC side to South Africa on the strength of one first-class match (Gents and Players at the Oval) and the fervent recommendation of 'Plum' Warner. When the Australians had come to Oxford in May Don, then in full cry for his thousand runs, had not enjoyed a prolonged look at this promising exponent of leg-spin and googly, having been bowled by a near-shooter by H. M. Garland-Wells for 32.

Now Ian, in his first Test in England, faced the run-machine with one important psychological advantage. At Manchester, strange to say, it had rained. The wicket, as all agreed, was in no way spiteful. It was, however, a slow turner, and the Don had made all his 728 Test runs so far in the dry. His first ball from Peebles, a perfectly-pitched leg-break, nearly bowled him. He struggled to 10, whereupon Hammond, of all people, missed him at slip. Then he edged another leg-break and this time there was no mistake: it was c Duleepsinhji b Peebles 14. The weather easily won this Fourth Test, but at least, if only temporarily, the spell of Bradman's invincibility was broken.

Two brief little cameos survive the passage of forty years. In the Old Trafford Long Room during a break for rain a rather bowed figure with an unrolled umbrella was inspecting the team groups on the walls, and he was pointed out to me as A. C. M. Croome, a cricket correspondent of *The Times*. I did not meet him, and there came no other chance, for he was a sick man reporting his last match. Before the end of the season he was dead.

Of all the pioneer figures in games-reporting, Croome and Sydney Pardon were, I think, the only ones I never knew – though from the latter I had at least a paternal handshake. 'Crumbo', curiously even for those less pressured days, combined the functions of cricket correspondent of *The Times* and golf correspondent of the *Morning Post*, having previously been a schoolmaster at Radley. He was one of the founders of the Oxford and Cambridge Golfing Society with my wife's father, R. H. de Montmorency, the famous 'Monty'. He had played a bit for Gloucestershire with W.G., and is reported to have been a repository of stories about the Old Man, including this one.

W.G. said to a young player, 'Remember we're playing against George Hirst tomorrow. Be sure to bring a box.' The abdominal protector, as it was termed with more refinement than accuracy, was not generally worn in the 'nineties. Nevertheless, the young man dutifully repaired into Bristol, and endeavoured to describe to a blushing lady in a sports shop what he was looking for.

Masculine assistance was forthcoming, and he eventually purchased a cumbersome metal contraption which he was assured was the latest thing. Came the Yorkshiremen, and in due course the young man found himself facing Hirst's fastish left-arm in-swervers with his captain at the other end. After a ball or two a resonant pinging sound announced that, both literally and metaphorically, Hirst had rung the bell.

A couple more pings, and W.G. squeaked down the wicket: 'I said a box, you know, not a musical box.'

When the game at Old Trafford restarted it came to Peebles's turn to bat, and as he strode smartly through the room a clergyman, also with a gamp, just reached him in time to say good luck. This one I did grow to know, for it was Ian's father, come south from the manse at Elgin for the occasion, and his son was to become my closest friend and ultimately best man.

Ian was at his best in 1930, before persistent muscular trouble in his right shoulder took the zip out of his leg-break. He had a beautifully smooth, rhythmical run-up and high delivery, great power of spin, and that perceptible dip at the end of the flight that made it difficult to judge the length. The best batsmen thought they were 'there', and found to their cost that they weren't. He had come south when only seventeen to learn the art of bowling from Aubrey Faulkner, of whose School of Cricket he acted as secretary. Faulkner kept Ian so hard at it that he taught himself to bowl left-handed to ease the strain on his right shoulder. He could wheel down practically anything, and I once took a slip catch off him bowling left-arm at a brisk medium-pace, in the second innings, after a one-day game had finished early. To this extent, I suppose, he was an even more versatile bowler than Gary Sobers.

Don Bradman set the seal on a prodigious season in the Fifth Test at the Oval where he made 232, and brought his tally for the rubber to 974, a number unapproached in a series either before or since. Yet having got this far his sights were set firmly on the thousand. Suddenly he was given out caught

behind off Larwood, it is said on a lone appeal from mid-on.
Don was not amused. The story went that the umpire concerned explained that he thought on reflection he had made a
mistake in his favour a hundred runs or so earlier, but that
was no doubt someone's flight of fancy. At all events Larwood
and Tate bowled 113 overs between them for this wicket and
that of the number 11, Percy Hornibrook. Peebles had one
of the more extraordinary analyses in Test cricket:

O	M	R	W
71	8	204	6

Perhaps I should pause a moment here to attempt some brief
evaluation of Don Bradman's astonishing achievements in 1930,
and this can surely best be done by answering the questions:
What was the bowling standard against him, and how did his
record compare with others? As to the first, well, England
could call on the identical attack (all of them already mentioned) which had retained the Ashes 4–1 the previous year in
Australia. In addition there were such prolific county wicket-
takers to choose from as Nichols, Goddard, Dick Tyldesley,
Voce, Robins, Peebles and Freeman. Neither the English bowling
nor their out-cricket generally could be described otherwise
than as of good Test quality. As to the second, Bradman for
seven completed innings averaged 139. The next figure in the
Australian list was Woodfull's 57. The wickets certainly were
for the most part good and easy-paced; yet no one else on
either side achieved anything remotely approaching Bradman's
devastation.

Old Trafford apart – and perhaps excepting, too, one dangerous spell after rain by Larwood at the Oval – Bradman batted
his way through the series with an easy dominance to which
I have experienced no parallel. The stranger seeing him for the
first time must have noticed the exceptional quickness of his
reactions, his speed between the wickets and the lithe fitness
that enabled him to take the longest innings in his stride.
He was smallboned, dapper, his power of stroke deriving from
strong wrists and an exquisite sense of timing. To give a
physical example from the present generation is not easy.
He was about the height of John Edrich, but lacking his chunki-
ness; a shade bigger all round than the Nawab of Pataudi.
Perhaps Doug Walters comes nearest to him in build and
height.

You saw all the strokes, the off-drive less frequently than the others. The precision and the variety of his cutting specially struck one. He was a most delicate glancer, and adept at playing the ball off his body at all the on-side angles. When he hooked he got into position so quickly that he could hit the ball early with a downward thrust of the bat aiming in front of square-leg. A stylist? Not indeed in terms of such contemporaries as Walter Hammond, 'Duleep', or McCabe. The bat was more of a sabre than a pendulum. But if perfect balance, co-ordination and certainty of execution be accepted as the principal ingredients of batsmanship, we who watched the Don in his early manhood will not hope or expect ever to see its art displayed in a higher form.

England lost the Fifth Test by an innings and the Ashes duly returned to Australia. Bradman had set fresh standards and opened up new horizons. But at the Oval another thing had happened which was more significant in the long run than the winning and losing of the series. During a long stand for the fourth wicket between Bradman and Jackson it rained, and when play was resumed Larwood made the ball fly.

The contrast between the play of these two young batsmen at this point is vividly clear still in my mind. While Jackson stood his ground and offered defensive strokes of classical straightness, Don exceeded even his own normal great speed of foot, improvising brilliantly and keeping his body well clear, one side or the other, of the rising ball. Whether or not he was happy that afternoon against Larwood's speed, with the short ball flying shoulder high and more, he did not look as though he was. In one or two minds the suspicion registered, and with it the thought that here might be a way of cutting the phenomenon down to size. The accident of the rain falling when it did, of Bradman happening to be batting – though the odds about that were pretty short, to be sure – and of Larwood being on hand to exploit a pitch that was soft on top and hard underneath: the combination of these circumstances sparked an idea that in due course led to the scourge that became known as 'Bodyline'. Though no one can have recognized it at the time, this Oval scene of 1930 marked the end of an era so far as Test cricket was concerned.

For myself on the other hand it was the start of a life-time of watching the world's best – of doing what I so greatly wanted to do, and of being paid for the pleasure.

5

The Bodyline Explosion

The English seasons of 1931 and 1932 seem, retrospectively, of a wonderful serenity in my eyes. There were Test Matches of a relatively unexacting kind, and the summer's cricket otherwise followed its orderly procession, from the MCC's opening games against Yorkshire and Surrey, past the time-honoured landmarks (the chief county matches had fixed dates, known and looked forward to year after year), the Lord's Week, comprising the University Match and the Eton and Harrow, and on finally to the Scarborough Festival and the game between the Champion County and the Rest of England at the Oval. With all the foremost players engaged on one side or the other, this occasion made an appropriate, nostalgic conclusion.

I in my middle-twenties was now the accepted cricket, as well as the Rugby football, correspondent of the *Evening Standard*, seeing and writing about the Tests – three in '31 against New Zealand, only one against All-India the following year – keeping a programme that took in most of the principal games in London and the south, and contriving to play myself, on Sundays, on every day of my summer holidays and generally whenever an odd game could be squeezed in. Ian Peebles and I had been infinitely lucky to find our set of rooms in the Temple, at 8 King's Bench Walk, which were sub-let by an elderly barrister of Dickensian appearance who had retired to the West Country. He used to write letters of hilarious formality and punctiliousness, and I fear we used to delay sending our monthly fifteen guineas for the pleasure of getting another missive beginning 'Dear Mr Swanton, In re the rental . . .' A truly angelic cook-housekeeper, Mrs Smallbone, still alive as I write, looked after us.

Ian was playing regularly for Middlesex – and likewise for England – and generally finding his way around town. The young journalist was installed within a stone's throw of Fleet Street. Altogether, winter and summer, one was very much in the sporting swim, and life was sweet indeed.

The cricket world, as I say, was very much at peace, enjoying indeed a tranquillity it has never known since. This, though, was the calm before the storm, and the storm was the biggest sporting row there has ever been – or, at least, that there was before the D'Oliveira affair, with all its repercussions, some of them still echoing on. Bodyline had its repercussions also, and it is a nice point which caused the bigger outcry. What bitter irony that the most pacific and courteous of games should have brought forth two such cataclysms!

There is a full, well-documented, definitive book that covers the whole momentous episode of Bodyline, from its hazy origins to its full translation into practice, and the dramatic consequences, written from first-hand by J. H. Fingleton. His *Cricket Crisis*, published in 1946 by Cassell, is a notably thorough and objective story, and as such, of course, a valuable contribution to cricket history. Several others in close proximity to the scene have published their impressions, including Hobbs, Bradman, Mailey, Freddie Brown, Bowes, Moyes, and, not least, 'Plum' Warner. And I must not forget Sydney Southerton's fair and forthright editorial analysis of 'The Bowling Controversy' in the 1934 *Wisden*. There is no lack of literature on the subject, with Jack Fingleton's account the fullest and best. The average young cricketer of today, however, may have no easy access to such sources. I hope therefore that the following reflections may have some interest and also perhaps some present value as showing how in the heat of international sporting conflict passions can cloud cool judgment, and blur the confines of fair play. The story has a moral and a lesson surely for the players and administrators of today.

The first signs of what came to be known as Bodyline bowling were to be observed, probably, around 1930 when two lusty young men of Notts, Harold Larwood and Bill Voce, were sometimes spurred on by their captain, A. W. Carr, to drop the ball short and make it fly round the ears of county batsmen. There was, for instance, the incident, recorded with much relish among cricketers at the time, of the Somerset batsman, C. C. C. Case, who, endeavouring to avoid a ball that rose head-high, simultaneously lost his grasp of the bat and trod back on to the wicket. Such was poor 'Box' Case's confusion that, according to *The Times*, he returned to the pavilion 'carrying one of the stumps instead of his bat'. With Carr's active encouragement the Notts fast bowling was inclined occasionally, shall I say, to become a little 'rough'.

As we have seen, 1930 was the year that the youthful Bradman first came, saw, and conquered, aiming at and achieving targets not hitherto considered, and in so doing destroying the English dominance of the later 'twenties. In the Oval Test of that year as I told in the previous chapter there came the episode of his unorthodox reaction to the flying ball. Mental notes were made, and the evidence stored up for future use.

MCC were due in Australia in the winter of 1932/3. Whoever had ambitions to lead that side must have seen his first and crucial problem as the containing of the batsman who had begun to set these new run-getting standards. Who were the candidates for the job? Well, there was A. P. F. Chapman, who had led England with such flair and success; but in that last Oval Test he had been superseded by R. E. S. Wyatt. There was Wyatt, then, and among other amateurs with Test experience there was also D. R. Jardine, who had had a successful tour of Australia in 1928-9 but had been little seen in first-class cricket since. When the selectors met in May 1931 to name England's captain against New Zealand, they had to acknowledge that Percy Chapman, only a year before literally and in every sense the blue-eyed boy, had just come home from an unfruitful tour of South Africa wherein he had altogether failed as a batsman.

There was Wyatt and there was Jardine, playing again now with some regularity for Surrey, and if they were not to go back to a much older man – for instance Fender or J. C. White, both forty or thereabouts and a little past their best – there was no one else of comparable qualifications. (The captain had, in those days, of course to be an amateur.) Wyatt was now captain of Warwickshire, whereas Jardine had had no experience of leadership since leaving Winchester twelve years before. The appointment however went to Jardine, and in view of the consequences it is important to note that it was made by the new selectorial triumvirate due to serve much together in the 'thirties – 'Plum' Warner, T. A. Higson, and P. Perrin. The decision of these three laid the fuse for the Bodyline explosion eighteen months later.

As was to be expected, Jardine sailed through the 1931 New Zealand series, and the following year at Lord's in the one Test accorded to India redeemed much otherwise paltry England batting by scoring 79 and 85 not out. His position was now secure, and to the public it seemed a mere formality when he was duly named as captain of the MCC team bound for Australia. Douglas Jardine was too aloof to commend himself in the same way as the gay, ever-boyish Chapman. He made no concession to popular sentiment: rather the reverse. The Harlequin cap he almost invariably wore seemed a conscious badge of superiority. Yet in the mind of the average follower a tough fighter was needed to play the Australians at their own game – and the new man was certainly that. To this extent at least the choice was widely approved.

It was only Jardine's contemporaries and those who had been closest to him who had doubts. The Oxford XI's of the early 'twenties had seldom broken through a certain sardonic reserve, and had accordingly never considered him as captain. The MCC team of 1928–9 had chiefly noted in him, beside his habitual fierce determination, a particular antipathy for the Australians. In pavilions and dressing-rooms the better-informed were asking one another what MCC had let themselves in for. Rockley Wilson, who as master in charge of cricket had come up against Jardine's inflexibility when he was captain of Winchester, delivered the prophetic verdict: 'Well, we shall win the Ashes – but we may lose a Dominion.'

In the summer of 1932 the Notts bowling had elicited a few more grumbles, as had that of Bill Bowes for Yorkshire. I recall watching him bowling at the end of August at Bournemouth in the match that won Yorkshire the Championship. He let go some fast bouncers at the Hampshire captain, Lord Tennyson, who (then aged 42) was manifestly not amused, and ostentatiously marched up the wicket and smacked at imaginary marks around half-way. A more significant protest had been made earlier in the month at the Oval when Yorkshire played Surrey, in a match I didn't see. Bowes bowled fast and short at Jack Hobbs, who protested both on the field and in print. As I have related earlier, so too, in emphatic terms, did 'Plum' Warner, who was actually combining the chairmanship of selectors with the cricket correspondentship of the *Morning Post*. Warner, who thus early declared his hand, was not only chairman of selectors but was to be manager of MCC in Australia. Hobbs was to travel, too, complete with 'ghost', as correspondent of the *Star*. One wonders whether Jardine, now captain of Surrey, speculated, during that Oval scene and its aftermath, on probable conflicts of view lying ahead.

Whatever premonitions anyone might have had, MCC sailed in September with four fast bowlers, Larwood, Voce, Bowes, and, to the surprise of the critics, G. O. Allen. As luck would have it they started well in their planned subjugation of Bradman by getting him twice on a wet wicket at Perth, once for 3 and then for 10. Bradman had made a royal progress by train from Sydney right across the continent. Fingleton, also on the trip to the west, says, 'No prince could have had a more regal entry into Perth. As the long and dusty eastern train jolted to a halt thousands crammed the station, the adjoining roofs and buildings, the exits and the streets outside. Police had to force a passage for Bradman, and the Palace Hotel, where we stayed, was in a constant simmer by day and night.' Such was the atmosphere surrounding Bradman in Australia; needless to underline the implications of success and failure – or, surely, to point to the danger to peace and harmony of employing against him tactics in any way suspect.

Jardine brought his fast bowlers gradually into top trim, and against the Australian XI at Melbourne in November Woodfull was hit by Larwood with a short, fast ball. Larwood here had three short legs and one back on the boundary for the hook. At Sydney Voce's leg-trap was increased to four or five, and a full-length press picture showed Fingleton with a dozen cricket balls indicating the places, from thigh to shoulder, where blows had struck.

Jack Fingleton says that the MCC bowling in this game took the majority of the New South Welshmen completely by surprise. By the First Test on the same ground the Australian team must have had more than an inkling of what lay ahead, and Warwick Armstrong, the day before the series opened, sent this in a cable to the London *Evening News*:

'As to England's attack I say frankly that I fear there will be trouble if the fast bowlers go for the body instead of the wicket . . . In Australia bowling at the batsman is generally considered unsportsmanlike.'

Well, Larwood and Voce in the First Test took ten and six wickets respectively, alternating between orthodox methods when the ball was new and the short, fast stuff to a strong leg-side cordon. Stan McCabe, showing the utmost courage and supreme hooking skill, played one of the great innings of history (187 not out in just over four hours), but England won by ten wickets, needing to score only one run in their second innings. It was a convincing win, but gained against a side from which Bradman had dropped out through illness.

From Jardine's point of view there was in that conclusive victory only one note of discord. Before the game he asked Allen, who had previously declined to bowl to the leg-side field, whether he would now do so. Allen again said no, and as a result of his refusal did not positively know he would be playing until shortly before the start. Gubby Allen, unlike most other protagonists in the affair, has never put his views on Bodyline in print. On the other hand he has always maintained in conversation his unequivocal objection to it. What is not perhaps generally known is that he jeopardized his Test place by his refusal to co-operate.

For the Second Test, as history records, England, with Bradman now due to oppose them, underlined their intentions by augmenting their fast bowling strength to four, bringing in Bowes and dropping Verity. I suppose that Larwood, Voce, Allen, Bowes and Hammond made up the worst balanced attack ever to take the field for England until Bedser, Statham, Tyson, Bailey and Edrich comprised the bowling against Australia at Brisbane in 1954. However, the Melbourne curator, whether by accident or design, produced an unnaturally slow pitch for the Second Test, the result being, of course, less resort to the short, fast stuff, and, incidentally, the best game of the series. (Australia won it by 111 runs.)

The scene moves to the fair city of Adelaide, where in the Third Test rancour reached its climax, and whence the sad exchange of cables was begun by the Board of Control's first unfortunate volley:

Bodyline bowling has assumed such proportions as to menace the best interests of the game, making protection of the body by the batsmen the main consideration. This is causing intensely bitter feeling between the players as well as injury. In our opinion it is unsportsmanlike. Unless stopped at once it is likely to upset the friendly relations existing between Australia and England.

It is easy in the light of history to fault the text of this grim pronouncement, and in particular the use of the word 'unsportsmanlike' which MCC seized on and, inevitably, repudiated. One must, however, try to imagine the circumstances of the moment in the heat of the battle – and that is the word. Larwood and Voce were whistling the ball round the batsmen's ribs, shoulders and head to a thick cluster of close leg-side fielders. Both Woodfull, twice, and Oldfield were hit, and though Woodfull was struck while Larwood was bowling to an orthodox field, as soon as the batsman recovered and play was resumed Jardine at once switched his men across to the leg-side placings. This was the incident which did more to damn him in the eyes both of Englishmen and Australians than any other, and it was, incidentally, the only one which Jardine long afterwards said he regretted. The spectators were in constant uproar, while outside the ground, behind the long pavilion stand, mounted troops waited in readiness in case the field should be invaded. What those in authority feared above all else was that Bradman should be laid low.

The Board's cable set more than the cricket world by the ears. In England as in Australia it was the news of the day, and at home it was only natural that the criticisms were bitterly resented. I have told in my opening chapter of the assorted trio of evening paper writers on the spot, on whose comments the public had to form their judgment: Jack Hobbs (assisted by Jack Ingham of the *Star*), Warwick Armstrong, and Bruce Harris, who at the last minute had been preferred to me. The morning papers, almost a day behind with the news, had to make do with second-hand comments from old players such as MacLaren, White, Tennyson, and Chapman which, read retrospectively, were generally miles wide of the mark. MacLaren before the Third Test, for instance, was saying that the English bowlers would have to pitch the ball farther up in order to save themselves punishment from Bradman's 'telling back-play'.

While it was not easy for those far away to appreciate the perils presented by Larwood's great speed and accuracy when he dropped the ball short, there were a few percipient remarks from well-known personalities. Nigel Haig said he was glad that Allen had taken his wickets 'without resorting to intimidation'. A. E. R. Gilligan said that 'cricket is supposed to be fair, and this does not savour of it in the least.' He proposed, very sensibly, that leg-theory should be investigated by an Anglo-Australian committee.

Neville Cardus was highly dubious, and asked why, if there were no valid objection to the bowling of Larwood and Voce, Australia's protests had not been emphatically denied by those on the spot. He could only have been referring to Warner and his co-manager R. C. N. Palairet.

Not least the Jam Saheb, K. S. Ranjitsinhji, pronounced: 'Although the batsman has a bat with which to defend himself, I disapprove strongly of the concerted leg-side attack. I would rather lose the rubber than win over the bruised bodies of opponents.'

But such sentiments found no echo at Lord's. Although by this time Warner must have reported back, the MCC reply was a complete disclaimer:

We, Marylebone Cricket Club, deplore your cable. We deprecate your opinion that there has been unsportsmanlike

72

play. We have fullest confidence in captain, team and managers and are convinced that they would do nothing to infringe either the Laws of Cricket or the spirit of the game. We have no evidence that our confidence has been misplaced. Much as we regret accidents to Woodfull and Oldfield, we understand that in neither case was the bowler to blame.

If the Australian Board of Control wish to propose a new Law or Rule, it shall receive our careful consideration in due course.

We hope the situation is not now as serious as your cable would seem to indicate, but if it is such as to jeopardize the good relations between English and Australian cricketers and you consider it desirable to cancel the remainder of programme we would consent, but with great reluctance.

As Fingleton points out, the suggestion of the tour being cancelled with two Tests still to go caught the Australian Board in a tender spot. Whatever the unpleasantness, big profits were accruing. The Board's next cable was mighty close to a volte-face. It protested that the sportsmanship of MCC was not in question, and in continuing bitterness therefore the tour dragged out its length. England won the last two Tests, and when it was all over not a single Australian player bade them farewell. No record is available of what Woodfull and his team said or thought when, on the rubber being decided, the MCC manager, quoting Lord Roberts, declared that 'the men were splendid', while the captain turned to Kipling.

What of the aftermath? First, the MCC Committee – who in the estimation of all had won the verbal contest hands down – called certain of the principals to testify: Warner and Palairet, the managers, Jardine, the captain, and the two bowlers chiefly concerned, Larwood and Voce. The views of Palairet, the Surrey secretary, a taciturn man, have never been disclosed, so far as I know. His function on the tour was largely financial, but his nature was in some ways akin to Jardine's. Of the five interviewed, Warner probably spoke with a lone voice.

But whose opinion was *not* invited? Firstly that of the vice-captain, Wyatt, who while remaining loyal to his captain, as all were, disapproved of the tactics in question; secondly Allen, the remaining fast bowler, who had refused to use them. Nor was Herbert Sutcliffe, the senior professional, brought in. Nor Jack Hobbs. No one likewise wanted to hear what Walter Hammond felt about it all – though they were to know, as it happened, very shortly.

73

If with the lapse of years the MCC minutes were one day to be made available to some responsible historian, the result might be illuminating. Meanwhile the impression must remain from the available evidence that the anti-Bodyliners in the team – who formed a strong majority – were given the minimum of attention. It might have been different had not the fourth Lord Harris, that shrewd, fair-minded autocrat of cricket, died in harness as Treasurer the year before.

However, a more or less chance event was to open people's eyes in England that following summer of 1933, for on an Old Trafford pitch vastly slower than those of Australia two West Indian bowlers somewhat less fast and accurate than Larwood, Learie Constantine and E. A. Martindale, gave England a dose of their own medicine. Hammond retired with a cut chin, and on returning to bat was soon caught in the leg-trap. He announced without prevarication that if this was how Test cricket was going to be played he wanted no part of it.

Jardine however, whose courage, either moral or physical, was never in dispute, seized a heaven-sent chance to prove his point by batting as steadily as a rock for 127, his only Test hundred. I can see him now, playing the dead-bat back stroke with the utmost coolness as those two fine bowlers strained every effort to get some response from the docile pitch – and it was an academic point noted only by the experts that Jardine's methods could scarcely have availed him against Larwood in Australia, since from those classical back strokes the ball would have carried to the short-legs. To succeed in 1932–3 an Australian batsman needed to possess the hook in his armoury – and Jardine was never a hooker.

The Old Trafford Test was something of an eye-opener to cricket-lovers in England, and they had other evidence that helped to jolt the complacency of those who had begun by concluding that Australia were in the wrong. Hobbs, once the team was home, roundly condemned Bodyline, as, among others, did Reg Bettington, a formidable Anglo-Australian sporting figure who had been a contemporary of Jardine's at Oxford and wrote as 'a very close and valued friend'. In July 1933, Warner himself gave his unequivocal views in a letter to the *Daily Telegraph*:

July 1933

Mr James Agate's letter in the *Daily Telegraph* of Thursday last demands a reply. I was 'sorry the West Indies had recourse to leg theory', or 'Bodyline' (Australian), because

74

I had hoped that my countrymen would avoid a type of bowling which I believe to be against the best interests of cricket.

But I agree that its exploitation at Old Trafford will serve a useful purpose in giving Englishmen some idea of what this bowling is like, though it is well known that Constantine is at least two yards slower than Larwood, and also lacks his control of the ball . . . What is objected to by a great many cricketers is fast leg-theory on hard, fast wickets. A bowler must be fast to carry out this plan of attack, but it requires not only speed, but accuracy of direction and control of length. No batsman objects to fast half volleys on his legs, however many fieldsmen may be placed on the leg side. What is objected to is when the ball is pitched short. It is the length of the ball, not so much the pace of it, to which exception has been taken.

Short-pitched very fast deliveries on hard wickets on the line of the batsman's body look – even if the bowler is acquitted of all intention to hurt the batsman – as if the bowler was 'bowling at the batsman', in the sense in which that expression has hitherto been understood by cricketers.

It is akin to intimidation. At the end of the last century, and at the beginning of this, English cricket boasted many fast bowlers – every county had at least one; Surrey two, the renowned Richardson and Lockwood. Some hard blows were received at times.

Sir Stanley Jackson, for example, had a rib broken by E. Jones, the Australian, but these bowlers did not give the impression of bowling at the batsman, and the short very fast 'bouncer', on the line of the batsman and which caused the batsman to duck, was certainly not defended, or encouraged.

At all events, fast bowling was very much in vogue at that time, and no cry was raised against it, whereas today we have practically every Australian cricketer of every generation definitely opposed to what they call Bodyline bowling.

This vast mass of opinion deserves the deepest thought and consideration. To suggest that the Australians are 'squealers' is unfair to men with their record on the battlefield and on the cricket field. Rightly or wrongly they believe that such bowling is contrary to the spirit of the game.

Mr Agate hopes that 'the Australians are now raking the bush for some Hercules who can bowl faster than Kortright, in order that, without regard to length and aiming solely at the batsman's head and heart, he shall, next season, try on the English goose the sauce that has been deemed proper for the Australian gander'.

I should be sorry indeed to see 'a Red Terror' from the 'Never-Never', some Saltbush Bill of Richardsonian proportions, exploiting this bowling against England in a Test Match at Lord's, or anywhere else.

The courtesy of combat would go out of that game in ten minutes: and one of the strongest arguments against this bowling is that it has bred, and will continue to breed, anger, hatred, and malice, with their consequent reprisals.

Admitting it is within the law – there are many things in cricket which by the laws of the game are right, but which are 'not done' – is it worth while if, as a result of Bodyline, England and her greatest cricketing Dominion are to 'fight' each other?

It was not thus that cricket gained its great name, a name synonymous with all that is fair, and kindly, noble, and upright.

Some would urge that the laws should be altered. I do not agree. This is a case where one should rely on the spirit, kindliness, and good will which should be inherent in cricket. But if a change in the law there must be, why not draw a line across the pitch and no-ball any delivery pitched the bowler's side of the line? The cricket pitch might look somewhat like a tennis court, but would that matter greatly if we got back to the old happy state of affairs? For the cricket world today is most decidedly not happy.

Always have I been opposed to this bowling which has aroused so much controversy, and, right or wrong, I am only pleading for what I honestly believe is best for the great, glorious, and incomparable game of cricket. I am not the least of the lovers of cricket.

Gradually, in the 1933 summer, what was involved in the contentious word 'Bodyline' (invented, by the way, almost accidentally, by an Australian journalist using telegraphese) came to be appreciated by men in authority for something like what it was, and in the winter MCC ruled:

That the type of bowling regarded as a direct attack by the bowler upon the batsman and therefore unfair consists in persistent and systematic bowling of fast short-pitched balls at the batsman standing clear of his wicket.

This amounted to a directive to the umpires to act under Law 46 (Fair and Unfair Play), and it made the way easier for

Australia to agree to come to England according to schedule in 1934. But the doubts as to their coming were being debated with equal intensity at both ends of the world, and it was not until 12 December 1933 that a final cable from Lord's made it clear that Australia would be welcome. And the text of that message was passed, as 'Plum' Warner indicates in the following letter, by only eight votes to five. That is how near it came to a rupture of relations. The 'Sandy' to whom he wrote in Adelaide was Sir Alexander Hore-Ruthven, afterwards Lord Gowrie, at that time Governor of South Australia. He had been in England during the Bodyline tour, but when on returning to his post he gauged the strength of Australian resentment, and realized that a just case had been unfairly presented in England, he had tried to put the record straight with J. H. Thomas, the Dominions secretary, asking him to use his good offices with the principal London editors. In fact the English press had already begun to show the other side of the picture.

Conservative Club

Dear Sandy,   Jan. 3rd 1934

Thank you very much for your nice and very interesting letter, and for your good wishes for 1934 which I heartily reciprocate. Well, I am delighted 'the row' is over – but cannot imagine why after 8–5 in favour of Peace, the chairman allowed the Minority to run the show. Much comment on Oxlade's CBE in the New Year Honours. Personally I think it will do good. It is a gesture, but fancy they don't much like it at Lord's, think it a little premature. Some construe it as saying the Board were right in their view though everyone here is certain that their original cable was a terrible blunder. Anyway Australia will no doubt take the CBE as a friendly gesture. The Press and Public will give the team a good reception and a circular (entre nous) will be sent to all the Counties urging them to stop at once any sign of barracking of which there may be some danger in Yorks (Bowes) and Notts (Larwood) if he is able to bowl fast again, which I doubt. The real trouble is Jardine. Is he to be Capt.? At present I say 'No' unless he makes a most generous public gesture of friendliness and then I am not sure I would trust him. He is a queer fellow. When he sees a cricket ground with an Australian on it he goes mad! He rose to his present position on my shoulders, and of his attitude to me I do not care to speak. It is hoped he may retire at the end of the Indian Tour, but in many quarters here – where they do not know the truth – he is a bit of a hero. If he is captain in First Test and is not friendly he will not capt. in the 2nd but I would not have him at all . . .

We start a New Year here on a wave of optimism – things look good – and they say Income Tax will come down. I trust so.

Would the 1934 Test selectors (F. S. Jackson, P. Perrin and T. A. Higson) bring the embers into a blaze by inviting Jardine to be captain against Australia once more? That ticklish decision at least he nipped in the bud when he cabled from India, where he was leading MCC in their first Test tour of that country, saying that he had neither the desire nor the intention of playing against Australia in the summer. He then forthwith signed to write about the Tests for the *Evening Standard*. Wyatt led England, and Australia regained the Ashes by winning the concluding Test at the Oval.

The tour passed off without much untoward incident except at Trent Bridge where Voce's bowling and the behaviour of the Notts members caused an uproar, and the county were accordingly required to apologize to the Australians by the Advisory County Cricket Committee. The scars of Bodyline were far from healed. Jardine forsook first-class cricket for journalism, while Warner continued to write for the *Morning Post*, and after its decease for the *Daily Telegraph*, and, again, to act simultaneously as Chairman of Selectors.

From Warner's letters his agony of conscience in Australia, when he had to watch a team under his authority carrying through with ruthless efficiency tactics which he so abhorred, can well be imagined. At Adelaide, if not before, where on entering the Australian dressing-room to commiserate upon Woodfull's injury he was coldly snubbed, he must have considered resigning the managership. To have done so – as it appears at this distance – would almost certainly have caused the tour's abandonment, and relations so severed would not have been easily restored. The irony was that he, a man of peace if ever there was one, should have been embroiled in the most momentous row in the game's history by the man he himself appointed.

It was true of 'Plum', I think, that he could never think ill of a fine cricketer, an amiable characteristic but dangerous in a man of such authority who had to make important judgments. Unfortunately for English cricket, this was not the last time that this propensity of his led to unfortunate consequences.

6

The Gay 'Thirties

Gay at any rate they were to me as I look back on the scene, sporting and social, of the years before the war. For me, as for most of my generation, the black cloud ahead was still beyond the horizon.

My reflections on the Bodyline affair concerned events at which I was not present. They seemed worth inclusion in a personal book because they formed the watershed between eras. Test cricket against Australia – which had been and continued to be the highest expression of the game – was never quite the same again. Yet when I published the gist of the last chapter in *The Cricketer* two or three years ago it seemed to be news to all but a very few. The middle-aged and elderly had forgotten, the young never knew. But let that be the end of what is second-hand. From now onwards, for the next forty years or so (except for the war) I have Badminton diaries which record every match, tour, dinner or other engagement I attended. They are the spur to a memory of variable quality, clear on some episodes, impenetrably foggy on others.

In the first category comes the Cahn tour of August-September 1933. Julien Cahn, as I mentioned earlier, was a conspicuous figure in the cricket world of the 'thirties with his own team and two superb grounds, one more or less in Nottingham at West Bridgford, the other in front of his house, Stanford Hall, Loughborough. The wickets were perfect, and the out-fields were like bowling greens. Hospitality was on a lavish scale with no shortage of champagne; but there were those who took undue advantage of a bountiful host, and latterly therefore drinks had to be signed for. He had a first-class side, most members of which were accommodated in his furnishing business when they were not playing for him either at home or abroad. He took teams to Jamaica, to the Argentine, to Denmark, to Canada, USA and Bermuda, to Ceylon and Singapore and to New Zealand. His purse was apparently bottomless, and, of course, he gave a vast deal of pleasure to very many people, even though his sides were much too strong for most of their opposition. This didn't worry 'Sir J' – he was first knighted and then accorded a baronetcy for 'service to agriculture and a number of charitable causes' – whose idea of a good game, I suspect, was to see his stars make three or four hundred and then bowl out the enemy quickly enough to avoid too long a spell in the field.

For he played himself, in a manner of speaking, bowling when he felt inclined and sometimes putting himself in first. As a bowler his style is best described as parabolic. It can perhaps be imagined from John Gunn's answer – or it may have been 'Tich' Richmond's – to the question how Sir Julien was bowling that year: 'up and down, I suppose?' 'Not so mooch oop and down, I'd say, as to and fro.' When I took Crusoe to play once at Stanford he remarked that the chief evidence that Cahn was bowling was a faint whistling in the trees. He was probably hit higher and farther than any bowler before or since, runs, of course, being no object as there were always hundreds to play with. But sometimes he got a wicket, and high was the merriment.

The brilliant players who surrounded him made some astonishing catches, one of which at London, Ontario, comes back to me as I write. The batsman hit the cricket equivalent of a full brassie shot, low, down wind, and practically straight. Walter Robins – I think one of the best half-dozen all-round fielders I ever saw – came sprinting in full pelt from the sight-screen as the stroke was made and took the ball right-handed down by his boots. Done in a Test at Lord's it would have won imperishable fame.

It was said, no doubt erroneously, that when the side's averages were made up at the end of the season the scorer by a simple manipulation of the decimal point brought the captain up to the top of the list.

He was the sort of man around whom revolved many such stories. For instance, his pads, which were very large, were said to be blown up with a bicycle pump. The ball certainly bounced readily off them for leg-byes which the umpire some-times conveniently forgot to signal; but I never saw them inflated, though I did once see the butler, who was in attend-ance to accoutre Julien in the changing tent at Stanford, rush out with the fielding pads which he had forgotten to strap on. Not a bit abashed, his master paused from leading his team on to the greensward, pulled up his trousers and allowed the matter to be rectified.

Even with his legs thus encased it has to be admitted that

Julien was not a brave fielder as many will remember. But if this little weakness is mentioned I must add that as Master of the Pytchley and of the Fernie is was said that no fence was too high for him, and that his intrepidity in the hunting field cost him several broken bones. He was, in fact, even more of a mixture than most of us, with an innately kind side to which many a cricketer was indebted, myself included.

Thanks to him I made this first tour of seven weeks, sailing from Southampton in the *Empress of Britain* across the Atlantic and up the St Lawrence river to Quebec, proceeding south down the eastern seaboard of Canada to Chicago and New York, and thence to the climax of the expedition in Bermuda; a week's cricket there, return by sea to New York (through a hurricane, the worst thirty-six hours I ever spent in a ship) and then home in a dead calm all the way in the old *Aquitania*. Our side had four Test cricketers, R. W. V. Robins, I. A. R. Peebles, D. P. B. Morkel (South Africa) and R. C. Blunt (New Zealand), and one to become so, P. A. Gibb; G. F. H. Heane and S. D. Rhodes, soon jointly to lead Notts, and seven others all of whom either before or subsequently played varying amounts of first-class cricket, C. R. Maxwell, H. R. Munt, F. C. W. Newman, T. B. Reddick, E. P. Solbé, G. F. Summers, and myself. Plus, of course, Julien Cahn.

We won sixteen matches (all one-day) and drew four, most of the North American games being 11 against either 12 or more. In the States there was a preponderance of West Indians against us, this being my first close acquaintance with people from the islands one of which, many years later, was to become a second home. I write as one who has scored fifties in Ottawa, Chicago and New York, but to tell the truth the difficulty on our side was not so much in making runs but in getting in.

Until we got to Bermuda. The excitement that greeted the first English side to visit England's oldest colony was, to us, staggering. Our first appearance on the Prospect ground, proceeding round the field in carriages (no cars were allowed on this microscopic mid-Atlantic speck until in war it became of major strategic value), was like a royal procession. And it was at once evident that on a lively pitch of matting over concrete we might be hard pressed. The climax came with our game against Somerset, the champion side, when in front of five thousand people crammed into the little ground (about one in five of the total population) we were bowled out for 85. The chief destroyer was a fast left-arm bowler called Arthur Simons, who on this surface was like Bill Voce and 'Nobby'

Clark of Northants rolled into one.

Neither in the West Indies nor Australia have I known a greater hubbub than this whole game was played in, the noise growing, if possible, even greater as the Somerset score ticked up against Robins and Peebles. By the time the ninth wicket went down for 62 the half-Battalion of Northumberland Fusiliers who had backed us to a man, on English reputations, at odds of three to one, were feeling a little easier. But they had plenty of shocks to come. Another Simons, Obrien by name, chanced his arm, and the score rose by startling leaps to 82. At this point a well-hit straight-drive looked like going for six when George Heane from long-on dashed across the sight-screen and leapt up to make a marvellous catch, two-handed, above his head. Whereat the crowd thronged the field, and the soldiery threw topees into the air, and carried George shoulder-high to the pavilion, where Julien also was seized, somewhat to his alarm, and borne aloft likewise. Walter Robins always said this was the most thrilling game he ever saw or played in. I think I got 5 before falling to the Voce-ish Simons, and held a catch at extra-cover amid a noise like that which greets a goal in a Cup Final or the winning try at Twickenham.

It was more than twenty years later that the chance came to visit Bermuda again, when I captained my own side there on our way home from the West Indies, in 1956. The Bermudians were rather more sophisticated then, having had various visits including that of Len Hutton's MCC side *en route* to the West Indies. Nor did our game quite match the excitement of that earlier one. But one felt an echo of it when Frank Tyson, indubitably the world's fastest bowler, was hit for six for the first time in his life, it was said, and then for another, by a character rejoicing in the name of 'Cheesey' Hughes.

So much – or almost – for Julien Cahn, though I pass on with reluctance from this eccentric open-handed figure who (according to E. E. Snow, the historian of Leicestershire and author also of a slim book, *Sir Julien Cahn's XI*), being something of a hypochondriac, thought nothing of ordering a special train to bring from London the King's physician, Lord Horder, and who took his barber with him round the world. His grounds contained a golf course as well as lawn-tennis and squash courts, bowling and putting greens, swimming pool, besides a lake well stocked with trout, and – sublime touch! – a performing seal pond. The last addition to the house before war brought such vanities to a halt was a luxurious theatre seating 350, complete with Würlitzer organ.

He purchased from F. S. Ashley-Cooper, the distinguished historian, the best cricket library ever collected, but thereby hangs a melancholy tale. At his death Lady Cahn offered MCC any items they did not already have, which was a generous gesture considering her husband had enjoyed no more than two years of membership. Later the balance of this unique library was put up for auction, the sale being due to begin at eleven o'clock. However, a considerable collection advertised for sale earlier in the morning was withdrawn at the last moment, the Cahn sale began early, and, before serious purchasers arrived, much irreplaceable material went dirt cheap to dealers and has never been located.

When the Australians came, after all, in 1934 they were exuberantly received at the Savoy luncheon given by the British Sportsman's Club, though distinctly less so later on by the crowds at Trent Bridge and Headingley. A word about the BSC, which exists chiefly to greet in this way teams of all kinds from the Commonwealth before the serious business of their tours begins. Its members form a distinguished cross-section of British sporting life, with a chairman of appropriate eminence. At present it is the Duke of Norfolk, with Lord Wakefield of Kendal, the famous 'Wakers', as his deputy. The foundation of the BSC owes itself to the great drama of the sending-off at Twickenham of C. J. Brownlie in the England-New Zealand match of 1924. This happened in the presence of the Prince of Wales, who at half-time is said to have attempted in vain to bring about Brownlie's return. The All Blacks were so angry and upset that they refused to attend the Rugby Union dinner that night. Accordingly with the Prince of Wales's encouragement a luncheon was hurriedly arranged before their departure. Sore feelings were to some extent mollified at this, and the organizers thereupon formed the British Sportsman's Club.

At one period the chair was occupied by someone less at home in sports than politics, and when he remarked what a great honour it was for us to have the famous Sir Jack . . . with us, his memory went, and he kept repeating Sir Jack . . . Sir Jack . . . as though a gramophone record had got stuck in its groove. At last someone had to call out 'Hobbs'. Generally these are the smoothest occasions with all the right notes struck.

This is not a Test match chronicle – few readers, if any, would face the daunting prospect of digesting 230-odd of them

– but they must have their place. After all they have occupied upwards of a thousand of my working days: the best part of three years' concentrated watching time! England lost the first Test since Bodyline at Trent Bridge by 238 runs – and ten minutes.

There followed Verity's match at Lord's in which after a thunderstorm he took fifteen wickets in a day, and that was that. The Australians are always nervous, and naturally so, when they have to face the music on a pitch on which the ball stops and turns, but when they arrived on the Monday morning with 192 for two on the board it never occurred to them that they would not make the 99 more they needed to save the follow-on. They missed the target by seven runs, and those seven runs meant the match.

The Old Trafford Test was the one in which England made their then highest score against Australia, yet failed to win. One recalls O'Reilly getting England's first three wickets in four balls – those of Walters, Wyatt, and Hammond – and the uproar when Gubby Allen's first over was elongated to thirteen balls. In those days the groundsman was not empowered to renovate the foot-holes during a match, and Bill O'Reilly whose large feet and strong final stride were apt to dig deep holes had bowled 59 overs in the English innings. So what with running wide to avoid the pits and finding a ball that swung a lot, Gubby, in between a few legitimate ones, bowled four no-balls and three wides. He says the over also contained a couple of chances but they seem to have escaped historical notice. He also maintains that he missed a cushy hundred because he misinterpreted a wave from Bob Wyatt on the dressing-room balcony. He thought it meant the captain was going to declare, and so had a dip (he made 61, bowled McCabe). Perhaps Bob was just fanning his face – the heat was like Melbourne at its worst. He did finally declare, at 627 for nine, just before tea on the second day of the four-day match, but England never looked like winning.

Altogether it was an ill-fated year for England, with Jardine in the press-box, Larwood also unwilling to play, some ill-balanced sides chosen by Messrs F. S. Jackson, T. A. Higson and P. Perrin, and a final calamitous match at the Oval lost by 562 runs. For me the final indignity was, after Les Ames had been crocked, to see Frank Woolley in the last of his 64 Test Matches keeping wicket.

Sussex have never won the Championship, but 1934 under Alan Melville was one of the years when they very nearly

Around £13,000 can make your retirement as carefree as this.

It's very easy to make sure of a happy and secure retirement. You just take out a Prudential Endowment Assurance.

For example, if you're a man aged 30 next birthday, a monthly premium of £12.50 would give you a guaranteed minimum sum of £5,000 at age 65. But this sum would be increased by bonuses, and a £5,000 policy for a similar term maturing on April 1st, 1974, would have given you a lump sum of £12,970.*

Of course, bonuses can go down as well as up. But in the past the trend has always been a steady rise.

For the full story of how to make your retirement secure and happy, just fill in the coupon and send us the card. It won't cost you anything to find out.

And it could give you peace of mind. At the very least.

Prudential

Purely by way of interest, I'd like full details of your Endowment Assurance policies.

Name

Address

BUSINESS REPLY SERVICE
LICENCE NO. KE 1511

The Chief General Manager
The Prudential Assurance Co Ltd
142 Holborn Bars
London EC1N 2NH

Around £13,000 can make your retirement as carefree as this.

It's very easy to make sure of a happy and secure retirement. You just take out a Prudential Endowment Assurance.

For example, if you're a man aged 30 next birthday, a monthly premium of £12.50 would give you a guaranteed minimum sum of £5,000 at age 65. But this sum would be increased by bonuses, and a £5,000 policy for a similar term maturing on April 1st, 1974, would have given you a lump sum of £12,970.*

Of course, bonuses can go down as well as up. But in the past the trend has always been a steady rise.

For the full story of how to make your retirement secure and happy, just fill in the coupon and send us the card. It won't cost you anything to find out.

And it could give you peace of mind. At the very least.

Prudential

*Applies to U.K. only.

BUSINESS REPLY SERVICE
LICENCE NO. KE 1511

The Chief General Manager
The Prudential Assurance Co Ltd
142 Holborn Bars
London EC1N 2NH

did. They had a last chance when Lancashire came down to Eastbourne at the end of August 1934; but a draw was all Lancashire wanted, and amid spasmodic barracking they set out to achieve it. I remember arguing with Peter Eckersley, the captain, about the methods he had used, and being quelled by his reply, which was to the effect that in that age of low wages he knew how hard-pressed some of his chaps were in the winter and how much the bonus they'd get for winning the Championship would mean to them. That was a lot more important to him than pleasing a lot of holiday-makers sitting round the Saffrons. Not an easy attitude to refute! Strangely enough, I remember Arthur Richardson, of Derbyshire, also at Eastbourne two years later taking very much the same line when his side were fighting to win their only modern Championship.

In those days the best amateur captains, especially those of the largely professional sides of the north and midlands, stood in a somewhat different relationship with their sides from that obtaining today. They were very much the guardians of their flocks even though they were probably junior in age to half the men they led. Melville, Eckersley and Richardson were all still in their twenties at this time, as also were Brian Sellers, who brought Yorkshire six titles in eight years, and Walter Robins of Middlesex, Tom Pearce and Denys Wilcox of Essex, R. H. Moore of Hampshire, Charles Lyttelton (now Lord Cobham) of Worcestershire, and Maurice Turnbull of Glamorgan.

The fact that most of the captains in the 1930's were roughly of an age with myself meant that I knew most of them pretty well and so got a good idea of what was going on. Among those slightly older were A. P. F. Chapman (Kent), E. R. T. Holmes (Surrey), R. E. S. Wyatt (Warwickshire) and G. F. H. Heane (Notts). Looked back at through the rose-tinted spectacles of time they seem a capable and attractive bunch – which does not mean, of course, that they escaped the perennial criticisms that county cricket was dull and going to the dogs. It always has been, sometimes faster than others.

The diary tells me I moved along the coast that early August of 1934 from Hove to Canterbury, and I need no reminding of what I saw there. There had been a thunderstorm the night before Kent played Notts in the second match of the week, and Percy Chapman thought some while before deciding to bat. He did so, moving up Frank Woolley to No. 1 with the idea of rattling the bowling. Sure enough the ball flew at the start. It flew off the pitch, and it flew off Frank's bat – all ways. The quicker bowlers made the cardinal error of digging the ball in short, which suited the master perfectly. He hooked, of course, and he cut – how he cut! Along the ground, but also over gully's head; for that matter over cover's head likewise. Imperious, disdainful, commanding. The superlatives were never so quickly used up as when Woolley was in the mood.

This sunny day (all August days in the 'thirties were sunny) and on this awkward wicket he and Bill Ashdown made 109 for the first wicket in under the hour. 'Actually starting with 52 runs out of 71 in 33 minutes,' says *Wisden*, 'Woolley with sixteen fours got 101 out of 155 in a hundred minutes.' 'Dazzling', they called it. I wonder what description would fit the case in the 'seventies when a man is said to have 'flayed' the bowling when he reaches his hundred not twenty minutes before lunch but somewhere around tea-time. Of course, the Notts bowling having been demoralized, Kent plundered at will – 445 for six before the close. Next day 'Tich' Freeman had seven wickets, 'Father' Marriott eleven, and all was over.

When, watching with Frank at Canterbury a year or two ago, I reminded him of the innings he couldn't recall it. If this seems extraordinary remember that he did make 145 hundreds, and, for that matter, 35 scores in the nineties. Perhaps the innings would have stuck in his mind if Notts had bowled a little better. By the way, the older he grew the more he liked going in first, saying that the red one was easier to see. He was 47 in 1934, and had still four more summers to go.

Descending with a vengeance to lesser cricket matters I this year began qualifying for membership of MCC by playing. After your cricketing qualifications had secured your acceptance as a candidate you engaged for either ten or twelve days' cricket spread over two years. Assuming you made a few runs or took a few wickets, and behaved with reasonable decorum, you were then elected. The whole process from the time of being put up took four years – as opposed to merely waiting passively, which took about twenty or thirty. I was proposed by Major E. G. French and seconded by D. J. Knight, and on 9 March 1936, in a document from Lord's, the Secretary, W. Findlay, had the honour of informing me of my election and assuming I would 'have the goodness to sign the subjoined order upon your Banker or Agent' he remained my obedient servant. A red-letter day!

But here I was pushing off to Wisbech in late April for a two-day match with a dance in the middle and much hospitality and all things civil, except the weather. For the wind that blows over East Anglia seems sometimes, as I discovered in the early days of the war, to sweep straight from the Urals. We had three Gilligans, no less, and several Cambridge undergraduates, and the captain of Lincolnshire, one Major C. Wilson. Why I specially remember the last-named is because on the second morning, after a notable party overnight, our manager and captain, H. D. Swan, set him to bowl uphill and into the piercing wind. Now 'Swannie' was one of those captains who made his changes by the clock, and it so happened there was no clock. He was forgetful when there was a clock, and much more so without it. So the gallant major went on and on, breasting the wind and the slope, while we gave him a little facetious encouragement and avoided the captain's eye. At last when collapse from a combination of exhaustion and exposure was clearly imminent the wind grew full of sleet, and we all gratefully retired.

'Swannie' was one of quite a collection of middle-aged men who between the wars helped to run wandering cricket. They had plenty of money and leisure, and great zeal for the game, and much kindliness to the young – and were no earthly good whatever. Some of them had been once: others never had. They used to proceed to the nets at Lord's with red and yellow scarves to keep their trousers up, and the ground-staff bowlers used sometimes to amuse themselves with bets as to who would hit the stumps most often. 'Swannie', a large and heavy man, used to field at mid-on very straight, so that he was almost behind the bowler's umpire. There was no question of his running after the ball, and he used to convey the impression that it was well out of reach even when it was whistling past his boots. He went in, when he had to, at No. 11, and I never heard or read of his making double figures. In short he was distinctly the worst cricketer I ever saw, and since both he and his charming wife are long since dead, and were without issue, there is none to take this judgment amiss. He collected strong sides, and went to endless trouble, and loved the company of good cricketers. I expect the happiest time of his life was when he accompanied Archie MacLaren's MCC team to New Zealand and Australia as honorary manager.

Another of a like kind was Captain T H. Carlton-Levick, who went with MCC to the West Indies, to Canada, and to South America, paying his way in a similar capacity. Carlton designed his own blue cap with the letters MCC entwined on the front, and is to be seen wearing it, and complete with 'co-respondent shoes', squatting at 'Plum' Warner's feet in the MCC South American group of 1926/7. It was said that Carlton used simply to arrive to catch the boat train at Euston or Waterloo and say, 'Hullo boys, I'm your manager.'

Gerry Weigall was in that side of 'Plum's' and was of similar vintage, except that he hadn't a bean to take himself anywhere and moreover had been a good cricketer when young. The Weigall saga is as rich as that of Rockley Wilson, with the difference that Rockley was both a wit and a scholar. Apart from some fondness for the horses Gerry's life was rooted utterly in cricket which he played whenever possible and talked 365 days of the year. He was never without a walking-stick or umbrella, since one or the other was in constant use to illustrate his remarks. He always had a few pet bees buzzing around in his bonnet, and used to inveigh against the criminal folly of selectors and authority generally if their views did not match his own. When in 1928 Woolley, despite making 3,500 runs, was omitted from Percy Chapman's team to Australia his anguish was terrible to see. To think that they had preferred that 'cross-batted village-greener', Maurice Leyland !

He used to inflict on *The Cricketer* articles in which the golden deposit of truth was apt to be obscured by grammatical difficulties and an absence of punctuation. Remonstrating gently with him on this account 'Plum' Warner said, 'Gerry, you ought to take a course of Macaulay.' 'What, sir,' he exploded, 'the Yorkshire bowler?' Christian names were scarce with him; everyone was 'sir'. He pronounced various rules or axioms. 'Never eat veal and ham pie for lunch' was followed by 'Never cut in May' and 'Never run to cover on a fast wicket.' The Kent 2nd XI which he captained knew these don'ts well enough. One day young Leslie Todd was in with Gerry and going nicely, when the latter hit one to cover and called for a fatal run. As poor Todd passed him ruefully on his way to the pavilion, the captain consoled him with, 'Only shows you, sir, only shows you !'

Altogether running between wickets was rather a sore point, for although G. J. V. Weigall in the University Match of 1892 took out his bat for 63, the score-book also records that three of the best Cambridge bats were run out while he was in, including his captain, the immortal F. S. Jackson. When from Gerry's square-cut, half-stopped, it was likely that one of them would have to go Gerry is supposed to have sacrificed his partner with the words, 'Get back, Jacker, I'm set.' Apocryphal, no doubt. George Fenner, a splendid character himself, who was a stalwart of Kent 2nd XI before he became head pro at Lord's, was a repository of Weigall stories, and they were warm friends. On one of the Minor County grounds one day they were surveying a very dubious wicket, Gerry having won the toss, and wondering what to do. 'I think I'd bat, sir,' said George, 'before the flowers come up.'

To the reader who never knew Gerry Weigall he may well sound a rather preposterous fellow. To such I can only say that every cricketer was his friend, and that he never spoke an unkind word about anyone.

I had quite a successful season, as may be judged from A. W. T. Langford's opening paragraph in his notes in *The Cricketer* of 8 September 1934, concerning the annual two-day match between MCC and Eastbourne at the Saffrons:

MCC included H. L. Wilson, the former Sussex captain, and Major C. B. Rubie, who has done so much for cricket in India, but their outstanding player was E. W. Swanton, who these days must be ranked as one of the best opening batsmen in club matches. Only the other day he scored two separate hundreds for the Cryptics v. Lancing Rovers, and was on the way to repeating this feat for MCC when he had to retire hurt for 61 in his second innings, after making 102 in his first.

The injury was nothing worse than a cut ear that needed stitching, the ball running up my bat as I aimed to pull. In my time I tore a few muscles inevitably, and had some trouble with knee cartilages and achilles tendons, but in forty summers of playing this was the only time I was incapacitated by the ball. Incidentally, club cricketers were much luckier, in those times of cheaper newsprint, than their counterparts today in the space their doings commanded in the press. The full scores of both the matches mentioned by Arthur Langford in which I got runs were printed in *The Times*. When the Arabs toured the Channel Islands the complete scores made a *Times* column. *The Cricketer* printed many pages of full club scores in each issue. It was interesting, of course, to see what one's friends were doing, while the publicity seemed to bring club cricketers somewhat closer to the first-class game. They were closer, too, in a real sense seeing that county amateurs, so many of whom spent a month or less in first-class cricket, were for the remaining time playing with clubs. This was good for all concerned.

1934 was notable for me as the year in which I first broadcast, and in which my activities were also widened by regular writing for the *Illustrated Sporting and Dramatic News*. In

1935 we had founded the Arabs, and I wrote my one and only Test series for an English paper other than the *Evening Standard* and the *Daily Telegraph*. The South Africans, under H. F. Wade, came over, and I did the Tests for the *Sunday Express* under the pen-name of Michael James. I don't know why Michael, or for that matter why James. This was the year when the leather jackets invaded the square and caused such havoc that one first-class match after another was finishing between lunch and tea on the second day. These insects – the larvae of the cranefly – ate away the grass, so that the surface was rendered bare and loose. A certain Xenophon Balaskas, the most improbable name surely among the thirteen hundred Test cricketers listed in *Wisden*, took notable advantage of the occasion by taking nine wickets in the Lord's Test and so enabling his side, after striving for 28 years, to gain their first victory in a Test in England. Balaskas bowled leg-breaks and googlies, was Greek by origin and by trade a chemist.

I had my first game at Lord's in this year of the leather jackets for MCC (as a candidate) against Indian Gymkhana and was baffled not so much by the pitch as by the difficulty of picking up the brown arm and swift, swerving flight of one of the best bowlers in the world out of the background of the Committee Room windows. His name was Amar Singh, and I was LBW (N) for 7. Two young cricketers named Edrich and Compton did a little better and we won the match.

Amar Singh came to England with the Indian sides of 1932 and 1936, and in the two Tests at Lord's of those years his bowling in company with a big strong fellow, Mahommed Nissar, reduced England to impotence. Amar Singh was tall and slim, but broad in the shoulders, long in the back, and loose in the wrist, the ideal recipe for a bowler of pace. His speed from a short run was fast-medium, and he had a command of swing and cut, and a life off the pitch that brought comparison with Tate in his prime. I never saw a finer bowler of his type before or since. With an Amar Singh and a Nissar to make their opening attack the present Indian team would be about twice the side they are.

What's this, you may say, about LBW (N)? Well, for the years 1935 and 1936, when a change in the LBW law was a matter for experiment, umpires were instructed to raise their right hand, palm pointing upwards, after first signalling their decision, if the ball had pitched outside the off-stump and the pad was between wicket and wicket. Previously, of course, the ball when struck had to pitch between wicket and wicket.

Wisden records that in its first years the amendment increased the number of LBW victims by more than 40%. After these two seasons – and to the long-term detriment of the game, as many of us believe – the experiment was made law. This book is far from being a technical treatise, so that must be enough of that.

I've told how chance led to the forming of the Arabs and our first tour to Jersey in 1935. Our side was a strong one. It included two Oxford blues, Robertson-Glasgow and Tindall, two from Cambridge, Bartlett and Hotchkin, and one soon to become one, Brocklebank. The rest were average or better-than-average club cricketers, except Eggar, that summer's captain of Winchester. Wreford-Brown was a Harlequin. Only Crusoe and I were older than 23, he a veteran of 34, I 28. The full party was: R. C. Robertson-Glasgow, R. G. Tindall, H. T. Bartlett, N. S. Hotchkin, J. M. Brocklebank, J. D. Eggar, A. J. Wreford-Brown, J. S. O. Haslewood, A. A. Muir, J. C. Bune, and myself.

We were a young, gay, irresponsible bunch who in due course proved altogether too indecorous for the Palace Hotel, Jersey. But subsequent case-histories suggest certain underlying qualities. Crusoe's genius as scholar, writer, and friend will be known to many readers of this book. Richard Tindall was a brilliant person and an almost uniquely popular master at Eton during the few years before the war accounted for him, as it also did for John Bune soon after he had been called to the bar. Of the rest Hugh Bartlett, after going to South Africa with MCC in 1938/9, won the DFC at Arnhem and the rank of Lieut.-Colonel before returning to captain Sussex and pursue a livelihood on the Stock Exchange. There, too, is Neil Hotchkin, who was a gunner major in Burma, is a deputy-lieutenant for Lincolnshire, the owner of Woodhall Spa, one of the great inland courses, and President of the English Golf Union. For seventeen years he was our secretary. John Brocklebank was another gunner major, and rose to be chairman of Cunard. Eggar was a major in the Sixtieth, became a house-master at Repton, and is now headmaster of Shiplake College; Tony Wreford-Brown, also in the Sixtieth, has just given up a house-mastership at Charterhouse. John Haslewood, MC, commanded an Irish Guards Battalion during the advance into Germany, an almost unique distinction for 'an amateur', is the director of Watney's who is credited, in company with his chairman, Simon Combe, with the thwarting of the Clore take-over bid, and is a member of the committee of MCC. Alec

Muir, one of the original 'Trenchard Boys' at Hendon Police College, is chief constable of Durham. Retrospectively it looks as though I made a pretty fair pick.

But around Brocklebank's coming hangs a story. I was having a net at Fenner's, as I enjoyed doing when I went to Cambridge, and John's quick wrist-spinners were far too good for me. He was in his second year, and had been brought to meet me by Neil Hotchkin, and I invited him soon afterwards by post to come to Jersey. I got no answer, and eventually picked someone else, who at the last moment had to cry off. Then at Lord's a mutual friend remarked how Brocklebank was looking forward to touring with us, so I made contact again and it turned out that John had written accepting, though the letter had never found its way to me. I mention all this because John carried all before him on that first Arab tour, and it occurred to Hugh Bartlett, who was due to captain Cambridge the following year, that here was someone who, if he were nursed carefully, might win him the University Match.

Hugh next summer decided that his secret weapon might not be accurate enough to make his mark against county batsmen on the superb Fenner's wicket, and kept him up his sleeve until the last match of the term. John took only one wicket in that, and none could understand why this unknown fellow was chosen to go on the University tour. (In those days amateur sport was given a fair coverage in the national press generally.) In the five matches on tour John Brocklebank proceeded to take no less than 32 wickets, finishing with 10 against Oxford, and so having the biggest share in the win. It was a great coup for Bartlett, and it was a rare piece of luck all round that I ran into that friend at Lord's. But for that John would never have caught the captain's eye, nor subsequently, I dare say, have gone on to play for Lancashire and the Gentlemen. He was also chosen to go to India with MCC in 1939/40 on the tour that perforce was cancelled. On a hard wicket, especially one with a spot of dust, he was a match for the best.

I often recall the case of J. H. Human to illustrate how a slice of luck at the right moment can make all the difference to a games-player, and especially perhaps to a cricketer. John Human, a freshman from Repton, had had no trial for Cambridge during the term although no one had got many runs. With only two matches to go before the University Match someone picked up *The Sportsman* in the Cambridge dressing-room at the Oval, and said, 'Listen to this. John Human's just made 231 out of 324 for Berks v. Herts.' So a wire was sent summoning John to Eastbourne where next day, going in at No. 7, he made 158 not out for the University against 'Shrimp' Leveson-Gower's side, and was promptly given just about the swiftest blue on record. Doing well against Oxford, John was forthwith made secretary, which was the invariable stepping-stone to the captaincy. This, in turn, led to his being chosen for E. R. T. Holmes's MCC side to New Zealand and Australia.

It happened on the boat out that John fell in love with the daughter of the Lord Mayor of Sydney, whom he married after the tour. So his life was charted, starting from the inconspicuous game between Hertfordshire and Berkshire at Douglas Crossman's ground at Cokenach. But when he was in single figures, as the fielder used to tell and the lucky batsman has often confirmed, John Human gave the easiest possible catch to 'Tommy' Crossman, captain of Herts, on whose father's ground the match was being played. If that catch had been taken John could not have had his blue as a freshman, and therefore could not have proceeded step by swift step to the captaincy, and thence into the Middlesex XI. Thus he could scarcely have put himself in the running for the MCC tour. So no Lord Mayor's daughter and no successful business career in Australia. Mind you, John Human was a highly talented cricketer who but for the war might have played for England. But it needed 'Tommy' Crossman's gaper to set him on the path.

What with writing almost every day in the *Standard*, and for other people as well, and broadcasting, and playing every single day I wasn't working, life in my late twenties was agreeably full. I seem to have made some more hundreds including one which I would always remember even if it did not happen to be the highest of my life. I always used to get to the ground early, partly, I expect, because I loved going in first, but this particular day some chore detained me, so I rang Brian Egerton, secretary of the Thespids, to say I was afraid I'd be late. 'It doesn't matter, old boy,' he said, 'I've got a marvellous batting side.'

When I got to Woodford Wells, where we were playing in the Home Week, the Thespids were batting, and however marvellous they were the first seven were out for 35. I scrambled in at about 50-odd for eight to join a red-faced major on leave from the East. He lasted a while, and then made way for our No. 11, an actor with small pretensions. However, by this time the ball was looking very big, and 'Egie' ultimately declared at 250-odd for nine, E.W.S. not out 143. We then bowled out the opposition for not very many and returned to London for a celebratory dinner. I hope this egotistical memory may be excused. At least it gives me a peg on which to attach some mention of the Thespids, an unusual club which fulfilled a wandering role on non-matinée days, and played certain 'home' matches on Sundays by an amiable arrangement with Wimbledon CC.

Basically they were actors, and there were some very good ones – such as Gerald du Maurier, Owen Nares, Basil Foster, Nigel Bruce, Basil Rathbone, Oliver Gordon, Anthony Bushell, and the Liveseys, Roger, Jack, and Sam. But they were fortified with certain lay members, including Donald Knight, C. H. Taylor, Dr T. C. Hunt, Alec Waugh, and a few more plus myself. At the end of that season we dined at the Café Royal under the august chairmanship of our President, the venerable Sir Aubrey Smith, a Test cricketer of the 'eighties, and now half a century later the doyen of the Hollywood film community. (Does anyone remember 'Bengal Lancer'?) All sporting institutions, if they are to prosper, must have at least one tireless, selfless person to do the work, and in the case of the Thespids it was, to give him his full name, B. Egerton Todd. When in the fulness of time dear old 'Egie' passed on so did the Thespids.

There has always been a singularly close affinity between cricket and the stage, helped no doubt by the fact that actors are apt to have plenty of leisure during the day. Henry Ainley, Oscar Asche, Godfrey Tearle and George Robey were a few other famous names often to be seen at Lord's in the 'thirties. Such men as Ian Carmichael, Harry Secombe, Trevor Howard, and Richard Attenborough, among many others, perpetuate the tradition today – and in their cases support cricket in a wonderfully practical way by working for the Lord's Taverners, the first object of which is to give financial support to the National Playing Fields Association.

Oliver Gordon, by the way, was the stage name of O. G. Battcock, who at a conservative estimate took 6,000 wickets in club cricket for a variety of sides but chiefly Incogniti, Datchet, where he lived, MCC, Butterflies, Thespids, and also Bucks in their halcyon days among the minor counties. E. M. Grace, 'The Coroner', is credited in his life with 11,906 wickets (besides 75,762 runs). But he bowled for sixty successive seasons, mostly as captain, and is said seldom to have taken himself off. In modern times I know of no one of whom it could be claimed that they took more wickets than Oliver. He had something like fifteen hundred of them, incidentally, between the ages of fifty and sixty. He was producer-manager of the Repertory Theatres of Windsor and Salisbury and continued to give great satisfaction in those positions without allowing them seriously to interfere with his cricket. In his prime his pace was a brisk medium (a bit below Amar Singh) with a very late out-swing, and I would rate him by a long way the best bowler of my experience who never – so far as I know – played any first-class cricket. He also just about wins the prize for the keenest cricketer.

As a member of a year's standing I attended the 150th Anniversary Dinner of MCC at which Major the Hon. J. J. Astor presided, and the speeches were made by the Duke of Gloucester, the Rt. Hon. S. M. Bruce (afterwards Lord Bruce of Melbourne), Sir Stanley Jackson, G. O. Allen and Lord Hawke. It is irritating that I can conjure no memory of two such illustrious figures from the past as Hawke and Jackson, but presumably the eight courses with wines to match were overwhelming. They might even conceivably have been over-much for the orators, for 'Plum' Warner in his *Long Innings* records that the speeches were unworthy of the occasion, and that the names of Grace and Harris, incredible to say, went without mention.

I only recall sitting between two members of the family of Purdey, the gun-makers. Since my knowledge of field sports was nil this was scarcely a felicitous right and left by who-ever was responsible. I do however recall Major (afterwards Lord) Astor, and I suppose there can be few who ever met him with whom he did not leave a vivid picture. Shortly after the war I was bidden to lunch at *The Times* – whether I was being vetted for a staff job I have no idea – and at first hand had an impression of utter integrity behind a diffident charm of manner which scarcely any other individual has conveyed in quite the same degree. He was one of the transparently good men.

How serene then to all outward appearance was the ancient institution of Marylebone! How far away were the political strains and the financial stresses of today! Even Bodyline, whatever its effect on the game at its higher levels, had left little permanent mark on the Club itself. No doubt there were some inner tensions, but the outward impression was of a bland, benevolent autocracy. Everything was ordered smoothly by the secretariat – no less so when Colonel R. S. Rait-Kerr brought a military precision to his office in succession to William Findlay. The Committee still met in the mid-afternoon at the Carlton Club, where the arrival of tea and crumpets was said to signalize the end of the proceedings.

Writing for a London evening paper I naturally saw much more of Lord's than I did subsequently. Moreover, since my work finished around four o'clock what more pleasant than to have a net in the evening with friends coming up from the city? So the scenes and the scents of Lord's were fresh in memory however long the war lasted, and in whatever uncongenial circumstances one found oneself. The people likewise.

There is a long tradition of warm friendliness between members of MCC and the staff. I dare say it may go back much farther than the middle 'twenties when Ronny Aird went to Lord's as assistant-secretary, but I always attribute to him much of the credit for the spirit of the place, for he had a way of his own with the staff, and they were so evidently fond of him. 'Jimmy' Cannon, the chief clerk, was a little cockney red robin, spruce and sharp, and with a rare twinkle. When he retired in 1944 he had been 65 years at Lord's, beginning in 1879 under the Prime Ministership of Disraeli. As a boy he fagged the tennis balls and held the heads of the horses of members who had ridden to the ground. Jimmy seemed to know every member, and was said to be able, by weighing up all possible factors, to pronounce at breakfast-time almost to a man the size of the crowd; which was naturally of much benefit to George Portman, the caterer.

Here was another cockney, shrewd and full of banter. He did a mere 48 years at Lord's, and if there is one thing above any other that the older members miss today it is Portman's catering. Behind the Long Bar reigned Mrs Barrow, and that is the word. She had a slight look of Queen Mary, and scarcely less dignity of manner and carriage. She would have looked well in a toque. When, after the war, one enquired after Mrs Barrow it was no surprise to learn that in a bombed street in Peckham she was at one time the only resident. The Germans didn't shift her!

The Gabys, Dick and Joe, now Ground and Pavilion superintendents respectively, were working their way up under the eye of their father 'Old Dick', whose connection with Lord's began in 1875 (so Lord's is only three years short of a Gaby centenary). Charlie Wray is another faithful who came to Lord's in the mid-'twenties. Until a few months back he was king-pin of the ticket office (which in fact is rather more than that and was called by 'Plum' Warner when he served as Deputy Secretary throughout the war the 'Engine-room'). Charlie, by the way, always thought this appropriate enough as it is a bit below the water-line and used to be the stoke-hole!

Archie Fowler, who came with the Arabs to Jersey as our umpire, was head pro, and old Sam Beton in charge of the dressing-rooms. This reminds me of a pleasant little story. Some years ago Roy Harrington, now the chief dressing-room attendant, said: 'You won't remember this, but you were once approached by a young lady at the pavilion door and asked whether you could get Denis Compton's autograph. You brought her book up, Denis signed it, and I took it back to her at the door.' Roy said he thought I'd be interested to know because the girl waiting there was now his wife, and they were accordingly grateful! Which can serve as a signal for bringing another of the central characters into the story.

I had my first all too brief taste of cricket with Middlesex in the middle 'thirties, Walter Robins having the flattering idea that I might be useful as an opening bat. This didn't work out, but my games both for Middlesex II in the Minor Counties' Championship in 1936 and against Oxford twice and Cambridge once in the two years following were full of interest for me. The experience, fleeting as it was, likewise had some value. As it happened, my first game for Middlesex II was Denis Compton's last, and it could be said, without stretching the truth, that I may have had some minor share in the prelude to his first appearance for the county at Lord's a day or two later. As I have told before, I went in first, against Kent at Folkestone, and with the score about 20 for four was joined by this eighteen-year-old with the loose-jointed, slightly way-ward walk which was soon to become so familiar. We put on 100 together, each getting just under 50, and in the second innings Denis again made about 40.

On being asked by Robins, when I returned to Lord's, for my impressions of the game I said I hoped I'd seen an embryo Test cricketer. 'Denis Compton?' said the captain. 'Funny, we're just going to have a look at him in the nets.' The upshot is well known enough, how Denis came into the Whitsuntide match against Sussex, how Jim Smith was promoted from No. 11, as always when Middlesex were in trouble, how Denis therefore went in last to join Gubby Allen with 34 still needed for first innings lead. We know, after his partner had given him the firmest instructions, whatever he did, to play forward to Tate, how Denis went back to the first ball which flew half an inch over the bails, and how, following this escape, he batted with so much assurance and skill that the runs were got.

Needless to say the 'Golden Boy' never looked back, and I dare say that if in August the selectors had taken the risk, as Allen says they nearly did, of sending him to Australia with MCC his star would have risen even more steeply in the cricket sky. If ever there was one Denis was a natural, needing no critical genius to pick him out. Under the eye of Fenner and Fowler he had shown his aptitude from first arrival on the Lord's staff at the age of fourteen. The eye and co-ordination were there, the physique was there. They gave him the strokes and kept an eye on the bowling action, and sharpened the fielding. To the great credit of both coaches they allowed due play to his individuality, rather than schooling his cricket into an over-rigid orthodoxy. The one thing that only experience could determine was whether such talent was complemented temperamentally. Within a few games for Middlesex there was no room for doubt on this score. In short there was never a more swift, inevitable burgeoning.

Meanwhile Denis's partner at Folkestone was treading a more modest path. Bill Watkins (due after the war to succeed Fowler as head pro) and I made 100 together in scarcely over an hour at the Oval against Surrey II, Bert Lock, the famous groundsman, who had a lovely medium-pace action, being one of the bowlers. I generally got a few but against good bowling was apt to grow fatally careless when set. At Fenner's I went in first with George Mann in his first first-class match, and got a horrible lbw – neither N nor M nor anything else. We won very easily, Bob Felton, a very good bat but just short perhaps of the required class, making a double hundred, and Pat Hendren negligently (or kindly) allowing himself to be bowled a yard or so down the pitch by a very slow leg-break from R. B. Bruce-Lockhart. Rab Lockhart was soon to get a Scottish rugger cap, and is now headmaster of Loretto. But he was less brilliant as a cricketer, and this most illustrious wicket was his only one in first-class cricket.

In the Parks, playing against Oxford, Jim Smith went in with a brand-new bat. His innings lasted three balls, and he returned grumbling about the bat. This seemed a rather premature judgment since he had hit a six to square-leg, a four that might have been caught by a long-stop, and sent the third ball steepling to the keeper. So we inspected the bat and found three marks, one on the splice, one on an extreme edge and one on the back!

Big Jim in the 'thirties was the best entertainer in the business, his lumbering entry guaranteed to empty the Tavern, and indeed every bar on every ground. He seldom batted for long, but there was never a dull moment, for he aimed exactly the same ponderous heave at every ball he received. It was just a question of which portion of the blade, or the edges, or the back the ball would connect with. If he got it in the middle of the bat on the up-swing the ball flew to a vast height and disappeared not only over the boundary but probably clean out of the ground. It was the less precise hits, however, those that might fly to any point of the compass, that caused the most hilarity. The way to bowl to him was to pitch the ball an absolutely full length, preferably a long half-volley or, of course, a yorker. The mistake was to bowl short, for the good length was his favourite meat. He simply drove at long-hops with primeval relish, and sometimes hit them great vertical distances.

The most celebrated of these blows I saw. It happened at Lord's against Kent for whom 'Hopper' Levett was keeping wicket. As the ball disappeared into the stratosphere 'Hopper' confidently shouted 'right' – which must have been a relief to the fielders nearby. For what seemed an age the ball remained a speck while the keeper stood static, peering upwards. Suddenly 'Hopper', judging he was not exactly underneath it, shifted. Then he circled again – and again – and again. Finally, and inevitably, he lost his balance and fell with a thud at about the same time as the ball came to earth two or three yards away. It was some moments before order was restored, and the game could be continued. Frank Woolley, dignified and aloof, laughed so immoderately I thought he might be going to fall over too. At slip he had a grandstand view.

It would be stretching the truth to say that I recall much more about the 1937 New Zealand tour than Jack Cowie's admirable bowling and Len Hutton beginning his Test career at Lord's by falling to him for o and 1. The young hopeful, however, made amends with 100 at Old Trafford, while Denis Compton first appeared in the Oval Test and got 65 before being run out, in the unluckiest of all ways, through a deflection by the bowler. But two incidents that August of 1937 are vivid enough. One was in the second game of the Canterbury Week with Notts against the visitors. On the last afternoon Kent set their opponents 310 to win in 3¾ hours: a lot of runs but feasible enough with everything going right. It went better than right, for Joe Hardstaff – known as 'Young

Joe' to distinguish him from his revered father – tore the attack apart and made his 100 in 51 minutes, which won him the Lawrence Trophy for that year and is, incidentally, the fastest first-class hundred I ever saw. Perhaps he recalled that George Gunn, his father's contemporary and the oracle of Trent Bridge, always said he batted better to the sound of music. The band of the Buffs would have been playing that August afternoon, and I sat under the old tree at the top of the ground with a bag of cherries watching this ever-elegant fellow dismissing the Kent bowling to all parts. In particular, with that generous back-lift and both hands very high on the handle, he drove with perfect timing into the pavilion geraniums at one end, and up to the tents at the other. To me at least a fine innings in the matchless setting of Canterbury is just a little more of a collector's piece than if it had been played elsewhere – except, of course, at Lord's.

The other occasion I recall was, as it happens, at Lord's: Pat Hendren's last match, Middlesex v. Surrey. There was never a more sentimental nostalgia-filled moment than when before a very large crowd the little man reached his hundred, and again as he walked back just afterwards in the late August sunshine, with everyone on their feet applauding the hero in, that shy grin hiding the emotion that was surely near the surface. Hendren (E.) christened Elias, 'Patsy' to the man round the ring, Pat to his friends, had been part of the Lord's scene for thirty summers, bar the war years. He had an impish, Irish sense of the comical that communicated itself to the crowd, with whom he was a favourite almost without rival. With them he was as popular at Melbourne and Sydney, Bridgetown and Port-of-Spain, as he was at Lord's. Here now was the old actor taking his last big curtain – to be exact his last but one, since on the third day he had to bat a second time, and made a duck. So he ended his career exactly as he had begun it.

If that was an anti-climax of its kind, another and a preventable one followed it. Errol Holmes wanted to take a new ball (which in those days came at 200 runs, not after 85 overs) when on the third evening, with seven wickets down, Allen and Robins for Middlesex were struggling to save the game. He accordingly, to quote *Wisden*:

> bowled an over that, consisting of deliveries tossed high or wide of the wicket, yielded 24 runs from byes and wides while a fieldsman in the deep made no effort to prevent the ball reaching the boundary. Protests came from the crowd, but before the new ball could be brought into use, a success-

ful appeal against the light ended the unhappy proceedings. As the sun shone, it was ridiculous to suggest that the light was unfit for cricket, but a farcical situation was ended by this pretence.

I wrote that this episode was a deplorable way to bring Hendren's great career, let alone the Lord's season, to an end, and was duly critical of Errol Holmes, who had engineered it. It was strangely unlike Errol, who stood out even in a more liberal age as a notably generous-minded opponent. I suppose there was some special 'needle' in the game which at this distance escapes me. Anyway Errol took my remarks very much amiss, which worried me, as I had a great liking and admiration for him. It was well on into the following summer when he made a brilliant hundred at the Oval against Sussex in 65 minutes. I naturally enthused over this in print, and had a note of thanks asking me to come to the dressing-room and 'bury the hatchet' over a glass. We remained friends, and fellow-members of the Bath Club, until his sadly sudden and early death at the age of fifty-four.

The possibility of antagonizing people one holds in high respect, or even affection, is, naturally, an occupational hazard of journalism. In fact one's relationships within the subject of one's writing are inevitably just that bit more delicate than normal. The sporting critic can only strive to see games and situations in perspective and to be objective and fair in his judgments on all who take part. Even so, human nature being what it is, he will occasionally offend someone, whether knowingly or not. Some otherwise rational people are sensitive beyond all reason about references to them in print. One can only follow one's conscience and carry on. It is an early lesson for the writer that with some people recollection of the warmest, most consistent praise can be obliterated altogether by a few words of censure.

It was in the middle of February 1938 that H. S. Altham opened for me a new area of work, and an obvious chance of advancing my reputation, by asking me to collaborate in a second edition of *A History of Cricket*. 'I should like to have the last say in any general verdict on major issues, e.g. Bodyline and the policy of the MCC, but I don't think we should often be at variance,' wrote Harry in the letter of invitation which I gratefully accepted. That we were never at odds he testifies in the preface when he says: 'For all the sections in which we have collaborated we have been well content to accept jointly the first person singular whenever it occurs.'

On the leader-page of the *Daily Telegraph* J. B. Firth, writing of the new material in the book, said, 'This has largely been undertaken by Mr E. W. Swanton, also an accomplished critic of the game, and possessed of a pretty Theophrastic touch in delineating the character of a cricketer.' The accomplished critic was duly flattered once he had ascertained that Theophrastus, the disciple of Aristotle, was so named by the latter because of his divine eloquence. If this may seem to have been laying it on a bit, it must be agreed that the *Daily Telegraph*'s first mention of my work was auspicious indeed. Anyway, the book was well received – *The Observer* called it 'a sparkling history' – and this revision formed the basis of the third and fourth editions and a fifth impression in 1947, 1948 and 1949 respectively, which in turn preceded the enlargement into two volumes in 1962.

It sheds a revealing light on publishing timetables then and now, by the way, that only eighteen weeks elapsed between Harry Altham's suggestion asking me to co-operate in a new edition and Firth's review timed to coincide with the Lord's Test against Australia. It looks as though Allen and Unwin must have done their stuff inside two months, as distinct from the six or more of the 'seventies.

I suppose the thing that most people recall about the visit of the 1938 Australians was Len Hutton's marathon at the Oval. As a piece of cricket his 364 in 13 hours 20 minutes did not compare with two great innings in the series, Stan McCabe's 232 at Trent Bridge, which to my eternal regret I missed, and Wally Hammond's 240 at Lord's, the best innings I ever saw him play. However, there was no doubt which of these performances most enthused the public. The Don was a legend, with every record in the book. Here was an Englishman snatching one back – and the highest Test score at that. The Oval pitch was of a wonderful docility – O'Reilly maintained 'You could smell the cow-dung on it as you came out of the pavilion gate,' and the Australian opening attack of Waite and McCabe was pretty docile too. But O'Reilly was O'Reilly, and in the everlasting duel with Hutton gave nothing away (85–26–178–3!).

I was broadcasting for the Empire Service, and have a picture in my mind of Hutton coming up the ladder to our BBC perch on the roof of the Ladies' Stand after he was out, to be interviewed by Howard Marshall, his trousers grey with the Kennington dust. Some months later, when we were golfing together in South Africa, Len told me something of the strain of his vigil. For three nights, including the Sunday, he was not out, and he had practically no sleep in any of them.

The crowning irony came when with the score pushing 900 Bradman bowled and badly wrenched his ankle in O'Reilly's footmarks. His carrying-off was the end of the match as a contest, though it was said that Hammond practically wanted a doctor's certificate confirming Bradman's inability to bat before he called off the slow ritual murder at 903 for seven. Australia's swift collapse owed nothing to the pitch. Fingleton as well as Bradman was injured and unable to bat, and the rest tacitly accepted the utter hopelessness of the position. So Australia toppled twice, and the timeless match – timeless because the rubber was undecided when the last Test started – was over in four days after all.

One very small thing about the 1938 Australians was that for the only time I remember they wore English-style green caps instead of their usual baggy ones, and somehow gave a slightly less formidable impression in consequence. They were weaker in bowling than usual, with no speed to speak of apart from the erratic McCormick, and no Grimmett at the other end from O'Reilly. Moreover the English batting just before the war was mighty strong. By the time they had finished playing after the war the first seven men in that Oval order, Hutton, Edrich, Leyland, Hammond, Paynter, Compton and Hardstaff, had made 713 hundreds between them, and if Ames had not been unfit the first eight would have totted up 815!

Yet even in that company Hugh Bartlett very nearly forced inclusion for the Oval Test. His 175 not out for the Gentlemen at Lord's a month earlier was the second highest innings ever played in the match. He batted only *two hours and three-quarters*, hit four sixes and twenty-four fours, and gave no chance. One of his sixes off Nichols (from the pitch next door to the middle one) hit the topmost corner of the Grand Stand nearest the pavilion. Another from the other end – remember that he was a left-hander – disappeared into the highest recesses of the Mound Stand. No one seemed to be enjoying it all more than Frank Woolley, who had coached Hugh as a Dulwich boy, and who was leading the Players in this, his farewell season. Altogether this 'G and P' stands out marvellously clear. Ken Farnes's eleven for 103 is described by *Wisden* as 'the best fast bowling seen in the match since Arthur Fielder dismissed all the Gentlemen at a cost of 90 runs in 1906'. Ken had just been dropped from the Test side, and was relieving his feelings by what I think is the fastest bowling I have ever seen in England. Larwood was fast in 1930 (though the pitches drew his venom), Lindwall and Miller in 1948, Hall and Griffith in 1963, and at their peak all these were probably faster than Farnes. But he could be roused by an occasion to a different degree of speed. When he was absolutely flat out he seemed, at the moment of delivery, to be almost shaking the head off his shoulders. This, by the way, was always a sign, too, that Alec Bedser was in the mood and scenting blood.

Not least this match at Lord's was the farewell to Woolley that I best remember. Wherever he played that summer the spectators rose in salute, and he seldom failed those who had come to pay their final homage. At the age of fifty-one an aggregate of 1,590 runs, average 32, is no mean note to end on. Here at Lord's, after the crowd had applauded him all the way to the wicket, Frank on arrival stood for a moment firmly at attention, bat at his side, and slowly took off his cap. It was natural, and charming, and unique. Then, this brief ritual over, he proceeded to make 41 lovely runs showing, as ever, his taste for fast bowling, by playing with more apparent time against Farnes than anyone else. At the Folkestone Festival in September Frank went to the wicket for the last time in a first-class match, and so after 33 seasons less the four years of war, the account was closed with the figures reading –

Innings	Not out	Runs	Highest	Average
1,532	85	58,969	305*	40·75

In addition there was a little matter of 2,068 wickets at 19·85 each, and eight summers when he did the double, plus 1,011 catches, a number unapproached by anyone. In the history of the game only Jack Hobbs made a few more runs, and not even he stirred the crowd in quite the same way. No cricketer ever gave so much happiness to so many for so long.

During the autumn of 1938 I was trying to organize the trip to South Africa with MCC on which I was determined, but though the only other English journalist to go was William Pollock of the *Daily Express* Fleet Street were uninterested, and I therefore sailed off on 2 December on the old *Balmoral Castle* with orders amounting to £188.6.0d., of which I was getting £126 from the BBC for 20 broadcasts. As I was to talk back home twenty times for an aggregate of 6½ hours this was not a lavish reward, though in line no doubt with BBC scales of payment in the 'thirties. I took a chance, of course, of finding more work in South Africa, and was not disappointed. For the first Test the South African Broadcasting Corporation, which had never before broadcast live cricket, merely took the bits I was sending to London; but there was such a quick demand for more that I was soon doing two hours a day over the South African air during Test Matches, and also writing for the Argus newspaper group. In the end, thanks to the final Test lasting ten days and me being remunerated by the day, I showed a small profit on the enterprise. If this seems surprising remember that travel and hotels were then marvellously cheap. For instance my return first-class fare by Union Castle to the Cape was £103.10.0d., on which my kind uncle in the shipping world succeeded in getting me a 'professional' discount of 20%. So a glorious month at sea cost £82.16.0d. – plus drinks!

The first day of the first Test at Johannesburg was the first occasion when a live cricket broadcast had been sent back to England, besides being my own first Test effort at running commentary. So I was keen to put up a performance. However the commentary box held only one (no scorer), I had not had time to get acclimatized to the 6,000 feet of Johannesburg, while on the field the action was minimal. It was the last half-hour of the day, and Paul Gibb was playing some very slow leg-breaks from Bruce Mitchell with vast circumspection. This was on Christmas Eve, and it was much the same on Boxing Day with Mitchell now batting with utter passivity against Hedley Verity. As I sweated in my tiny enclosed box I imagined English listeners by the thousand falling asleep over the Yule log. Then suddenly, with about ten minutes to go before the close, Tom Goddard got a wicket, catching and bowling Dudley Nourse with those enormous hands of his for 73. The night-watchman arrived, Gordon by name, stretched at his first ball and was stumped. So Tom was on a hat-trick.

Here was a situation the drama of which even this tyro at the mike couldn't miss. Somnolent fathers were obviously now being aroused, especially around the west country. Young Billy Wade, the South African wicket-keeper, a good bat but a beginner in Test cricket, came slowly in, went nervously through the business of taking guard, looked around – and was promptly bowled.

Only five Englishmen in Test history had ever done the hat-trick before Tom Goddard, and incidentally only one, Peter Loader, has done one since. So it was quite a story, and altogether the lucky commentator felt very much set up, especially when at the end of the game Michael Standing wired – 'Congratulations on commentaries. Everybody pleased.'

Altogether those first two days brought it home to what extent one is beholden to one's material. With experience, naturally, it became easier to make bricks without much straw, and indeed I came by a fair dose of experience in the last Test of this same series when I had to woffle two hours a day for ten days, or, to be accurate, for nine, since one day mercifully it rained and there was no cricket.

This 'Timeless Test' was a fairly ridiculous game of cricket, made even more so by the fact that, whereas the whole point of its being played (theoretically) without limit was so as to ensure a finish, in fact it had to be left drawn. This was because in order to catch the *Athlone Castle* leaving the Cape a thousand miles away on a Friday the team were obliged to leave Durban by train on the Tuesday night. They could have finished the game by flying, but English cricketers were thought too precious to be allowed in the air, and strangely enough there was at once some slight evidence for the official view since the plane they would probably have travelled on, having landed at Mossel Bay on the southern toe of the continent, on its way to Cape Town, had to be dug out of the sand. I know because I was on it, as also was Walter Hammond, who presumably dispensed himself from the rules.

The key to the extraordinary lasting power of the pitch – and therefore to the course of the game – was that one of the playing conditions empowered the groundsman to roll before a day's play began any time after rain, if the pitch might be improved by so doing. Accordingly before the third, the fourth, the sixth and the ninth days Vic Robbins, the curator, as he was called, at Kingsmead, used the heavy roller at dawn, and in effect made a new cake which the tropical sun had dried out by the start of play. As the poor, sweating bowlers grew more and more weary so they were faced with a pitch becoming ever easier. Since South Africa had started the game light in bowling, and seeing that their best man, A. B. C. Langton, had to bowl his 56 overs in the England second innings lame and at half pace, what would normally have been an utterly impossible task – 696 were needed to win – began as the hours unfolded to look first conceivable, then likely, and finally almost a certainty.

Bill Edrich, whom Hammond had persevered with in the face of continued failure in Tests, came good at last to the tune of 219 in seven hours, 40 minutes. (He had actually played eleven Test innings against Australia and South Africa in the preceding nine months for 88 runs, with such other young men at Bartlett and Norman Yardley pining for a chance.) As day followed day even the commentator's stamina was taxed. But one of the singularly pretty girls in which Durban abounded used to pick him up at lunch and take him for a swim, while in the evening one could always make do with the oysters at Umshlonga Rocks. There was no shortage of amusement and hospitality.

Just after lunch on the tenth day after a session on the air I was rung up by a listener of English sympathies who said I'd better tell Hammond to buck up as it was raining where he was, down the Natal coast at Isipingo. I duly informed our manager, Flight-Lieut. A. J. Holmes, who, using the usual pretext of a batting glove, sent Wally, out in the middle, a message to this effect. Eddie Paynter thereupon had a go and got out (611 for four!) and the captain was ultimately stumped (650 for five), but Les Ames had scarcely been joined in mid-afternoon by Bryan Valentine when the heavens opened for the last time. England were within hail of what would have been a wholly extraordinary victory, while South Africa must still have had at least some slim hope of capturing the last five wickets for fewer than 46. Yet the fact is by that time neither side seemed to care a jot. The game in the steamy heat of March had left them drained and exhausted.

The pity was that this freak affair, following closely on Hutton's match at the Oval, turned everyone decidedly away from timeless matches. People blamed the lack of a limit instead of the root cause of the ennui, which in both cases was the pitch. Thus it came about that Australia, where Tests had always been played to a finish, after the war reverted to a 30-hour limit.

Before I leave Durban let me tell of a passing strange meeting which had an important sequel. We had come up the coast to Durban for the Third Test from East London on the *Warwick Castle*, which like all the Union Castle boats, if I remember aright, had a gymnasium below decks. When I repaired to this, possibly to work off the effects of the usual prodigious hospitality, I found a little chap climbing about on the wall bars and generally displaying much agility for his middle-age. He told me he was on his way from England to Australia, and was going to be in Durban for the first couple of days of the Test Match. He asked what chance there was of getting a ticket. I said that if he would tell me his name I would introduce him to our manager.

'That's very kind of you,' he said. 'The name is Nuffield.'

In that case, I said, there was very little doubt about it. Jack Holmes gave the great car manufacturer and philanthropist (who had been accorded a viscountcy in the preceding year) a seat on the players' balcony. When he went out to have a look at the pitch he was recognized and warmly applauded. This pleased him, and so did his reception at the Saturday night dance at the Country Club, which saw him in good form on the floor. Stimulated by the Palais Glide and the Lambeth Walk Lord Nuffield got up and said he'd like to make a gesture towards South African cricket – if £10,000 would be any use to them.

He was sailing, however, on the Monday morning. Could they submit a scheme before then? The SACA rather shrewdly persuaded Walter Hammond to chair an *ad hoc* meeting on the Sunday at which the notion of an annual schoolboys' tournament was formulated, each province fielding a team. Lord Nuffield thought the encouragement of youth an excellent idea and before continuing his journey dropped in a further £500 so that the plan could be initiated right away without waiting for the interest to accrue. Hence the annual Nuffield Schools Week, held ever since at a different centre each year, which has done so much to stimulate the game in South Africa. Most of the post-war Test cricketers have first come to notice in this way.

Sad that no far-sighted person thought of bringing non-Europeans into the scheme! The fact is in the climate of that time it would not have occurred to anyone; but equally if it had done so there would have been no government objection. I hope those who hold that I have taken too liberal a line in the recent grievous troubles may put to the credit side the fact that by chance I happened to set this particular set of Nuffield wheels turning.

My first tour to South Africa was wholly pleasurable. The visit of an MCC side was a great social highlight, and one was young enough to enjoy everything to the hilt. In addition to our side, most of whom I knew fairly well before I started, Alan Melville and Pieter van der Bijl had been friends since their Oxford days and I saw plenty of them and of their families. Alan was as elegant a bat as any of his generation. Having captained both Oxford and Sussex he returned home to lead his country, not having played in a Test match. After a modest start he blossomed richly, and in the Fifth Test ᴜ~ (78 and 103) and Pieter (125 and 97), going in first together, kept the England bowlers at bay for hour after hour. This, as it turned out, was the first of four Test hundreds in a row for Melville, the other three coming in England in 1947; but Pieter van der Bijl was badly wounded in the desert, and after the war had to restrict his energies to teaching the young at that great school, the Diocesan College, Rondebosch, commonly called 'Bishops', whence came the Van Rynevelds, 'Ossie' Newton-Thompson, 'Tuppy' Owen-Smith, and a host of other names famous in Oxford sport.

Looking back on the South Africa of thirty-odd years ago I can recall no impression of stark social injustice. No doubt I was young and heedless. In my twelve-week stay I also had plenty to do. Probably the only non-Europeans one came in contact with were the servants in friends' houses, and they would have been treated well enough. Within these narrow contacts the atmosphere, both then and when I returned ten years later, seemed to be of a benevolently strict paternalism. It would have registered had things been otherwise – as it did when one encountered the very different climate of the third and last of my MCC tours in 1956/7.

When we watched Cape Town recede, framed in its noble mountain, in March 1939, throwing coins into Table Bay as a pledge of our return, the coalition of Herzog and Smuts was still enduring. But the Ossewabrandwag was no doubt already recruiting its heroes to practise their U-boat signalling and otherwise give active aid to Germany. Herzog and Smuts were soon to split, and when Smuts, after a bitter debate, carried South Africa narrowly into the war he could only do so at the cost of a deeper rift between those of English and Dutch stock. The South African tragedy was taking another step on its fateful course.

The last summer of peace provided a good store of memories to help carry us over the following years. The West Indies came, and George Headley in the Lord's Test made a hundred in each innings, while at the Oval Learie Constantine put up a virtuoso performance possible perhaps to no one else : five for 72 in England's first innings followed by a whirlwind of an innings – 79 in about an hour with fifteen fours, not to mention an almost belief-defying straight six off the back foot at the expense of Perks down to the Vauxhall End. As it happened this was the West Indians' ultimate gesture, for on Colonial Office advice they returned home while they could still get a sailing, and perforce abandoned the tour with seven matches to go.

Yorkshire under Brian Sellers won the championship as usual, and as usual Middlesex, now with Ian Peebles as captain after four dynamic years of Walter Robins, were runners-up. Oxford won the University Match which for the first time in history started on a Saturday, when 9,000 attended. (But this was rated a disappointing gate!) The last game I broadcast was at Bournemouth where Yorkshire finally clinched the championship by winning in two days. I remember nothing of it, but very well recall standing with George Mann on the Middlesex balcony, after they had with equal emphasis disposed of Warwickshire, and as the Lord's crowd dispersed wondering when we should see them next assemble. The answer, apart from the war games when we were far away, was, of course, seven years; but the wonder was not so much that most of us in the Middlesex camp survived those years but that Lord's itself was to emerge a little shabby but largely unscathed.

From Munich onwards the premonitions of war led many, I suppose, to a sort of 'last fling' attitude. This had, for me and many friends, one special expression which perhaps I may recall on the theory that what is still amusing to write about may strike an echoing chord or two with the reader. I mean the regular, almost ritual, attendance at that most extraordinary of musical melodramas called Young England. It started at the Victoria Palace which, so R. H. Gillespie, the kingpin of Moss Empires, afterwards told me, Walter Reynolds, its octogenarian author, rented from him in the off-season for £40 a week. It was said that Noel Coward saw an early performance, and was reduced to quiet sobs of mirth. Word went round that this reincarnation of the style and language of the most lurid Victorian melodrama was far too bad to be missed. Longhurst, Peebles and I were initiated early, and followed the great drama round its several theatres in 1938/9, from the Victoria Palace to the Kingsway, to the Piccadilly, to Daly's, and lastly back to the Kingsway, which was a bit off the beaten track, and in the view of the real afficionados its spiritual home.

There were certain conventions. One never arrived for the first scenes, since the start was inconveniently early. Legend had it that the curtain went up to the wail of a (first war) air raid siren, to which grisly accompaniment and in the shelter of the underground an unfortunate girl gave birth. My recollection is that she had been brought to platform, as one might say, by the Boy Scout leader, robustly played by

Guy Middleton, but it could have been the rascally Mayor of Carlingford in the person of John Oxford, for whose performance, night in and night out, no praise could be too high.

The author, hard though it was to credit, had written the play in a mood of high crusading patriotism, and the mayor played it dead straight, stroking his long black moustaches and looking suitably sinister. The chief 'goody' was called Dr Capt. Frank Inglehurst, VC; there was someone who made frequent references to 'my mother, the Duchess', and a highly decorative sister, whose acquaintance some of us made off-stage, known as Lady Mary.

One turned up any time in the first act, paying 3/6d. (?) for a seat in the pit, and a further florin or so if required to the attendant at the junction between the pit and the stalls. The success of any particular evening depended upon the volume and quality of the audience participation. At its worst, on Saturday nights, when rugger toughs made it the vogue, the noise spoilt the enjoyment, the single sound from the stage that penetrated the uproar on one occasion, it was said, being the revolver shot with which in the last act the mayor finally did the decent thing.

Interruptions were welcome at any time, so long as they were thought funny, and at some of the impromptus the cast must have been hard pressed to keep straight faces. There were certain traditional interjections such as when the caddish Middleton stole the funds from the safe in the Boy Scout hut. Stealthily he tiptoes away until he stops in his tracks and to cries of 'Wipe it! Wipe it!' returns and removes the fingerprints with a handkerchief. Sometimes he would feint to stop, and get the audience shouting too soon. But this was the extent of the collusion across the footlights.

At the end, after the grand finale featuring Boy Scouts, Girl Guides, and the rest, John Oxford would step gravely forward and thank the audience for their magnificent reception. One night in doing so he apologized for his own performance, saying that his throat was bad and he was afraid he was a little hoarse. Whereat Leonard Gullick, proprietor of the XIXth Club and a regular, stood up, a dapper monocled figure, and enunciated clearly in a moment of hush: 'How *can* a mayor be a little horse?' Henry Longhurst in *My Life and Soft Times* has paid his tribute to Young England and even mentioned this particular interjection by his old friend Gullick. But the great drama can surely stand a double exposure from two of its most faithful patrons. Henry, incidentally, had a quelling way with sub-standard comment. 'Now then, sir,' he would say sternly, 'funny or not at all.' Utterly infantile, was it? A deplorable waste of time? No doubt, but I can only plead that in the prevailing mood it all seemed very funny at the time. In any event the frivolities were all but over: the west-end lights were soon to give way to the long black-out.

7

One Man's War

The Eighteenth Division, of which 148 Field Regiment, RA (Bedfordshire Yeomanry), formed part was, I expect, pushed around and generally mucked about little if any more than most Territorial Army units in the war of 1939–45. Our first rôle was an essentially static one, since we had no transport to speak of, defending the coast of Norfolk and Suffolk from any foray or landing from the other side of the North Sea. In conjunction with our friends of the Norfolks and Suffolks in 54 Brigade we fulfilled this unexacting rôle for the whole of 1940. In the bleak mid-winter of 1939–40 we manned the wind-swept promenades of Great Yarmouth and Lowestoft. When the phoney war ended we formed the anti-invasion force for the area east and north of Norwich. After Norfolk we repaired north to the borders of Scotland where our training and equipment were due to be completed.

Having endured some months of Hawick and district, as I remember it almost permanently under snow, we wended south again, armed now to the teeth, and supposedly ready to sail. But no, the summer and autumn of 1941 found us still training, first in Lancashire, where we had a grandstand view of the Liverpool raids, and I got an unexpected bonus of half a season's tough, admirable cricket on Saturdays for Liverpool in the Liverpool and District Competition, and latterly in Monmouth.

When the King came down to see us there, and we paraded in the courtyard of the castle, it seemed that this time we really must be off, and so it proved. But where? Back at Liverpool 148 Field embarked on that lavish cruise ship the *Andes*, and as we crossed the Atlantic due west depleted its cellar almost to extinction. After a little more than two years we were off at last.

Until now our war had been unexciting and, as wars go, relatively comfortable. We were essentially, for the most part, Territorials, and the chief happiness I personally found was in getting to know well the sort of sterling fellows who had had the guts and the push to involve themselves in matters military in the middle and late 'thirties well in advance of the scramble when the inevitable finally became fact. I say 'we' though as I explained at the beginning I had the luck to be smuggled in at the outbreak, without the benefit of OCTU, and despite the lack of any Bedfordshire connection. From the area of Dunstable and Leighton Buzzard most of my battery came, from Luton the other: altogether a fair assortment of town and countrymen, to whom there came to be added the conscript batches, later absorbed without detriment to the character and spirit of our close community. I had great respect for the qualities of the men of Bedfordshire, and there was no sadder moment for me on returning from the Far East than to meet the next of kin of the many who never returned, and to fill in, so far as it was known, the detail of each pathetic story.

'Very flat, Norfolk,' as Noel Coward reminded us, and to soldier there is to discover just how lacking it is in anything that could be called a hill. For most of 1940, now rather more mobile, we occupied constantly-changing positions in the area to seaward of the Yarmouth–North Walsham road, digging gun-pit after gun-pit, and climbing church tower after church tower (negotiating a good deal of rather dangerous dry-rot in the process), since only from them could one get any sort of field of view. Were we so naïve as not to realize that there was nothing tactical about these dispositions? All that digging was designed to impress German intelligence through their aerial reconnaissance with the thought that East Anglia was bristling with guns. What a hope!

One of the depressing things about the period after Dunkirk was that one's equipment, instead of becoming more modern, was always being changed for the worse as the BEF units, devoid of arms, were being reformed. In September 1939 I had taken charge of a troop of four eighteen-pounders, actually with pneumatic-tyred wheels. By the time of the Cromwell alert (Invasion Imminent) a year later these had given way by stages to the possession of *two* 4·5 howitzers, marked DP – for demonstration purposes – and dated 1915! These were dug in, in the garden of The Grange at Ingham, supposedly covering a mile or two of foreshore. My observation post where one 'stood to' at dawn and sunset with a sprinkling of 5 Suffolk infantry was a hollow in the dunes overlooking the beach a little north of Palling. If the Führer's forces had chanced to descend on this portion of our sea-girt isle one autumn morning of 1940 he could have declared by lunch-time. Which reminds me: just one game of cricket I had managed to get in that summer, on the pleasant Ingham ground, where we ran into a team half full or more of Edriches. At the age of three I suppose John might have been an infant spectator.

By this time, sadly for me, Ian Peebles had applied successfully for a transfer, having innocently fallen foul of the divisional CRA or Commander, Royal Artillery. I laugh now to recall how this happened, though at the time it seemed serious enough. The day came in Norfolk when under the piercing eye of this formidable Brigadier the young officers of 148 Field were summoned one by one to the Observation Post to conduct their first shoot – with live ammunition. It came to Ian's turn, we who had been through the mill staying on to watch.

'Peebles, eh? Anything to do with the cricketer?' Ian pleaded guilty, and was duly given his target of copse or hedge somewhere well to our front. Calculations were duly made, and the orders given over the telephone to the troop of guns in rear – range, bearing, and so on, ending with the magic word – Fire!

So far on this day of days all had gone smoothly. We had seemed to know the drill reasonably well, and the shells from a range of somewhere between 4,000 and 6,000 yards had fallen in roughly the right area. But now! As the guns fired we raised our binoculars looking hopefully for the burst. Next second there was a fearful cr-r-r-ump and the OP was enveloped in dirt and smoke as the first shell exploded about a couple of cricket pitches in our rear.

'Stop!' bellowed the Battery Commander down the line. 'Stop!'

Yes, but would he be in time to prevent the next round, which might even now be whistling towards us in advance of the sound? In a word would near-miss be followed by direct hit? They were awful seconds before the cancellation was confirmed by the Gun-Position-Officer, and we breathed again.

The CRA's wrath at this escape was terrible to behold – as, for that matter, was the anguish of poor Stanley Harris, our CO. The verbal rockets spared no one. Mr Peebles had made a gross error in the range, giving the distance from guns to OP instead of from guns to target. His Ack. was guilty of being a party to it. The GPO and his Ack. had failed to check and were equally guilty. So were all the officers at the OP, from the colonel downwards. Thus the day's sport terminated abruptly, and the CRA and his staff departed in a gleam of field-boots and fury.

Maybe an anonymous-sounding culprit would have got away with it to the extent of time blurring his identity in the CRA's mind. But the name of Peebles was seared deep, and the story went that whenever it appeared on lists of promotion candidates it was as regularly struck out. Hence Ian's ultimate transfer, and the irony of his proceeding to Intelligence was not lost either on the regiment or on him. Photographic security, as I recall, was his special province. It was illegal to take a picture of the Thames without a pass signed by Captain (at last) I. A. R. Peebles. As it happened he was engaged one night in rescue operations during a raid outside his MI5 department in Queen's Gate when a bomb dropped even nearer than his own shell had done on the Norfolk flats, and with far greater effect. It killed twenty-three, considering which Ian was lucky to lose merely the sight of one eye and a certain amount of mobility in one leg.

The CRA, I might add, Geoffrey Franklin by name, when one came to know him was the most brilliant soldier in my limited experience, a master at seeing everything that mattered through the fog of a training exercise, and summing all up without a superfluous word. Franklin, his complexion matching the scarlet of his tabs, looked like *Punch*'s idea of a general. He demanded high standards, not least of personal comfort, the duties of his G III, Harold Cassel (now Sir Harold, Bt., QC), including the instant provision on demand of a dry martini, very cold and very dry.

But to return to 1941: here we were now in a vast convoy crossing the Atlantic due west. We were scarcely half-way when an extraordinary thing happened. The American Navy took us over and the British turned and went home. The date was October 1941, several weeks before Pearl Harbour brought the United States into the conflict. When we docked at Halifax, Nova Scotia, another surprise: with the USA still nominally non-belligerent, we trans-shipped into large American transports, a brigade to a ship, and proceeded south.

It would be idle to pretend that the spirit of the Grand Alliance prevailed in the *Wakefield* as we zig-zagged our way close to shore, past the West Indian islands, before leaving the South American coastline to starboard and making across the South Atlantic for the Cape. The Americans who had sailed under sealed orders to Halifax were, not surprisingly, astonished and resentful at what they found themselves doing, while we were crammed so tight in cabins and on mess-decks that exercise, other than static PT, was almost impossible. There were long queues for meals in shifts – and the ship, according to American naval custom, was bone dry. After the *Andes* it was steerage travel for all ranks with a vengeance – and a mighty long voyage to an unknown destination at that.

The news of Pearl Harbour, coming when we were off the Cape, made little difference to the attitude of our new allies. Relationships continued frosty. As to the outrage itself the American attitude afforded us some wry amusement. 'The little yellow bastards!' they said. 'Now they'll find what's coming to them. Reckon about three weeks'll settle their hash.' The extent and significance of the Pearl Harbour losses, of course, remained long hidden. Ten years later, returning from New Zealand and Australia via Honolulu I made the sombre tour of the battle scene in the Admiral's barge and heard how at dawn of the morning after the great annual football game the Jap planes had flown in out of the sun and caught the American Navy with their trousers down.

After a couple of leg-stretching, superbly hospitable days at the Cape the convoy moved into the Indian Ocean at the time the Churchill–Curtin exchanges were going on wherein our fate was being decided. Off Durban the *Mount Vernon*, carrying 53 Brigade as well as 50 Hurricanes, peeled off east to Singapore, while we sailed north to land just after Christmas at Bombay. The fate of 54 and 55 Brigades was still in the balance, as we afterwards knew, as between the Middle East, which was our original destination, and Malaya. Leaving the *Wakefield* gratefully behind us we entrained and after a comparatively short journey looked out to see on the station of our arrival the magic name Poona.

After so many long weeks at sea the three weeks we spent in the dry, bracing heat of this place which was the popular symbol and epitome of British rule in India, were a blissful interlude, even if the dowdiness of the Poona Club on New Year's Eve was a surprise and disappointment. The pukka sahibs, of course, were far away on sterner business. My chief memory is of bowling all afternoon better than I ever did before or since against the pick of two Yorkshire regiments, the KOYLIs and the York and Lancaster, full of gritty league cricketers. Not long ago one of the KOYLIs came up and reminded me of this match, and remembered that I'd brought my cricket bag with me thus far. As a matter of fact I don't swear I didn't take it on with me to Singapore. What would our gallant allies of the *Wakefield* have made of this strange object, I wonder!

There was a big match on that magnificent Poona ground between two Indian teams whereon I saw a certain D. B. Deodhar after a fine innings garlanded with flower-necklaces in the traditional manner. After which halcyon interlude we were back in the train again, heading for Bombay, and – dammit – the blasted *Wakefield*. Same cabins, same arrangements. As we headed south and then east on rounding Ceylon there was only one place we could be bound for.

The 18th Division, less the Brigade already engaged in Malaya, approached Singapore round the wicket – that is from the south through the Sunda Strait dividing the vast islands of Sumatra and Java rather than direct which would have exposed the convoy to air attack from Malaya all the way through the long and narrow straits of Malacca. In the Sunda Strait we were spotted, and the sea swallowed a bomb or two, and in the remaining two days before we docked we were naturally expecting more. But we were unmolested.

As the *Wakefield* berthed, and became a sitting prey, quite a large bomber force came straight at us in diamond formation. The moment had surely come. Then when they were almost overhead the bombers wheeled right and unloaded on a target nearby. Naturally we were soon hustled ashore, and the ship was empty of troops before they returned. This was our first insight into the Jap mentality. The leader must have seen the target of his dreams suddenly dead ahead. But his orders specified otherwise, and in the Jap priority of virtues obedience presumably came before initiative.

The date was 29 January 1942 – the day on which the Churchill Government won its vote of confidence by 464 votes to one. Would the margin, one wonders, have been quite as massive a few weeks later? There is little that an insignificant gunner troop commander can add to the story of the Battle of Singapore at a remove of thirty years, but a brief comment may perhaps be acceptable. At any rate the episode cannot be ignored, if only out of respect for one's comrades in the regiment and division who had little enough reason to be ashamed of their own part, however deplorable was the whole tragic affair.

The early chapters of volume IV (*The Hinge of Fate*) of Churchill's history make, of course, fascinating reading to anyone involved in the Far Eastern theatre at that time. Thus one finds him in a minute of 19 January 'staggered' that 'the gorge of the fortress of Singapore, with its splendid moat half a mile wide, was not entirely fortified against an attack from the northward. What is the use of having an island for a fortress if it is not to be made into a citadel? . . .' I can only add that the Prime Minister's astonishment was no greater than our own when on taking up position on the north-east coast overlooking Johore and Pulao Ubin island twelve days after this date, and only two after our landing, we found not so much as a roll of wire let alone a trench or pill-box in the way of preparation for the defence.

My first – and only – communication from Command head-quarters at Fort Canning closely following our moving under canvas on arrival was a request from the Deputy Provost Marshal for particulars, with photographs in duplicate, prior to the issue of an identity card . . . This with the enemy at the very gates! The signature looked, and, sure enough, was familiar: Brian K. Castor, Lieutenant-Colonel. In the 'thirties he had been secretary of Essex, and in the future was to fulfil a similar function for Surrey. In the first forty-eight hours one gathered more positive signs that confidence regarding the control of affairs by Fort Canning was limited, to say the least. Referring to the lack of defences on the north of the island, the same Churchill minute goes on: 'By such neglect the whole security of the fortress has been at the mercy of 10,000 men breaking across the straits in small boats. I warn you [the Chiefs of Staffs Committee] this will be one of the greatest scandals that could possibly be exposed.' The invasion by small boats, not on our front but on the Australian on the north-west side, was to happen, of course, three weeks later.

In Churchill's words 'The 18th British Division, which after three months on board ship, needed time to get on their tactical feet, had to be thrown into the losing battle as soon as they were landed.'

Losing battle? 'At home,' wrote Churchill of the last days of January, 'we no longer nursed illusions about the protracted defence of Singapore. The only question was how long.' Another minute by him of 21 January questions whether the naval base and guns should not at once be blown and all reinforcements concentrated on Burma. At that date, of course, our precious convoy could still have been diverted to Rangoon. In the end the moral effect all over the world, and not least in Australia, of a British 'scuttle' outweighed strategic considera-tion, and our Division 'went forward on its way'. But the great man added: 'There is no doubt what a purely military decision should have been.'

In other words the two fresh brigades of the Division which General Beckwith-Smith had trained for so long, and in which he had such pride, 'newly landed from their ships in strange and unimagined surroundings', were sacrificed on the high altar of Allied morale. Maybe then we were not utterly wasted, but we would not be true to ourselves if we did not maintain that with other dispositions to meet the Jap attack affairs on the island might have gone very differently.

The Jap was expected to come in on the Changi side, and reconnaissance up to the last minute suggested he would do so. From long POW post-mortems it seemed to emerge afterwards that that was why General Percival had put us there. The 8th Australian Division, involved in the latter stages of the long withdrawal down the peninsula, had, like the British and Indian troops engaged, in Churchill's phrase lost their punch. The Japs, gliding in on the Australian front at night through the mangrove swamps, made swift progress down the Bukit Timah road and towards the reservoirs upon which the city of a million civilians completely depended.

Not a man had landed east of the Causeway by the time our brigades were withdrawn intact to protect the perimeter, with the reservoirs, and therefore the city, already doomed. As the troop dispositions stood, the issue was decided from the time the Jap gained a firm foothold on the island at the first attempt. Whether our fresh troops could have succeeded where the Australians failed is mere conjecture.

What can be said, surely, is that the defence of Singapore would have been conducted with greater efficiency and spirit if the 18th Division (either with or without the residue of 53 Brigade) had been allowed to fight as such. The heartbreaking thing for everyone, from the General downwards, was that units were sent off piecemeal to plug holes at different points of the retreating front. Poor Beckwith-Smith had to endure the humiliation of seeing his proud Division disintegrate before his eyes. The Prime Minister, in a message to General Wavell of 10 February, wrote: 'The 18th Division has a chance to make its name in history.' But that very day, and the next (my birthday) we were being dispersed. We never had that chance.

It would be wrong to suggest that the morale of the troops outside our own Division, whether British, Australian or Indian, was all it might have been by the time we came on the scene just seventeen days before the surrender, and this could be attributed to two things. One was general unfamiliarity with the special techniques of jungle fighting, in which the Jap had apparently been well trained. The other, which was fatal surely in whatever theatre it occurred throughout the war, was the complete absence of air support. In the seventeen days I do not believe I saw a single friendly aeroplane. Bombing apart, in my small sphere what would we not have given for a few reconnaissance aircraft to spot targets for our 25-pounders, as the Japs were doing at our expense all the time.

Granted the other essential supplies, all of which were failing, the crucial lack at the end was water. When I was wounded on the penultimate day, Saturday the 14th, the MacRitchie, the third and most southerly of the three reservoirs, was already in Jap hands. On the day of the capitulation I was moved to Singapore General Hospital, and was led through corridors lined with civilian cases on stretchers to what apparently was the last bed. I occupied it for twenty-four hours, and got only one cup of water. That was the standard ration.

My recollection of the three and a half years spent as a prisoner is still in parts remarkably clear; it is fortified also by a brief account I wrote on the way home in the SS *Corfu* in October 1945. In fact during the quieter spells at the Siamese end of the Burma–Siam railway late in the captivity I did a fair amount of writing on odd scraps of paper which I had hoped to smuggle through to the end. But all this priceless prose literally went up in smoke. What happened was this. It was forbidden to write, and consequently difficult to take anything away when one moved camp. Once it seemed particularly risky, and so I left a packet with a trusted sergeant who hid it away. Months later someone offered me a 'cigarette paper' and some of the strong Thai tobacco which was known by various rude names. I do not smoke, but in declining I caught sight of some handwriting on the paper. It was mine. Every scrap of paper was valuable to the smokers, and someone had discovered the sergeant's hideaway, cut up my careful prose, page upon page, and sold it. At the time I was rather disgruntled!

The first thing the Jap did after the capitulation was to march everyone to the Army area at Changi, throw a wire fence round the perimeter, set a number of Sikhs who had defected to guard it, and deposit an occasional lorry-load of rice (sweepings quality). Vegetables grown ourselves by degrees augmented the rice and made it more palatable. Possibly a few cattle and poultry had escaped looting. At any rate those early days of hunger were the worst, and the abrupt change of circumstance, coupled with the hunger, made this almost a more miserable time than any following. One day, on their way to the Naval Base, there steamed past Fairy Point in line ahead a succession of heavy Jap cruisers – they had a class with an 11" armament not far inferior in power to the British capital ship. We counted eleven, and the sight of them drove sharply home the realization that liberty was a mighty long way off.

Some, chiefly the more elderly, spent their whole captivity at Changi. Most of the 60,000 white troops who were on the ration strength at the capitulation were sent by batches in train-loads of closed metal goods trucks to Thailand to build the railway. Many of us went up there, as I did, via the River Valley Road camp in Singapore which had been built in days of peace for Displaced Persons. The rumour was that the DPs struck, and refused to be accommodated there, and it was certainly not attractive, though being in the middle of the city it offered opportunity for barter through the wire.

It was in that first summer in Singapore that I was able to inaugurate something that became a vast boon to the whole POW community in Thailand. The troops who worked by day cleaning up the city brought back quantities of books which were the only things that had not been looted from the European houses. So we built a library containing at its height not far short of ten thousand volumes, every man in order to join having to pay a subscription of two.

When the various parties left – no one knew where to – it was impressed on everyone to keep their books whatever else they had to cast away. Generally they did so, and this held wherever they went, so that once a new camp was built an early priority was some primitive sort of library. The books were the sort that might be expected on the shelves of expatriate Englishmen: a good deal of Galsworthy, Priestley, Buchan, Evelyn Waugh, Gunther, and H. V. Morton. Not a POW but by the end had read Arthur Bryant's *English Saga* and Richard Llewellyn's *How Green was my Valley*.

When the books began to disintegrate tattered remnants of gas-cape strengthened the original covers, and rice makes a good paste. My chief contribution was a 1939 *Wisden*, which, lovingly rebound several times by skilled men, and having been duly de-bugged and disinfected, is with me still. Marked with the Jap stamp (i.e. not subversive!), and with the letters AD in pencil before 1939, it claims to be the most-read copy of *Wisden* ever published.

My own journey through Malaya up to Thailand under the auspices of the Imperial Japanese Army took place in September 1942. Other ranks were packed thirty or forty to a truck, and so could only huddle and lie down in turns. There happened to be only twenty-two officers in our batch, so we enjoyed the luxury of being just able to lie full length head to tail like sardines in a tin. Talking of sardines, a few of us brought a tin of them which we soon ate, and the smell of fish and tomato sauce lingered in our airless corner for the four days of our journey. We must have been travelling backs to the engine! From time to time the train stopped at a station, and we were served rice and water from pails on the platform. We tottered out at last at the railhead of Banpong, and forthwith set out, with such belongings as we could carry, on our backs and slung on bamboo poles, to march westward towards the distant hills.

For two days in much heat we were on the tarmac road leading from Banpong to the town on the edge of the jungle at Kanchanaburi. It seemed longer than twenty-five miles, but I know that is the figure because rather more than twenty years later in company with Ken Taylor, of Yorkshire, while staying at Bangkok on my side's Far East tour, and by courtesy of Shell, I made the journey in an air-conditioned car.

It was now that most of us were first obliged to come in close contact with the Jap – or, as he was universally known, the Nip. In Singapore, they had left the camp admin to our own officers. Here, on the march, they were thick on the ground, halting us for interminable roll-calls, and generally getting excited. On the third, fourth and fifth days our route led through jungle tracks, and we were no sooner enclosed in these than it came on to rain cats and dogs. Drenched to the skin we slipped and slithered on. Our cup of woe, in every sense, it might have been thought, was full and brimming over, but as if spontaneously a strange thing happened. The men had borne the heat with terrible curses. Now suddenly they began as one to sing. Everyone grew cheerful. Maybe they were reminded of home. Anyhow I will never forget the look of utter, fearful mystification on the face of our own particular Nip. We were altogether beyond his comprehension – and so, in general, were all Europeans outside the understanding of all Japs. And vice-versa. Apart from the language difference we were as much a mystery to them as they to us.

Sometimes a contact of minds seemed to have been made. For instance Harold Lilly, one of the shining POWs, now long dead, who commanded the 1/5 Sherwood Foresters, and was British commandant of the first of the river camps at Wampo, established a quite exceptional degree of co-operation with the Jap officer in charge, called Hattori. This relationship while it lasted worked greatly to our advantage, and saved many lives. But when a year later at Kinsayok farther up river we met up with Hattori again he ruled with the maximum severity and was completely unapproachable. What dictated their attitudes one never knew. But they were nothing if not unpredictable.

A gunner major named McKinlay, a whisky McKinlay, was in British charge of a party that shortly followed ours. His Nip counterpart was a bearded NCO who frequently lost his way. At this constant loss of face he grew so angry that he turned on the major and gave him a stiff smack on the side of the head. But the Jap gunso wasn't the only one who had had enough. To the horror of all, the Scots major sent his man reeling with a sharp crack on the jaw. The Jap thereupon drew his sword, and announced he was going to perform an execution. But the troops gathered round so menacingly and muttered so ominously that after much palaver he thought better of it, put up his sword, and continued the march. To everyone's astonishment there were no repercussions.

Some months later at Tonchan Camp, McKinlay was called up by the IJA camp commander, and was alarmed to find the bearded one beside him. 'You know gunso?' said the commander. McKinlay shook his head and went on denying it. But the Japanese gunso knew his man, and eventually he admitted they had met before. This, he felt, was the end. But not so. Both the Japs promptly roared with laughter, produced omelettes, wine, and so forth, and insisted on the major taking part in the feast. But hitting a Jap was about the next most risky thing to being found with a wireless-set. Next time I heard of a British OR – under great provocation – hitting one, he was very badly beaten, taken away on a halter and was never seen again.

With life under the Nips comedy and tragedy were seldom separated for long, though it would have been more bearable if their respective proportions had been reversed. Talking of wireless-sets, those who worked them, using the most ingenious subterfuges, were the really brave men, knowing as they did what hideous things lay ahead at the hands of the Kempe-tai (secret police of whom the Japs themselves went in holy terror) if they were caught.

Every so often there was a camp search when all hell was

apt to be let loose. At the alarm prisoners had to stand at the end of the particular 2′3″ of the raised bamboo platform running the length of the hut which for the moment represented both bed and home. Once at Kinsayok, when one of these affairs started, Peter Fane, a brother-officer of 148 and my sleeping neighbour, realized that the hottest of all bits of property was sitting nearby in an old trunk. To leave it there seemed crazy, to attempt to move it only a little less so. However, helped by Barney Hotchkiss, a Northumberland Fusilier, Peter, with the Japs rushing around in much excitement, carried 'our' set out of the hut and, while we who were in the secret watched and sweated, calmly deposited it in an adjacent hut which had already been searched. Thereafter when not in use the damned thing was buried!

Happily the Nip private was generally a stupid chap, and the Koreans, who had most to do with looking after us and were not even accorded the dignity of any rank at all, were even thicker. So when on a search one of the latter discovered an oil-compass – which would have carried a penalty only a little less grievous than a wireless-set – the simple fellow put it to his ear, shook it, and merely said 'Watchee no good.' What a grotesque world to look back on!

If you were caught out of camp you might be shot for trying to escape, or you might get off quite lightly. At Chungkai – one of the biggest camps – in the early days it was quite a common thing to slip out at night to the Thai houses nearby. About three in the morning some guards were surprised to hear raucous noises coming from one of these houses, and on entering found a British OR in fine fettle. The OR was put in the 'no-good house' for the night and next morning brought before the Jap Commandant. After a long lecture the sentence was pronounced. A board was hung round his neck with the remarkable legend: 'I took whisky. This very bad thing.' Then the POW band was called out – I don't think it amounted to much more than an accordion and a trumpet – and ordered to play the prisoner round the camp. Thus was his disgrace to be made clear to all. Off started the procession, headed by guards with fixed bayonets.

The story went that the band played 'Roll Out the Barrel', 'Here's to good old whisky, mop it down', and finally 'Colonel Bogey'. The camp of several thousand turned out and, of course, roared with laughter. The Japs, thinking it was the prisoner who was being ridiculed, laughed as loudly as any – so everyone was happy. Everyone forgot for a moment that the huts were verminous, the food terrible, and that that day might have seen half-a-dozen burials. It was such comic relief that made life bearable.

Generally speaking, our troops outwitted the Japs, and were particularly good at making capital out of their fear of losing face. Nippon could never admit that he didn't know. The Aussies in this respect were second to none, and it was an authenticated story how down in Singapore two or three brazen fellows, set to work on a steam-roller, solemnly demanded petrol to make it go. The Jap was puzzled but couldn't admit he had no idea how the thing worked. 'No petrol – no go,' they told him, in the queer lingo that sprang up. 'Engine very thirsty – drink plenty petrol.' And so solemnly each day the Jap would issue forty gallons. The Australians just drove away and sold it to their Chinese friends round the corner for good hard dollars! There was another petrol racket at Bukit Timah, and again it was the Australians who did the trick. This time it was merely a case of their working in a camp which happened to contain a petrol dump. The Chinese would come to the fence and behind the sentry's back the dealing was done. The trade grew so brisk that this method was too slow. So the Aussies laid a pipeline to some point out of sight of the guards, and then the Chinese just brought their tins along and carried the stuff away.

But no one, I expect, will be persuaded by this farcical light relief that the joke, broadly speaking, was anything but on us. At the worst time in the wet weather of 1943, in the frenzy to obey the Emperor and get the Bangkok–Moulmein line finished before the end of the year, disease and weakness were so widespread and the food so scarce and revolting that in some places the expectation of life of the other ranks could be measured in terms of a few weeks.

The most graphic of the Far-East POW books is the Australian, Russell Braddon's *The Naked Island*, and for anyone who is looking for a vivid impression of the captivity (and has a strong stomach) it is required reading. Glancing through it again recently, one marvelled at how any of us survived, but I hasten to add that though I inhabited most of the same up-river places on the railway-line as he did either before or after him he generally chose the worse times. Also things went harder for the other ranks than for the officers because although, when the worst 'speedo' was on, the officers did their fair share of work on the railway, they had previously had much less of it. Their work, building and maintaining the

126

camps and undergoing the various camp chores – the latrine quarters were the least savoury but the most important area – was arduous enough, but less soul-destroying.

Talking of latrines, whenever I go to Sydney and meet two highly prosperous and distinguished figures in the financial world, Dick Allen (cousin of G.O.) and Claude Healy, I think of the pair of them, 6'3" apiece, wafer-thin, clad only in 'Jap-happys' covering the essentials, marching about the camp from loo to loo, one at each end of a horizontal bamboo pole from the middle of which was suspended a large bucket. To maintain an aura of dignity in such circumstances is surely a test of character.

The fact of the officers being in general a little older was another reason why their casualty rate was so much lower. It was the youngest, barely out of their teens, who were apt to succumb first. Some looked after themselves better than others, naturally, and, knowing a man's home background, one was able to gauge his prospect of survival with some measure of accuracy. But luck was not the least factor in the scale, and for the poor wretch who while suffering from acute dysentery went low with severe malaria, or vice-versa, the signs were adverse to a degree.

Again, resistance varied astonishingly, so that the phrase turning one's face to the wall was being illustrated literally all the time. Two men might be more or less identically ill and weak. To A you would give no chance while B, you felt, might have the will to pull himself through. Of all the sad cases that come to mind I will select that of Francis Millward, a young signaller of my own troop, a Derbyshire lad who at some stage of our training had been drafted to us as a recruit.

He was a practising Christian, and we had no nicer man or more reliable soldier. He went down at the worst time in Tonchan South, one of the worst camps where to the usual scourges cholera was added, the infection coming from a Tamil camp a little way up-river. One tried to keep touch with one's own men as far as possible, though gradually they became scattered far and wide, and the story of Millward's amazing cheerfulness and prolonged fight for life came to us at the main Tonchan camp. Though there were several deaths each day, and everyone was working from dawn to dusk, Millward's refusal to give up long after complete debility had set in became something of an epic. On 7 July 1943, I got Jap permission to walk the few miles between camps to see him. As it happened I was an hour too late, but was in time for the funeral. They were such regular occurrences as to attract little notice. Often all that could be done was a mass burial, with no accompanying words from the prayer-book. But for this one every man in camp seemed to have turned out, and to have saved a clean if tattered shirt for the occasion. It was as though we were all expressing our gratitude for a shining example of quiet courage which had put heart into the whole community.

My own battery – I was its titular commander from the time Major Merry was killed on the morning of the surrender – lost 66 men in captivity out of 202, and of these deaths one other comes specially back to me. It was of a man who had volunteered for the most dangerous of all jobs, orderly in the hut containing the worst of the dysentery cases. He invested this most gruesome of occupations with much zeal and humour until his own condition was so bad that he had himself to take to the bamboo slats which formed one's bed. The specific for amoebic dysentery was Atabrine, and though the doctors had none there were sometimes a few tablets to be had on the black market. I caused enquiries to be made, and was brought some which, I was told, had come from some Australians who admired his guts and would take no money.

When I gave him the news the relief was a joy to see. It was literally a reprieve from death – in ninety-nine cases out of a hundred. The injections were duly given, but this was the hundredth case of the man who was impervious to the drug. So hope went out, almost as swiftly as it had been engendered. Why I specially remember this case is because this fellow, who held a key rôle in the battery, was one of the only ones who during his brief experience of battle had reacted badly under fire. Maybe, given time, he would have faced the music as well as the next. As it was, everyone knew it. I believe the work among the dysentery cases which cost him his life was a deliberate act of self-redemption.

I found one could never begin to gauge in advance individual reaction to danger. During the sea passage through Sunda Strait I happened to observe at an air-raid alert that a timid young signaller was plainly petrified, and made a mental note. The first thing I heard on rejoining the battery after being wounded was how this same man had shown the greatest courage manning his post hour after hour while his truck was under constant shell-fire. Conquest of fear is surely the height of bravery.

There were twenty-thousand deaths on the Burma–Siam railway, and there must have been vastly more but for Boon Pong, the Thai trader who, with funds provided by the Swiss consul in Bangkok, as we subsequently discovered, provided all the railway camps with periodic canteen additions to the bare basic ration of rice, jungle vegetable, and tea. He also smuggled in certain priceless drugs and medicines. The railway followed the line of the River Menam-Kwa-Noi, and it was up this – broad, brown, swift-flowing – that Boon Pong hauled his laden barges by panting motor-boats known, onomatopoeically, as 'pom-poms'.

In the rainy season the pom-poms could scarcely make headway against the current, and for weeks at Tonchan none got through. Suddenly with morale at rock bottom the cry went up that Boon Pong had been sighted. We turned out, and there he was, this little, round-faced man, a topee on his head, beaming down at us from the back of an elephant! His staple food offering was eggs. They came a long way slowly, and by the time they arrived their freshness was usually a thing of the past. One fact one discovered however was that, high or rank bad as an egg might be, it retained its nutriment. So it was swallowed regardless. Another observation on the subject of eggs : if the ration augmenting the rice has been one in three days, and it suddenly becomes one (however bad) a day, everyone is in heaven. It's surprising how in necessity values adjust themselves.

Elephants, by the way, were sometimes used to fell and carry timber. One day when we were engaged on a 'speedo' job on a bridge I noted the various heterogeneous constituents of the bunch. There were British officers and ORs, Dutch officers and ORs, Tamils, Malays, Chinese, Jap engineers – and elephants.

But my regular occupation was welfare or 'Entertainments' officer, under which broad phrase went anything from organizing nightly lectures, running a book-binding shop as well as a library, arranging occasional sing-songs, and, when as was very often the case there was no padre, laying on church services.

The evening talks were a God-send, especially perhaps for those too sick to leave their huts and who were obliged to lie hour after hour with their thoughts in the dark. Where a thousand or so are gathered together there are experts on every topic under the sun, and great was the variety of subject. Sport was naturally popular, and cricket often well catered for, since I recruited Colonel D. V. ('Hooky') Hill, ex-captain of Worcestershire, and also Len Muncer, then of the MCC and Middlesex staff, but destined to have a big part in bringing their first championship to Glamorgan.

The church side of the job got me into trouble because of the most trifling occurrence. Someone had the idea of a Harvest Festival, though there in the jungle up-river at Kinsayok we had little to thank God for at that particular time beyond the fact that we were still alive. Anyway a Christian Korean, of whom there were a few, brought to our 'church' in a clearing a bunch of wild bananas.

Whereupon there was a great to-do, and I was hauled up and accused of undermining the loyalty of the Korean to the great emperor, Hirohito. Such an evil influence I was apparently considered by the Jap NCO in charge that I must be expelled from the camp altogether and sent down to the headquarters at Tarsao for punishment. So I was packed on to a pom-pom and taken there under guard. The leisurely progress down river would have been rather a treat had it not been for the prospect of a session with the Kempe-tai at the other end. One couldn't know what sort of charge might be trumped up, and the noises coming from the police hut told eloquently of their methods. But I was in luck. When I got to HQ the Jap CO apparently saw the matter for the trivial thing it was, and took no action.

In fact I kept on the move, being sent to the newly-built hospital camp at Nakom Patom, which lay through Bangpong and most of the way to Bangkok. After eighteen months enclosed in the jungle it was something to enjoy sunrise and sunset. There were as always virtually no drugs at Nakom Patom, but there were doctors and there was rest, and it would have been a satisfactory interlude if I hadn't contracted a mild form of polio. It left me, luckily, with no more serious a legacy than a withered left shoulder and upper arm which latter could, and still can, only be raised a few degrees from the vertical. It hasn't improved a golf-swing which was hardly a thing of beauty in the first place, and it made me after the war a one-sided catcher on the cricket field, but it is the sort of minor inconvenience that one just gets to live with.

At the beginning of 1945, when things were turning against them, the Japs for the first time separated officers and men, the former being housed outside the town of Kanchanaburi. But in August we were again being moved, in batches, to somewhere deep in the interior where we could be quietly liquidated in the event of invasion. Of this we had little inkling, for some time after the defeat of Germany our wireless gave out, and in the last vital months we were without news. My party were due next to move when one evening, on Wednesday, August 15 to be precise, the hut commanders were called to camp headquarters. This was next to the one confined to field-officers (majors and above) which was politely known as the Imperial War Museum.

Looking through the ventilation gap between the atap walls and roof we saw the officers march in, bow from the neck in salute in the prescribed manner, then listen to a statement from a visiting Jap. Our men then turned and left without making the obligatory bow, and it was at that moment we knew they had been hearing the news that the war was over. We had been prisoners three and a half years to a day.

As is well known, the Japs were ordered to maintain their guards and be responsible for our safety until Allied forces could fly in, and so there followed a varying period before we could taste the full sweets of freedom. Small parties took it by turn to visit the café in Kanchanaburi which belonged to Boon Pong. When my turn came, a friendly Thai went to a large radiogram standing on the earthen floor, and twiddled the knobs to get the BBC programme in our honour. Next moment we were at Old Trafford, listening to a commentary on the fifth of the Victory Tests between England and Australia and, dammit, a fellow unknown to me called Cristofani was about to get a hundred. Now we really believed that life at home was returning to normal! But what about the commentator? It was a certain Rex Alston, a master at Bedford when I left England, for whose MCC side I had sneaked off to play a war-time game against the boys.

Excitements now followed apace, beginning with a mercifully short spell as commander of a camp at Petburi on the Kra Isthmus, several thousand strong, containing all ranks, British, Australians, Dutch, East Indians, and a particularly difficult bunch of Americans, this with no sanctions whatever for the enforcement of discipline.

I had endured some days of this when, as I was reading a news bulletin to the assembled camp of two or three thousand, an American Air Force officer burst in, followed by a Chinaman with a tommy-gun whom he introduced as his bodyguard. He asked leave to make an announcement, then clasping his hands above his head and shaking them like a successful boxer acknowledging a cheering crowd he told us that the American Air Force was flying in to the nearby airstrip right away to fetch us out of this goddamned place, yes, sir.

And so they did. In due course I thankfully stepped on the last of the planes for Rangoon, and next found myself in hospital there, under the brisk inspectorial eye of Lady Mountbatten. The staff boys were apologetic about our accommodation and arrangements generally, but added disarmingly that they hadn't expected to see us. The Emperor's orders for the elimination of all POWs in the event of invasion of Jap-held territory had been duly intercepted, and although certain rescue plans had been made they hadn't put much faith in them.

The Allied invasions were planned for early September, so our expectation of life was roughly a month when the atom bombs fell on Nagasaki and Hiroshima. Japan's defeat was only a matter of time when the decision to drop them was taken, but time must have cost many more thousand Allied lives, including in all probability our own. So in the arguments on the moral issue of dropping the bombs some of us find objectivity difficult.

My father met me at Waterloo when after our trip home on the *Corfu* we came up from Southampton by boat-train; but he walked straight past me on the platform. He hadn't expected quite such a slim-line version. My weight in fact was 10½ stone. When we had said goodbye four years before it had been five stone heavier. I'd lost something physically which, as it happened, would fairly soon be put right. But from the experience I had gained much that would always remain.

8

Australia Calls

Recollection of the first early months – indeed years – of peace produces a blessed euphoria which is still wonderfully strong more than a quarter of a century later. Many may chiefly remember the frustrations, the shortages, the general shabbiness – but not our ragged company from the Far East. Yet there was one moment for me which, though it can now be recalled with amusement, was far from a laughing matter at the time. What with Rex Alston broadcasting Victory Tests and others trying their hands at the job over the summer of 1945 I thought I should make my number with the BBC as soon as might be. When that autumn I went to see S. J. de Lotbinière, the head of Outside Broadcasts, and said I hoped I could carry on next year where I had left off in 1939 as one of the Test commentating team, he was kind but surprisingly cagey. All he would say was that he was keeping an open mind between a number of candidates, but that he would give me the first chance.

In due course this turned out to be the match between Gloucestershire and Lancashire at Gloucester early in May. It went all right – Wally Hammond made 134 out of about 200, which was always apt to make more than usually good broadcast material – and I was forthwith offered contracts for all the Tests. It was a while later before 'Lobby' told me that when I had presented my haggard self to him six months earlier he had been quite shocked, and thought my reactions wouldn't be half quick enough for running commentary. Not for the first time, or the last, I might have been the victim of my natural impetuosity.

As it was, I picked up well, first staying with my parents, and, from the New Year onwards, living in Oxford at Pusey House. This is an address which may need amplification. Pusey House is named after Dr E. B. Pusey, one of the leading figures of the Oxford Movement or, to give it a name that removes all danger of confusion with the activities of the Buchmanites and their Moral Rearmament, the Catholic Revival within the

Church of England. The House was founded in 1884 to further within the University the principles for which Pusey stood.

While a prisoner I had had the chance by reading and discussion to remedy to some extent my ignorance about the widely differing shades of Anglicanism. From being an instinctive but ignorant Christian – duly baptized and confirmed but in the 'thirties an indifferent churchgoer – I was able partially to educate myself, thanks to some appropriate books, and in evening talk round jungle fires. My acceptance of Catholicism during the years of captivity embraced also the position of the Church of England as an essential part of the one holy Catholic and Apostolic Church, as the creed proclaims. By great good luck a fellow POW, Lawrence Turner (later to be MP for Oxford), gave me an introduction to the Principal of Pusey House, Canon Frederic Hood, and when, after being home a month or two, I first went to renew Oxford friendships he was kind enough to offer me a set of rooms.

There, with the staff of four priests and a changing resident population of undergraduates, some about to be ordained, others not, I was due to be based for six happy years, abroad often, elsewhere in England often doing my job, but with Pusey as my only home, in the university but not of it, enjoying much of the life of Oxford at an amusing and stimulating period.

For the Diamond Jubilee of Pusey House the late Lord Halifax, Chancellor of the University, stayed with us, a fervent Anglo-Catholic like his father before him. My clearest recollection of the occasion is of a sermon commemorating Edward Pusey by the then Bishop of Oxford, Kenneth Kirk. He depicted Pusey's life in much detail without a note, in the clearest prose most beautifully spoken. For me Dr Kirk was in the Birkett class – that is to say perfect.

At one time or another half the Anglican hierarchy stayed with us when they came to Oxford. It was a privilege to live as a layman, and something of a Philistine at that, within those hallowed walls in St Giles next door to the Blackfriars and opposite St John's College, and I am eternally grateful to 'Freddy' Hood. Without claiming to be a prime authority I would hazard that there cannot have been many clerics of his time with better credentials who have not been made bishops. But both as Chancellor of St Paul's (1961–70) and in various diverse fields during the forty years before that he must have performed more valuable work than many who have been raised to the purple.

After which, to some perhaps, surprising deviation into matters ecclesiastical, let us tread the fresh green cricket fields of 1946. The early games were full of nostalgia with nearly all the same players striving, with a few creaks here and there, to find their feet as had left-off in 1939. But one game was such a poignant evocation of the past that one felt like pinching oneself. Woolley, Hendren, Tate, Sutcliffe, Sandham, Freeman, Jardine, Fender, Knight . . . Did these legendary heroes once again take the field together a decade or so, to say nothing of a World War, since nearly all of them had retired?

They did, and, with the King and 15,000 looking on, warmed a lovely sunny May day with memories of their skills. The occasion was a one-day match at the Oval between Old England and Surrey in delayed celebration of the centenary of the County Club, and of the Oval itself, which fell in 1945. Surrey, having made 248 for six with suitable panache against a side whose average age was over 50, eased off a little after getting out Sutcliffe and Sandham for a single apiece. Woolley and Hendren at least were not appealed against for lbw by Surrey's promising recruit, A. V. Bedser. Allowing this, it was still a miracle to see these two putting on a brisk 102 for the third wicket. 'Woolley, at the age of 59, drove with the same ease that delighted crowds before and after the 1914–18 war,' records *Wisden*. When he was out for 62, Pat went on to 94, he and Jardine making 108 together before the old 'uns achieved an honourable draw at 232 for five.

My own part in the occasion was, at Errol Holmes's request, to man the public address system, then a complete novelty on a cricket ground, so far as I can recall. I also made another contribution behind the scenes which had perhaps more to do with the success of the day, urging Errol to see that the pitch was covered – which so far as England was concerned was also a novelty. So the old gentlemen played on a wicket of benign pace and ease. Even they could not have rolled back the years if the ball had been lifting and turning.

But what of the younger generation which had been announcing itself with such promise at the end of the 'thirties? Happily all the youthful top-classers bar Kenneth Farnes had survived, though Hedley Verity, who would have been 41 in this first summer of peace, had perished in Italy. There were three Tests against India and two Test Trials as well as a full county programme to sort out the talent for the adventure which was to be the culmination of the season, the sending of an MCC side to Australia. It was a year too soon, of course, but Dr H. V. Evatt, Australia's Minister of External Affairs, speaking on behalf of the Australian Board almost before the ink was dry on the Jap surrender, had pleaded hard with MCC for a visit the following season.

The English batting, with Hammond and Hardstaff leading the older brigade and Compton, Hutton, Washbrook and Edrich already in or near the top flight, looked strong to most eyes, but the bowling was perilously thin, even though Alec Bedser, in the first post-war Test against India, took eleven wickets at Lord's, and in the second a month later at Old Trafford eleven more. Unfortunately both these games and most others of importance had to be played on wet pitches, and after a fine start the weather grew so bad that Hubert Preston, who had ascended to the editorial chair of *Wisden* three years before at the age of 75, likened the summer in his Notes to 1888! Not many were in a position to contradict him.

I had intended spending the summer broadcasting as much as I could, doing a weekly piece for *The Field*, writing a diary which was to have become a book, and, of course, playing when it could be fitted in. (A 60 for Incogniti against the Navy helped relieve my fears that a non-functioning left shoulder would ruin my batting.) But the cricket job on the *Daily Telegraph* soon proved too much for Sir Guy Campbell. On May 24, the day after the Old England match, I was seeing Lord Camrose's eldest son, Seymour Berry, and shortly afterwards was writing the Test Trial at Lord's under the name of A Special Correspondent. I was then hired on a monthly basis, and covered all the big matches from July onwards under my own name. The Old Trafford Test was my first for the *Telegraph*, and a thoroughly exciting one it was, with the last Indian pair holding out for quarter of an hour to save the game.

Walter Hammond led England against India, and between the First and Second Tests was appointed captain of MCC in Australia. His fame and seniority were such that unless the selectors (Sir Stanley Jackson, R. W. V. Robins, A. B. Sellers and A. J. Holmes) had taken a bold and what would have been a widely unpopular decision at the start of the season in favour of someone else the announcement was little more than a formality.

Remembering South Africa I had serious forebodings, which were the greater since the name of the manager had already been released. In the Long Room at the start of the season I had asked Lord Cobham, father of the present one and Treasurer of MCC, whether, hopefully, the captain might be appointed first and the manager afterwards. The man who might be ideal for one captain, I pointed out, would not necessarily be right for another. Lord Cobham was kind and thoughtful, but said, 'Oh, no, we've always done it this way round, and it's worked pretty well.' Just quarter of a century later, as a result of the *seventh* post-war tour of Australia, the Test and County Cricket Board have recently accepted the principle of naming the captain first.

Rupert Howard was a genial fellow, who had teamed up admirably as Gubby Allen's manager in Australia ten years before; but had he the toughness to handle Hammond? Like Jack Holmes in South Africa was he not 'too nice a chap'? 'Plum' Warner, as I have said before, could never believe that a man might be a fine cricketer and yet lack some of the important qualities needed in a captain, especially on a tour abroad – which was particularly strange since it was because of those very attributes of tact and consideration for other people (particularly his own side), to say nothing of a shrewd tactical sense, that he himself had twice been chosen to lead MCC in Australia over the heads of men senior to him in age and fame.

He, despite warnings, had picked Douglas Jardine in 1931, and it was he who promptly on Hammond's turning amateur in 1938 had appointed him captain in the Test Trial before the Australian series, over the head of Allen who by all account had led England admirably in Australia. In one of the tents at the Maidstone Week of 1946 I voiced my doubts about the tour set-up, already decided, in the presence of 'Plum' and his wife. 'Plum' was naïvely sanguine that all would be well; but Agnes Warner knew better, and understood just what I was talking about. Most people reckoned her a better judge of character than her husband.

The question was whether I should be sent to Australia. The time difference of ten hours in advance meant that early editions of the evening papers carried full stories of the play. Only one national paper (rather surprisingly, the *Express*) had sent their own man before. In the second week of August I took the Arabs to Germany to play the British Army of the Rhine, and from our starting-point at Harwich rang to hear the verdict from Frank Coles, my sports editor, who had proposed the idea 'upstairs' (the Berry seat of power was, and is, on the fifth floor). My luck proved to be in, and the prospect of Australia ahead gave the German tour an added relish. Incidentally, in the afterglow of victory it cannot be recorded that the Army admin was up to the standard of their hospitality. When we crossed the Dutch-German border at Bentheim an oriental-looking man in flowing robes approached and introduced himself as our interpreter. It was supposed that we were genuine Bedouin Arabs.

So on 31 August, less than a year after my return, I was at Southampton once more, embarking with W. R. Hammond's team and fourteen cricket-writers, no less, on the *Stirling Castle*, bound for Fremantle. This was the side that sailed under the MCC colours – W. R. Hammond (captain), N. W. D. Yardley (vice-captain), A. V. Bedser, D. C. S. Compton, W. J. Edrich, T. G. Evans, L. B. Fishlock, P. A. Gibb, J. Hardstaff, L. Hutton, J. T. Ikin, James Langridge, R. Pollard, T. P. B. Smith, W. Voce, C. Washbrook and D. V. P. Wright. The press party comprised L. N. Bailey (*Star*), W. E. Bowes (*Yorkshire Evening News*), Charles Bray (*Daily Herald*), Harold Dale (*Daily Express*), George Duckworth (Kemsley Group), Bruce Harris (*Evening Standard*), Vivian Jenkins (*News of the World*), John Kay (*Manchester Evening News*), J. M. Kilburn (*Yorkshire Post*), Vic Lewis (*Daily Sketch*), Norman Preston (PA-Reuter), Brian Sellers (*Yorkshire Evening Post*), E. M. Wellings (*Evening News*), and myself.

All shipping so soon after the war was controlled by government, and passes were necessary for travel which was on strictly austerity lines. Jim Kilburn and I shared a cabin so small that we literally could not stand up in it together – a trial of friendship which I'm glad to say survived the twenty-five-day journey. There were 200 English 'war brides' en route to join their Australian ex-service husbands – a sight to flutter particularly the tender heart of Bill Edrich, as I recall – but the ship was nearly as dry as the *Wakefield*. Only the crew had a beer ration, which they were often kind enough to share.

One starlit night I was leaning over the deck-rail with George Duckworth and listening to his reminiscences of Australia where he'd toured three times before. When we turned to discussing the prospect ahead George paused and then with great emphasis said: 'Bryan Valentine ought to be bringing this lot.' I was surprised at this unequivocal statement, though as I came to know so well on this and later tours it was typical of him.

George was warm, utterly sincere, and with a salty northern humour to soften the bluntness of his talk. There was no antipathy in his remark. He and Wally were friends who had been travelling-companions on those three Australian tours together as well as one to South Africa, and it was this that lent point to his judgment. He had never toured with Valentine, though the latter had been to India with Jardine and to South Africa with Hammond, and, incidentally, in seven Tests on those tours had averaged 64. Bryan, at the age of thirty-eight, captained Kent in 1946, as he had done before the war, and made 1,700 runs in that wet summer. He had also led the Rest in the first of the Test Trials.

So if not finally 'there' in the selectors' thoughts he was plainly thereabouts. No cricketer was more universally popular, and if not brilliant as a tactician (neither was Hammond) his side would have responded to his guts and cheerfulness with the utmost effort from first to last. Looking back, Anglo-Australian cricket would have been resumed on a far happier note, and probably a more successful one from the English point of view, if Bryan had been in charge in Australia. The significant thing was that no one saw this more clearly in advance than George Duckworth. As a judge of human nature he didn't make many mistakes.

The morning we landed at Fremantle a minor but not insignificant thing happened. While we were going through the immigration formalities on board, waiting to dock, a large, somewhat breathless, figure bore down on the captain and manager, having, it was said, shinned up a rope-ladder and surfaced like Neptune from the deep. This was Jim Mathers, a well-known not to say notorious Sydney sporting journalist who had thus stolen a march on his colleagues waiting on the quay. Mathers, with his fat, rubicund face, and disarming expression, was a faintly comical sight, and this first un-expected confrontation with the Australian press for ten years on their home ground seemed an occasion for a civil greeting, if not perhaps much in the way of exclusive interview. Hammond, however, had had his card marked about Mathers, whose pen could flow equally copiously with honey or with acid, and all he got for his enterprise was a frosty greeting, and the 1946 equivalent of 'no comment'.

Mathers was an old hand and far from thin-skinned. Perhaps he remembered that when Douglas Jardine had been besieged at Fremantle in 1932 for a press conference on arrival, and was reminded by a journalist from the eastern states 'Mr Jardine, Sydney and Melbourne are waiting,' he had answered, 'Tell Sydney and Melbourne they can bloody well wait.' The point was that in time the east is two hours ahead of Perth, and the evening newspaper fellows had editions to catch – as now did

Mathers. He may have reflected that Jardine's successor at least hadn't sworn. But, ribbed by his colleagues about the poor return on his enterprise, he didn't forget. A warmer welcome would have been so easy – to some but not to Wally.

There were press storms ahead all right, but before any cloud darkened the horizon there was the Australian welcome, and that is something the memory of which the years have not dimmed. Succeeding MCC sides have always been warmly received, but this was something rather different. The team symbolized 'the old country' which had come safely through the battle, bloody but unbowed. Beneath his tough exterior the Australian is very much of a sentimentalist, and there was an unmistakable wealth of affection in the greeting that met us at every point of our progress across the country.

It was not least evident in Perth where, because the ship sailings had demanded an early departure from England, we spent a full and valuable month. With time on our hands the augmented press party, English and Australian, formed a club, playing games against the West Australian schools and others, and christening ourselves The Empire Cricket Writers' Club. The 'Empire', soon dropped, was included at the insistence of Arthur Mailey, firmest of Anglophiles, but the club thus fortuitously set up grew to have an influence in the cricket world, and served as the prototype for similar clubs connected with other games and sports. I was installed as the first chairman, and, despite the presence of several illustrious cricketers, for some reason became captain of several of the teams which on that first post-war Australian tour played in every state.

When we got to Melbourne Dame Mabel Brookes, wife of Sir Norman Brookes, the great lawn tennis player, and a very considerable public personage in her own right, persuaded me to organize a match in aid of her pet charity, the Queen Victoria Hospital. So appeared a team, against Victoria Past and Present, containing also such names as Richardson, O'Reilly, Grimmett, Fingleton, Oldfield, Mailey, Sellers, Bowes, Duckworth, Wellings and Jenkins, the last two both Oxford blues. On the St Kilda ground 15,000 people produced nearly £2,000. My unexpected reward was the life-governorship – neither duties nor privileges were ever specified – of what turned out to be a maternity hospital . . .

However we are not yet at Melbourne, and I must record my only-ever train journey across the desert from Perth to Adelaide – a rather agreeable if dusty interlude lasting three nights with Dick Pollard beguiling the time on the piano in the train's drawing-room. Henceforward I have done this particular eighteen hundred miles either by air or sea.

At Adelaide – Bradman. The palaver over whether or not Don Bradman would play against us was almost as continuous as that surrounding the MCC team. Always fragile in constitution, despite his remarkable stamina at the wicket, he had been invalided out of the RAAF as early as June 1941, and had since suffered recurring bouts of acute fibrositis which precluded any form of exercise. When in the Australian spring the press were anxious to know the prospects of his playing, he entered hospital for an operation. Naturally enough he was not willing to commit himself unless satisfied of his fitness, and that could only be done by playing – which the doctors advised against anyway. Meanwhile everyone speculated.

For the Don the decision was a hard one. With the public he stood on a pedestal beyond reach of all contemporaries. The greater therefore the descent if he tried and – by the old standards – failed. Moreover he was shrewd enough to know that whatever the average man in the street felt there were those who would have been hard pressed to conceal their delight if he had come a cropper. More than one of these, he must have suspected, was in the press-box. Such is the strong love-hate with which Australians are apt to envelop their fellow-countrymen – in whatever sphere – who reach the top. He perhaps sensed there were some in the crowd who would have relished the chance of proclaiming that he was, as they say, 'over the hill'.

It was in this context that I jumped ahead of the rest of the party, which had stopped off north of Adelaide for an up-country match at Port Pirie, in order to get the earliest possible look at the great man in the nets. First reactions were that he was unusually frail and pale, second that, this notwithstanding, the old magic was still there. On a sluggish, unflattering net wicket he played the South Australian state bowlers with minutes to spare. The only doubt, to me, was whether he could get match-hard in time for the first Test five weeks later. In the event, thanks to his extraordinary determination he did – but with not much to spare.

Melbourne has the biggest cricket following of any place in the world, and, correspondingly, it has the largest cricket arena in the world. It's anything but beautiful – in fact it's a vast concrete bowl, far removed architecturally from the scenic charms of Adelaide on one side and the beflagged Victorian pinnacles and perfect cricket qualities of Sydney on the other.

But when the MCG houses a crowd worthy of its capacity an atmosphere is engendered which is all its own. So it was on that last day of October 1946 when some 30,000 turned up on a Thursday morning to welcome MCC against Victoria, and in particular to see the two great cricketers about whom they had heard so much but, thanks to the war, had not yet seen, Len Hutton and Denis Compton.

When Hutton and Washbrook came out to bat at the start of the day they were applauded all the way to the wicket. When Compton arrived at No. 4 he was similarly applauded until the moment of taking guard. These were sentimental days, and each Englishman in turn rose perfectly to the occasion. Denis in the first innings made 143 out of 220 in three memorable hours. In the second innings on a wearing pitch Len matched him with a superb 151 not out. MCC beat the strongest of the state sides by 244 runs, and for the moment at least the English party were happy enough.

Formal dinners, contrary to belief perhaps, are comparatively rare on Australian tours, but the NSW Cricket Association, feeling something special was called for, organized a welcome dinner to which all the great New South Wales cricketers of the past were invited: Macartney, Gregory, Collins, Mailey, Andrews, Taylor, McCabe, O'Reilly – it was a wonderful roll-call, and of course a compliment to MCC of no mean order. I found myself flatteringly placed between Dr Evatt and Jack Gregory. Sydney Smith, the NSWCA President, manager of the two Australian teams to England of the 'twenties, was in the chair, and the MCC captain was naturally down on the toast-list to reply to the health of the team.

Wally Hammond's name, need I say, was no less a household word in Australia than in England – this was his fourth visit and his run-getting on his first in 1928–9 was a legend. It still has not been approached. Something worthy of the occasion was palpably called for from him. But Wally did not speak, beyond getting up to say that the custom on this tour was to divide these social labours, and he would therefore call upon Laurie Fishlock. Poor Laurie, who held no official position in the side, had had no warning whatever and was put in such confusion that he could offer little more than a few mumbled words before sitting down. While he was doing so I saw Wally pointing at me and gesturing, and, sure enough, he next called on me, similarly without any previous notice. I hate nothing more than being asked to speak completely impromptu, however small the occasion, let alone one of such nostalgic moment

142

as this. I did my best, but am sure it was very poor. In any case the person everyone wanted to hear from was the captain, who was seemingly thinking it all something of a joke. The spirit of the evening could not, of course, be recaptured, the Australians were hurt, and the team and press embarrassed. Including, not least, George Duckworth.

For me, at least, this sort of thing, when insensitivity or sheer bad manners clouds the reputation of an MCC side abroad, is, and always has been, harder to bear than the most humiliating defeat. Generally speaking the hosts do their best to make visiting teams welcome and comfortable. It is merely stating the obvious to say they are entitled to the ordinary signs of appreciation.

Apart from all else, to make a good impression off the field is all part of the business of building up team morale. In the case of the 1946–7 side this episode was significant. They had arrived in Perth full of enthusiasm and eager for the fray. After six years of war they were as keen as could be imagined to get back to the game. Only three others besides Hammond – Fishlock, Hardstaff and Voce – had been to Australia before. They had been welcomed with open arms, and they possessed in their ranks fully enough talent to give the Australians what they wanted, a good hard fight for the rubber. All that was needed to bring the best out of everyone was inspiration and encouragement at the top – and it was this which it was not in the captain's moody, withdrawn nature to supply.

It has been the general verdict that England never had a chance in Australia in 1946–7 – it was too soon after the war, our side were not re-attuned, and so on. I never subscribed to this, and thought from the start that we should have had a level chance. Only three of the Australians had played before against England, Bradman, Hassett and Barnes, the last in one match. As things turned out they picked up some admirable recruits such as Miller, Lindwall and Morris. But when the series started these all had their way to make. On paper England were full of talent. The chief difference lay in the leadership. Also, it must be added, the luck went very much Bradman's way, especially in the First Test at Brisbane when the storms came after Australia had made their huge score. The weather finally decided the match.

I've written the cricket history of these times in another place, but must refer again to the ever-vexed affair of the 'catch' that Bradman survived on the first morning since the consequences of the decision were so far-reaching. He had made

28 rather scratchily when in his own words, in *Farewell to Cricket*: 'Voce bowled me a ball which was near enough to a yorker. I attempted to chop down on top of it in order to guide the ball wide of the slip fieldsmen. Instead it flew to Ikin at second slip. In my opinion the ball touched the bottom of my bat just before hitting the ground and therefore it was not a catch.'

Bradman stayed there, and on appeal was given not out. In those days the Brisbane press-box was at wide long-on from the end from which Voce was bowling, so none of us could possibly offer an opinion worth anything – though several tried to. I had my glasses on the stroke, and can merely record that when Ikin – raw to Test cricket – held the ball he first looked at Hammond, fielding at first slip, as though doubtful. Possibly if the ball had gone to Hammond he might have promptly pocketed it, confident it was a fair catch, and sat down, as he sometimes did. Whether such an attitude would have affected the umpire's decision can only be conjecture. The fact is that the question whether the ball has been trapped, or whether it has flown up on the top edge at the moment of the bat striking the ground, is seldom easy to determine. Certainly the batsman may not be sure, or he may be wrong in his opinion. On this occasion Bradman and the bowler's umpire thought one way, the Englishmen near the bat thought another. As the fielders crossed at the end of the over the captain of England said to the captain of Australia, 'That's a damned fine way to start a Test series,' the inference being, of course, that the Don should have 'walked'.

From this point the relationship between these two great cricketers, never exactly cordial, was at best chilly and formal, which was a thousand pities. Despite all the warm preliminaries goodwill had not survived the first morning. The effect on Don Bradman was to heighten his determination, if that were possible, and the longer he stayed in that day the better he batted. At close of play he had made 162, and was eventually bowled by Edrich next morning off his pads for 187. The most prolific batsman in history had returned to his old ways!

What if the decision, at 28, had been otherwise, making Australia 77 for three with only Hassett among experienced Test batsmen to come? Give Australia 400 if you like, instead of their record 645, and England should still have reached the point of saving the follow-on before the weather broke. In other words Australia, not England, would soon have been batting on a ruined wicket. It is at least very possible that

England would have won the game. Equally Don Bradman and the selectors might well have decided between them that the moment for his retirement had arrived. If they had done so Australia assuredly would not have won ten out of the next thirteen Tests and drawn the other three. The post-war Test picture would have taken a very different shape.

I can't leave Brisbane without a word about the worst of the storms because it seemed nothing less than a rehearsal for the Day of Judgment. Within a short while the Woolloongabba ground was a lake with the water level half-way up the picket fence. The stumps floated on the stormy deep, while the tarpaulin wicket-covers were ultimately recovered from the outfield. The worst affliction was the noise of millions of hail-stones literally the size of golf-balls shooting down on to the corrugated iron roofs of the stands. The scene was straight out of the Inferno, lightened only momentarily by the Queens-lander who, cupping his hands, bellowed into my ear: 'We often get it much worse than this.' Looking at the scene of bedraggled desolation and acres of water when at last the rain eased off it seemed to us that England had been saved from danger. There could be no cricket surely for the best part of a week. Little did we know of the strength of the Queensland sun. Next morning at the normal time the pitch was cut and rolled. At the normal time the game was continued! As, despite some batting of high skill on the treacherous pitch, England went down to defeat one couldn't help reflecting that, one way and another, the gods hadn't been terribly kind!

The Tests, after so long a cricket drought, drew very big crowds – the match attendance of 345,361 at Melbourne is the largest I have ever seen at a match, and only 5,000 short of the biggest ever there ten years earlier – and Australia did not have things all their own way. But the series was less satisfactory than it might have been because England failed to realize their full potential. Also the press 'war of words' further vitiated the early goodwill.

There were two or three dubious decisions which when they went against England were seized on by some of my colleagues in such a way that they – and, by implication, all we Pommies – were stigmatized as squealers when their indignant strictures on the umpiring were duly cabled back to Australia. The climax came when readers of the *Daily Express* were informed that Bill Edrich couldn't have been out lbw because he, the writer, had seen the mark on the bat that proved he had hit the ball. It was apparently just by the way that Bill had made

89, and the bat presumably was not still virgin white. This piece of detection raised a hearty horse-laugh all over Australia.

It was, of course, always this sort of comment that got cabled back, and the English cricket-writers generally were – indeed still are – apt to be lumped together as a bleating, biased lot. Sometimes the press abroad has been kind enough to mention honourable exceptions, but broadly the unflattering label sticks, and one has to live with it. In defence of those quoted back it's often true that their remarks are chosen out of context and without vital qualifications.

Thus early in my career with the *Daily Telegraph* I started an idealistic if naïve crusade against the criticism of umpires' decisions on the part of both players (by gestures) and press. Arthur Mailey saw my cable to London at the week-end of the Melbourne Test, and secured it for his paper *The Argus*, who introduced it by saying:

Because it is one of the fairest commentaries yet written during this Test series, and because, among its very pertinent suggestions to both sides, it contains a straightforward appeal to end the bickering which is spoiling enjoyment of Test cricket, *The Argus* has obtained Mr Swanton's permission to reprint it in full.

There is in the 'seventies a rather depressing topicality in what I wrote at the time of an England–Australia Test more than a quarter of a century ago:

It is a tradition in all sport that the findings of the umpire or referee are final and binding, and we cricketers are apt to claim, with not too conspicuous modesty, that specially noble virtues are inherent in and derivable from cricket. We must seem to many a hypocritical breed when the great question of the hour seems to be not whether England can win or save the match, but whether Edrich or Compton was or was not lbw.

There would be no point today in the classic reply of the late Bill Reeves to the batsman who, as he passed him, observed that he was not out: 'Weren't you? Well, just look in the paper in the morning.' Nowadays apparently the matter would depend upon which paper he looked in!

There is, perhaps, a special irony in the fact that the press-box in Melbourne, which is beyond mid-wicket and third man, is further from the play and at a worse angle than any in the world. It is sometimes possible, from a position directly in prolongation of the wicket, to form a private view as to whether the luck may have gone for or against a batsman in case of lbw or a catch, but the views of anyone looking from a slant are worth precisely nothing.

It follows that the only 'evidence' in such a case is the gestures or demeanour of the players on the field. Unfortunately both Edrich and Compton, in the heat of the moment, were unable to avoid giving the impression of being surprised when given out. Indeed, Compton has been read a little lecture in print by that striving, red-blooded cricketer W. J. O'Reilly, who, incidentally, until possibly the arrival of Toshack, exposed his inmost feelings to the public gaze with greater emphasis and frequency than anyone who ever stepped on to a field. The fact that there are certainly no two players more widely or deservedly admired in Australia for their buoyant and cheerful attitude towards the game than Edrich and Compton, is just an indication of what the stress and strain of a Test match means to all concerned.

Nor is the onus for constraint confined to batsmen. When Toshack, for instance, has an appeal answered against him, it seems as though he can hardly bring himself to the point of bowling the next ball. Again it is surely indefensible to appeal unless the bowler or fielders concerned are reasonably confident that the batsman may be out. There are degrees of probability in these things that have sometimes been raucously ignored out here in this series, perhaps rather more by the Australians than by the Englishmen. These things tend to make the job harder for the two wretched humans who have to stand up to the racket.

It is one of the fascinations of cricket that it is so clear and open a test of character, and no one wants to see the natural humours of a man subdued to the point of dull anonymity; but the truth is that these tremendous sporting affairs on which it might be thought the prestige of nations rested, can only be kept in any remote degree of perspective if all concerned, players, press, and public, do our best to see the 'other fellow's' point of view, and frankly, mind our manners. I wrote in much the same strain after the fracas in Sydney in February 1971.

At the end of the tour I sent back to the *Daily Telegraph* a long exclusive interview with Don Bradman which rated a double-column lead on page one, and was also syndicated in Australia. As usual Don measured his words carefully, and uttered shrewd judgment in various directions. He rated Evans as 'of the highest class', Wright the best of his type that MCC had sent to Australia for thirty-five years, and Bedser, the finest since Tate. He pointed out he was the only man who had played both Tate and Bedser in Australia, and he thought Bedser better than Tate in 1928-9. He thought he'd be even more formidable in England.

The Don praised the aggressive spirit of the new Australian batsmen and thought they had 'a team of great ability for some time to come'. He had a good swipe at some of the 'jealous critics' of his own performance – these were Australians – and said he preferred English pitches to Australian to bat on. The Don reminded me that for many years he had been in favour of amending the lbw law to include dismissal to a ball pitched on the off-side, even though the part of the person intercepting the ball be not between wicket and wicket. 'Padding up' to a ball outside the off stump – with the bat held over the shoulder – he condemned. 'It is negative, unattractive cricket, heart-breaking to bowlers and mainly indulged in by less competent batsmen.' He would like to have seen the change adopted immediately as an experiment. Here, of course, he was still well ahead of his time – twenty-three years to be precise.

He thought the best innings of his life was his 254 at Lord's in 1930 for the simple reason 'that I did not make a mishit of any kind until I was dismissed'. (I could vouch for that!) As to bowlers there had 'never been a bowler to equal O'Reilly. To play with him was an education – to play against him usually a lesson.' He thought the quick resumption of Tests had been wholly justified psychologically and pointed to the tangible financial benefits to counties and states.

It could be argued that in the light of a 3-0 series the psychological benefit was slightly one-sided; but there was no doubt of the value in cash terms. The MCC profit of £50,000 is still the largest ever brought back from Australia. The reason for this is largely to be found in tour costs. One figure sticks in my mind. A *suite* in the Hotel Australia at Sydney cost £2 a night!

In this hotel and in the Windsor at Melbourne (the latter then, as now, in my view, easily the best in Australia) I endeavoured to return a modicum of the lavish kindness I received – from, among others, some POW companions of barely eighteen months before. We compared our respective situations and thanked our stars. It's not the least of the pleasures and privileges of Test tours all over the world that the teams and their appendages are apt to meet many of the most interesting and important people in the countries they visit. I've mentioned Evatt. There was also a certain R. G. Menzies, then in opposition, with whom I spent the first of many subsequent sublimely happy evenings. There was General Grimwade of Frankston, Victoria, a famous Aussie soldier of the first war for whom the word 'grizzled' might have been invented.

The story went that when after the 1918 armistice in France some of his countrymen thought they were not being sent home quickly enough a situation developed among these troops (rated as tough a lot as any in the world) which was not a mile away from mutiny. The General was accordingly given a bristling armed escort to protect him as he went to recall them to order and discipline. Grimwade declined the escort, strolled into the rebellious area hands in pockets, and had no difficulty in making them see reason. He knew his Digger better than the brass-hat escort-provider. A monument of a splendid kind stands to this outwardly fearsome but at heart most benevolent of men in the Peninsula Golf and Country Club which he founded. He arranged for me to stay there, and in six subsequent visits I have never failed to do so, nor to pick up the strong strands of friendship with various Grimwades, not least his son John and Ginty, his wife, surely two of the most hospitable people in Australia.

When we got to Perth in 1946 it was discovered that for the first visit to Melbourne the entire English press were due to be put up twenty-five miles away – at Frankston aforesaid. We thought little of this, and, following the principle of going, if possible, always to the top, I wrote on behalf of all to Sir Keith Murdoch, owner of the *Melbourne Herald* and the biggest figure in the newspaper world in Australia. We not only got satisfaction as a result, but I came to know both him and his family. Keith Murdoch, who showed me much kindness, made his fame in the first war as a young correspondent in Gallipoli, with despatches highly critical of the administration. When he died with tragic suddenness in 1952 his stake in the newspaper world of Australia was inherited by his son. Rupert Murdoch was not long down from Oxford, but little time did he lose in expanding vastly his father's interests before moving in on London, with resounding effect.

I spent Christmas with Mabel and Norman Brookes at Mount Eliza, being driven down by Harry and Nell Hopman. In a company of lawn tennis players there were some who despite the spirit of the season were openly critical of Hopman. The reason, I discovered, was that in the *Melbourne Herald* this former Davis Cup player and future coach of many a great world champion had predicted that Australia were about to be deprived of the Davis Cup which they had held since it was last competed for in 1939. The sentiment that caused many Australians to hope that England would win the first post-war Test series did not, apparently, extend to their gallant American allies.

As it turned out Hopman was dead right. I reported the Davis Cup for the *Telegraph*, being on the spot, and the extra fitness and speed of two crew-cut, Teutonic-looking, impeccably-mannered Americans named Kramer and Shroeder swept the Australians off the Kooyong courts. Bromwich, Quist and Pails represented Australia, and it seemed symbolic that while the Americans bounded about in shorts and sleeveless vests one of the Aussies wore long flannels and a cricket shirt. If this rig represented the Australian lawn-tennis mentality at the New Year of 1947 it didn't take Hopman long to alter it.

A long slow haul back from Perth to Port Said on the (very) old *Largs Bay* gave one pause to relive six exciting, glamorous Australian months. The beaches, the bush, the superb golf courses of the Victorian sand-belt, the sophisticated cities of Melbourne and Sydney, all were new – while the standard of living, the food and the general air of plenty, were reminders of an almost forgotten past. One's chief impression – which later visits have only strengthened – was of the pervading friendliness. This Pommy was never made to feel a stranger.

The one cloud in the sky was the failure of the team to live up to its hopes, and the eclipse of its greatest player. As the last Test (in which fibrositis prevented his playing) drew to a close I wrote of Hammond:

He did a very difficult job as he saw it to the best of his capacity, and under one handicap which has beset none of his predecessors, in that there was no one at hand to whom he felt he could turn for critical advice.

This is no disparagement of Yardley, his vice-captain, who has been a notable success out here, both on the field and off it. But from the technical point of view the disparity in experience between Hammond and everyone else was apparently too great to be bridged. It is sad to see Hammond apparently slipping from the stage on anything but the very top note.

For one of the most gifted, commanding cricketers ever to play for England it was a melancholy end. He never played for Gloucestershire again (apart from one innings in 1951), settled in South Africa, and after trying his hand at the motor trade, ended with a coaching job at Natal University. He survived a severe motor accident in 1960, but was only 62 when he died in Durban in 1965.

9

The Boom Years

The summer of 1947 comes back to mind for the settled perfection of the weather for weeks on end, the visit of Alan Melville's South Africans, and the triumphal progress of Denis Compton, whose eighteen hundreds and 3,816 runs broke all records. Bill Edrich with 3,539 was not far behind him, and the efforts of these two coupled with Walter Robins's enterprising and altogether distinctive style of captaincy brought the championship to Middlesex at last.

It should almost go without saying that in 1947 runs were cheap – even Denis at his peak, as he was in this year before his knee began to give out warning signals, could not have achieved such figures otherwise. The pitches were hard and good, and, as the counties fulfilled their programmes of twenty-six matches each, apart from extras, it was mostly the old bowlers who had to do the donkey-work. Tom Goddard, just as old as the century, was complaining 'Haven't had a game of bridge for weeks.' But he did have one triumph at least when I happened to be on the spot. He took five wickets in seven balls at Bristol against Somerset, whose 25 was the lowest first-class score I've seen, just as Tom was the only man I've watched perform the hat-trick twice.

Yet, allowing all this, the brilliance of Denis's batting, day after day, both against the South Africans – over a thousand of his runs came off their bowling – and for Middlesex as they strove to make up by speed of scoring what they lacked in the way of a penetrative attack – was something I have never seen matched. Denis made his runs gaily, and with a smile. His happy demeanour and his good looks completed a picture of the beau ideal of a sportsman. I doubt if any game at any period has thrown up anyone to match his popular appeal in the England of 1947–1949.

I wrote a short biography at the end of the season called *Denis Compton: A Cricket Sketch*. It did rather well, and would have done even better if the subject hadn't absent-mindedly contracted for a ghosted book under his name to come out at about the same time. England was ripe to find a sporting hero to acclaim, and no one could have filled the bill better.

The great Lord's matches between the Universities and Gentlemen and Players were enjoying their last fine heyday in the late 'forties and 'fifties, their appeal immediately after the war owing not a little to the performance of Martin Donnelly from New Zealand, who emulated the distinction of Percy Chapman in making hundreds at Lord's on the three classic occasions. Donnelly in 1946 made 142 for Oxford in the University Match. In 1947 he made 162 not out for the Gentlemen in just under three hours in front of 17,000, and when he came in, the pavilion rose to a man – for the first time since Hammond's 240 against Australia back in 1938.

He completed the trilogy two years later with his 206 for New Zealand at Lord's. The war first and, later, business – he is as I write the boss of Courtauld's in Australia – prevented this beautiful player from building up the sort of weight of achievement over a period that surrounds the acknowledged 'greats'. Yet the best judges who saw him in his brief prime rank him in the company of the immortal left-handers, Clem Hill and Frank Woolley.

Talking of vintage Oxford batsmen, Alan Melville – high in the list for style and grace – got hundreds in his first three Test innings which, added to the one at Durban in his last Test innings in 1939, gave him four in a row and put him on a pedestal with Jack Fingleton who had done the same thing in the middle 'thirties. (Everton Weekes actually made five in succession shortly afterwards.)

The South Africans had not quite the weight of bowling to match England on good pitches, but they were extremely popular, and contributed their full share to the delights of a vintage season. They brought over a good deal of tinned food as a gesture of sympathy for the ration situation, but, despite the tins, the captain's efforts over the summer – and he was slim in the first place – cost him a couple of stone. Such hardships, all but forgotten now, were real enough at the time, and they struck no one more forcibly than our visitors from overseas. It was the Tory Government in 1951 that abolished ration cards. We needed petrol coupons even longer.

In the match between Middlesex, as champions, and the Rest of England at the Oval, Denis Compton (246) and Bill Edrich (180) between them made 426 out of their side's total of 543. This enabled them to win a handsome victory which in this match only one other county, Yorkshire, have ever achieved. In his innings Denis made what even for him was a phenomenal stroke. As he strolled out to play a ball from Goddard on the full pitch the studs of his right boot got somehow caught in the laces of his left and he toppled headlong forward. As he did so he remembered the ball and, in the act of falling, flicked it sweetly away for four. Have you ever tried walking on water, they asked him. But Denis played most of that innings with his right knee strapped. This was the beginning of a succession of trouble which ended ultimately in the removal not only of the cartilage but of the knee-cap. He was never so fit again as in that golden summer of 1947.

Just as 1930 belonged to Bradman, I wrote in the *Daily Telegraph* in a valedictory article at the end of the season, 1925 to Hobbs, 1902 to Trumper, 1895 to W. G., so 1947 was Compton's year. But I added that there was one English batsman very close to Compton in quality but at present in popular eclipse. 'If Len Hutton had been blessed with Compton's physical strength and vigour this summer he might have made 4,000.' I also went on to say that, as a legacy of war, bowling was on a lower plane than it had been at any time since the arm was raised above the shoulder. I thought there should be 'a central school of instruction, both to cater for promising individual players, and, possibly more important, to refresh the methods of school, club and county coaches. This would be best organized under the patronage of MCC itself, Lord's being the natural headquarters.'

Alas! that all these years later, while we have long had a costly Memorial Gallery at Lord's in tangible but not practical memory of the fallen, an Indoor School still has only just got as far as the drawing-board. The school was one of the three measures I suggested to ensure a general state of prosperity in the game. The others were the provision of artificial pitches after the Australian style in villages, parks, and schools where the maintenance of true turf was impossible; and the institution in the south of competitions on the league and cup principle similar to those that had long been general in the north. At this distance I am satisfied that these three proposals, all considered distinctly novel at the time, read pretty well.

After a break of three months or so I found myself winging off to the West Indies in the wake of the MCC, under G. O. Allen's captaincy, which was proceeding by sea – very roughly, as it turned out, on an empty banana boat. But if the MCC journey was hazardous in one way, so was mine in another. The only carrier making the air journey was British South

American Airways run by a noted RAF airman known as 'Path-finder Bennett'. They flew Tudors, which during the war had carried bombs. We spent the night at the Azores, and as this was not on the schedule I made enquiries. Weather not too good, presumably? Visualizing in my ignorance a string of weather ships across the Atlantic, I asked the pilot just how he had got the information on which he had based his decision. 'Oh,' he said, 'from a chap who flew in this morning.' Much shaken by this I was relieved to hear we were going to fly down to Dakar in North Africa, and thence across the narrowest stretch of the Atlantic to Natal on the Brazilian coast.

Apart from the fact that the natives were very far from friendly, we had no alarums, and plugging up the South American coastline arrived, very late but safe, at Trinidad. A fortnight later the next plane on this flight, called the *Star Tiger*, took the prescribed route from the Azores to Bermuda and was never seen again. All perished, including the pretty little air hostess who had looked after us so nicely on the trip before. Air travel in those early post-war days was rather a matter of by guess and by God.

As in Australia the year before, the prevailing first impression in the West Indies as Gubby Allen's team progressed from island to island was the warmth of the welcome. It was thirteen years since the visit of the last MCC side, and the war was still less than three years away.

No touring side had been there since 1935, so there was no yardstick by which to judge the several new players who had emerged since the West Indies had played in England in 1939. Judged by results this expedition of 1947–48 was something of a failure, since the side chosen did not carry quite the guns to extend fully the opposition they encountered. But there were extenuating circumstances, in the form of every sort of injury and illness, while, if MCC were not able to win, the cricket certainly stimulated the appetite of the most enthusiastic crowds in the world. The West Indies' triumphs in England two years later would probably not have been possible but for the experience they gained in this first post-war series. Also in terms of friendly relationships and the spirit of the cricket everything went admirably, and for this state of things Gubby Allen, with much aid from Billy Griffith, who acted as player-manager, was of course responsible.

Retrospectively, it could be thought that MCC might have sent a slightly stronger side, but at the time it was felt that with eighteen months of solid cricket, including fifteen Test matches, behind them and the challenge of the Australian visit ahead, most of the leading players must be given a winter's rest. So although the best side would probably have contained a dozen or so of those who had toured Australia with Walter Hammond, only three – Evans, Hardstaff and Ikin – were chosen. Because of the spate of injuries an SOS was sent during the second of the four legs of the tour (it comprised Barbados, Trinidad, British Guiana and Jamaica in that order), and Len Hutton promptly flew over and gave much-needed class to the batting.

On paper the MCC choice looked sensible enough – a largely young side with a captain of great experience and prestige in Allen. At the end Gubby felt, I think, that at the age of forty-five he had been wrong to accept the invitation. Yet the galling thing was that, though he broke down with strains once on the ship and twice on the field, when he was fit he looked a class above most of the rest. After all Wilfred Rhodes and George Gunn had lasted out the 1929–30 tour, and performed marvellously, despite the heat and hard grounds, when each was just on the shady side of fifty. It could be said, though, of them that their muscles were attuned by years of constant play whereas Allen in 1947 had been able to get very little cricket. He was also a bowler whose pace was still very much on the sharp side of medium.

As to the injuries they are scarcely worth cataloguing at this distance, except perhaps for one. Harold Butler, of Notts, a heavy, deep-chested fellow (known for no reason I can recall as Penelope!) was a master of late 'swing and cut with a reputation far below his deserts. He was not fit for the first Test, but in Trinidad was making the colony side look like children when he was struck down with malaria. He lost a stone in two or three days, and was something of a shadow of himself thereafter.

MCC were nominally fifteen strong all through, for as Hutton came one way poor Dennis Brookes with a broken finger departed for home. There were seldom fewer than four on the injured list and at one point, Gubby, something of an expert on the various ills the flesh is heir to, provided himself with a couple of lamps and augmented the work of the doctors by setting up a sort of clinic in his bedroom. 'Where do you feel it, Joe?' – or Jack or Johnny – 'Ah, yes, that's the one I pulled in '24' – or '31 or '37. 'Let's get the heat on it.'

Crawford White, on his first tour for the *News Chronicle*,

and I practised regularly with such of the team as were fit enough to perform, and were almost alone in maintaining a clean bill of health throughout. Crawford had played in the Lancashire League for Royton, and was a more than useful bowler of above medium-pace. He and I both played for MCC in a one-day match against South Trinidad, and when MCC flew down to Georgetown, the *Daily Telegraph* heading above a Reuter message was 'Allen has 7 Fit men : Reporter may be in MCC XI.'

Alas, though, the reporter was Crawford, I, probably for some frivolous reason, having lingered an extra day in Trinidad after ascertaining what the side against BG was to be. But at Georgetown others fell sick; hence the crisis. They included Godfrey Evans with a horrible attack of prickly heat. As the seven fit men included five or six bowlers the name of C. White was not in the final selection, but if I had been present before start of play, as distinct from a little later, I gather I should have been chosen instead of Godfrey Evans in hopes of my getting a few runs. As it was, Jim Laker went in No. 6, Godfrey, incommoded as he was, contributing 1 and 1. It has always been a regret that I thus missed the chance of playing in a first-class match for MCC on tour – and, who knows, of making some on the Bourda wicket, one of the best in the world.

The press party was the smallest in any of my fourteen MCC tours to date : just White, Charles Bray, Norman Preston, Brian Chapman (then *Daily Express*, afterwards *Daily Mirror*, now *Guardian*), and myself. 'Plum' Warner also travelled with the team, as did Charles Bray's charming wife, Marjorie. Plainly a small entourage of writers is easier to handle than a larger one, but even so the captain's happy knack with us all deserves notice. The journalists' abiding fear is that things of importance are being kept dark, and thus liable to be picked up by a rival and built into a scoop. It's exactly to prevent such a thing that popular papers send out their own men. But there is nothing of the oyster about Gubby Allen. It is in his nature to confide, and from his experience of the captaincy in Australia he knew that to let the press in on current plans was the best and wisest policy.

So, though the team's performance was disappointing, the press, well informed of the difficulties, recorded events with tolerance and sympathy. Gubby Allen has given most of a lifetime to cricket, and served it with the utmost energy in many fields, but I have a notion he would have made a particularly successful touring manager. He would have been a highly observant guide to any captain with whom he was *sympatico*, and he would have been helpful, as always, to any of the team, batsmen as well as bowlers, seeking technical advice. (It was his judgment of form – and reliance on 'class' – that made him so successful a selector.) He would have been a God-send to the press. Understanding with the opposing administration? Well, there his concern for English interests might have made him seem to them somewhat prickly. It would depend on his personal relationships. At the worst he would have had a substantial credit balance. I write in the past tense, since, seventy this year, he couldn't now be asked to undertake the job. So – a manager manqué.

But, of course, the Australians would likewise have had a formidable one in Sir Donald Bradman, who never considered the idea. When after the 1946–47 tour I asked him whether, if he did not come in 1948 as a player, he might do so as manager, he said 'In absolutely no circumstances.' It's a significant fact that, despite the obvious qualifications of many of them, so very few old Test cricketers of any country become managers. I suppose that, seeing the job at first hand, they have realized what a highly-demanding, never-ending, nerve-stretching one it is.

That first West Indies tour was a blissful time, so much more than living up to the apéritif of my Bermuda visit of the 'thirties. Our first port of call was Barbados, of which I shall have more to say later on, and this smallest of the Test territories (we didn't visit the smaller islands in 1947–48) remained perhaps the favourite of most of us. But Trinidad, British Guiana (now Guyana) and Jamaica all had their different points of attraction. There is no Test ground quite to equal the Queen's Park Oval at Port of Spain, with the vast spreading Samaan and Pride of India trees giving shade to the crowd, and the ground and arena framed in the mountains of the Northern Range with their tropical luxuriance and subtle colour changes. There were, too, for an evening's amusement the cosmopolitan delights of the city of Port of Spain, and the heady wonders of Carnival.

On the three days of Carnival, ending on the evening of Shrove Tuesday, all other activity ceases, and visiting teams are nowadays kept clear of Trinidad at and just before this time. But in 1948 we were in residence at the Queen's Park Hotel and from the balconies overlooking the vast green stretch of the Savannah got a grandstand view of the everlasting parade of the bands, each group in its own colourful, often bizarre costumes. We picked up something of the gay abandon, with everyone, from the highest to the lowest, letting his hair down to the beat of the music. For these three days and nights at least in this Caribbean island all men are indeed equal. I believe that those in authority in Trinidad – which has had its share of political tensions in the last few years – set great store by Carnival as a safety-valve. It is not the least extraordinary thing about Carnival that for all its hilarity and licence there is scarcely ever the slightest hint of trouble.

Just before the Carnival balloon went up we were watching the lively scene from the hotel when Gubby Allen cried 'there's old Tang Choon', and dashed out in time to greet one of our favourite opponents, at the wheel of a large open car festooned with little Tang Choons to the number of roughly a dozen. All were formally presented to the famous captain of MCC, a happy, grinning, group. There is no cricket community more diverse in origin than Trinidad, with its Chinese such as Tang Choon, Achong, and Lee Kow, those of French descent (Ganteaume), Portuguese (Gomez, Rodriguez, Dos Santos), German (the Stollmeyer brothers), and Indian (Asgarali, Ramadhin), in addition to the preponderant African stock and some Europeans (both Lord Harris and 'Plum' Warner were born in Trinidad).

This is the place to pay brief tribute to Sir Errol dos Santos, who has been the (on the whole) benevolent dictator of Queen's Park for countless years and with his inexhaustible energy and business sense has made the ground one of the best, as well as the most beautiful, of its size in the world. It is a feature of the administration of West Indian cricket that it is run almost exclusively by old cricketers – and, happily, often not so old at that. Errol was never a cricketer, but in his untiring work for the game he shows the stamina and determination that would have helped him to become at least a difficult man to dislodge.

The people of BG, as it was then, were inclined to be apologetic to visitors about the attractions of their country which surely is a contrast after the glamorous delights of the islands. Though the sea is on the doorstep of Georgetown it is still brown from the waters of the converging Orinoco two hundred and more miles to the northward of the South American mainland in Venezuela. The muddy shore attracts no custom over the sea wall that prevents the flooding of the city, which is actually below sea level. But Georgetown, laid out by the Dutch, with its wide, dyke-bisected roads and white-painted timber houses, has its own charm. while the trim Bourda ground is a completely worthy setting for a Test match.

An appealing thing about Guyanese cricket is that, more than any other activity perhaps, it brings the different races together in a common interest and patriotism even though the individual clubs tend to be sectional.

The other institution that transcends racial boundaries is the Christian church. The Anglican Cathedral is a vast airy church in the centre of a square, said to be the highest timber building in the world. The sight of two or three thousand men, women and children of so many types and colours wending their way to the High Altar to make their Easter Communions, men and boys in sub fusc, women and girls in white, is an abiding memory. One difference, incidentally, between England and the West Indies is that, while for so many English people Easter and Christmas are held nowadays to be enough, in the West Indies the weekly obligation is widely understood and accepted. The cathedral at Georgetown, with its several masses from dawn onwards, is comfortably filled every Sunday.

Another reflection on church-going in the West Indies : the roads on Sunday mornings everywhere are filled with children of all ages on their way to service or Sunday-school, their frocks and suits impeccably clean, ironed, and pressed, however small and modest the wooden, one-roomed houses from which they have emerged. There is a very strong self-respect in the average West Indian, and this is just one impressive and regular expression of it.

We came last to Jamaica, and this first time saw little more than the city and outskirts of Kingston where the matches were played. Sabina Park itself, with its gorgeous backdrop of the Blue Mountains, has that much in common with Queen's Park, Port of Spain, but it is small, square, enclosed, and with its high stands has a certain cockpit atmosphere. When the fast bowlers trudge back at the city end they come within a pitch's length of the press-box. You can see the whites of their eyes. There seems a special intensity about the cricket in Jamaica, partly induced by the configuration of the ground, partly by the fierce partisanship of the crowd. There is an ingrained toughness about the Jamaican, as it seems to me, that makes him either a good friend or a bad enemy. But, tough or no, he has the most attractive of all the Caribbean voice intonations, a Welsh sort of lilt – behind which perhaps lies something of the somewhat melancholy philosophy of the Celt.

1. Positively last appearance : the Fathers' Match, Wellesley House, Broadstairs, July 1971 ; with my step-grandson, George Carbutt

2. Coralita, St James', Barbados; with my wife, who made the garden.
3. (*below*) TV commentary from Lord's: with the late Roy Webber.
The occasion was England v. West Indies, 1957, and we are directly
above the home dressing-room balcony

4. (*above*) Kennington Oval as I first knew it, in the 'twenties
5. (*below*) The first Australian team I ever saw, Warwick Armstrong's famous side of 1921. *Back row, from the left:* W. Bardsley, J. Ryder, H. L. Hendry, J. M. Gregory, E. R. Mayne, T. J. E. Andrews, Sidney Smith; *seated:* A. A. Mailey, E. A. McDonald, H. L. Collins, W. W. Armstrong (captain), C. G. Macartney, H. Carter, J. M. Taylor; *on the ground:* C. E. Pellew, W. A. Oldfield

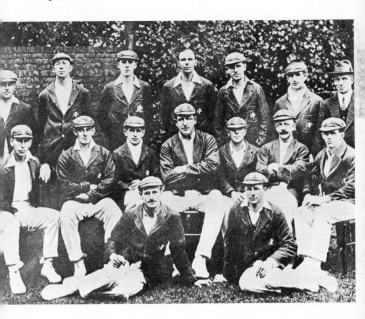

6. (*left*) J. B. Hobbs and H. Sutcliffe : the best of all opening partnerships. 7. (*right*) Headingley, 1930 : Don Bradman's triumphant return after breaking the world Test record with 334

8. Old Trafford, 1956 : the end of the game and Jim Laker's 19th wicket and 10th of the Australian second innings. *Left to right:* M. C. Cowdrey, I. W. Johnson, L. V. Maddocks, T. G. Evans, J. C. Laker, G. A. R. Lock, Rev. D. S. Sheppard, A. S. M. Oakman

9. (*left*) Keith Miller hits square. Sir Robert Menzies' favourite action picture. 10. (*right*) Denis Compton, idol of the post-war years

11. (*left*) Slater and Meckiff during the Sydney Test Match, January 1959, as portrayed in the *Daily Telegraph*. 12. (*right*) 'The Typhoon' – Frank Tyson at his peak in Australia, 1954-55

13. (*above*) With two stalwarts of Trinidad and West Indies cricket:
Gerry Gomez (*left*) and Jeffrey Stollmeyer. 14. (*below*) With
Sir Robert Menzies and Doug Walters at the launching of *The World
of Cricket,* Melbourne, January, 1966

15. (*above*) Far East Tour, 1964, at Kuala Lumpur; *from left;* Nick Pretzlik, Colin Ingleby-Mackenzie, Mike Griffith, Ken Taylor, Viscount Head (British High Commissioner), and Richard Hutton.
16. (*below*) H. E. Sir Solomon Hochoy, Governor-General of Trinidad and Tobago

8. Gary Sobers, now in the evening of his career, can look back on a record unsurpassed. No-one approaches the 8620 runs (average 51.84) that he has made in his 98 Test matches : only three men exceed his total of 256 wickets. Only Sir Donald Bradman has bettered by one his 28 Test hundreds. Only Colin Cowdrey exceeds the number of his appearances. Consider his virtuosity as a bowler in three styles, and his brilliance as a close catcher and you may conclude with the author that he has been the best and the most complete all-rounder in the game's history

By the end of the series (won by the West Indies 2-nil, with two games drawn) the 'three W's', Frank Worrell, Clyde Walcott and Everton Weekes, Barbadians all and born within about a square mile and eighteen months of one another, had firmly established themselves in the firmament of West Indian cricket. Walcott, tall, square, and one of the half-dozen hardest hitters of a ball I've ever seen, had announced his promise against MCC in the very first match. Worrell, graceful, languid, did so in the Trinidad Test. But for Weekes the road was a little harder, and he would not have played in the Fourth and last Test in Jamaica but for George Headley's withdrawal. There this squat, powerful fellow really came into his own, and henceforward never looked back. For the next fifteen years, though surrounded by many other fine players, these three great cricketers dominated the West Indian scene, the culmination of their effort being, of course, Frank Worrell's assumption of the captaincy and the acclaim won for his sides both in England and Australia.

Naturally one came to know the trinity of W's well, and their names will recur in this book, but on first acquaintance, so to say, it should be recorded that from their beginnings right through to retirement their deportment – a rather stuffy word, but I can think of none more fitting – both on the field and off it has never slipped, so far as I know, for a single moment. Though strong characters all, with minds and wills of their own, they never either did or said anything that was not completely appropriate to the situation. There was an instinctive sense of sportsmanship and good manners about the trio which is very much worth mentioning when it is realized that in the West Indies the cricketers are heroes of no ordinary degree. Their styles are aped, their attitudes imitated by every boy from his early schooldays. For this reason, if for no other, the awards that each received from the Queen were merited several times over.

A final reflection induced by this thought: in the 'seventies a sporting philosophy gains ground that is euphemized by the phrase 'professional' but for which there is much blunter language. It seems to suggest that the best way to win is to show a mean-spirited bloody-mindedness to the opposition. In cricket it is perhaps in part a reaction to the days when the amateur was the boss – though I hasten to add that it is only a minority of modern captains and players who subscribe to it.

The point is that this sort of outlook is miles removed from that of the West Indian, whose forebears learned not only the game itself but how to play it from British ex-patriates, from naval and military sides on their tours of duty, and from the various visiting sides from England. There is a tradition of good sportsmanship in West Indian cricket, long established, which has never weakened. Gary Sobers today is its perfect expression.

After four Test series, winter and summer consecutively, and with several more to come, and remembering maybe my adventurous air journey across the Atlantic, I arranged with the co-operation of my newspaper to fly to New York and then to put my feet up and return home on the *Queen Mary*. For me travel on a good ship and in congenial company touches the ultimate in human contentment, compared to which flashing about by air, with its tensions and fatigue, is a poor substitute. Nor is there any rest to compare with the leisurely life on a great liner – except the rather different and, incidentally, warmly recommended regime of the fruit juice 'cure' at Forest Mere or some other of the health hydros. 'Unwindings' both!

I returned to meet – and meet in a very special way – Don Bradman's 1948 Australians. In the anthology entitled *The Twelfth Man*, which the Lord's Taverners recently collected for the Duke of Edinburgh's fiftieth birthday, I contributed an essay about the early years of the Cricket Writers' Club which contained an account of our first dinner given in their honour and attended by the Duke. I expect that some who read these words may also have read those, but I must ask their forbearance, for I can scarcely gloss over in a personal book a function at which I took the chair with the royal personage on one side and the greatest of modern cricketers on the other.

We dined – and pretty well, too, by 1948 standards – at the Public Schools Club in Piccadilly. After an extensive experience of cricket dinners both before and since I still rate the talking that night, present company naturally excepted, as easily the best I have ever heard. What is more, so next morning did Peterborough of the *Daily Telegraph*, who opened his diary thus:

Cricket last night was the subject of as brilliant a series of after-dinner speeches as I have ever heard. The occasion was the Cricket Writers' Club dinner in honour of the Australian team. The speakers were Mr E. W. Swanton, Mr D. G. Bradman, Mr H. S. Altham, Canon F. H. Gillingham, Mr Justice Birkett and Mr R. C. Robertson-Glasgow.

As one at the studio end, as it were, of Bradman's broadcast speech, I can testify that he approaches the microphone not much less skilfully than he approaches the wicket.

Mr Swanton, *Daily Telegraph* cricket correspondent and chairman at the dinner, had bowled a perfect opening over. Bradman played after him under film arc lights with a short smile, a coolness and ease which the most polished after-dinner speaker might have envied.

The Don is often portrayed as a hard man, and no one who saw him play will deny that he was a tough competitor in the field. But in this return to the scene of his first and greatest successes after the intervening war years his mood, caught by millions over the air, was nostalgic and sentimental. The quality of his speech was such that the BBC in those less rigid days held up the nine o'clock news – and Don was deluged with letters by the hundreds, if not the thousand. Of the four speeches that followed I wrote in *The Twelfth Man*:

Sir Norman, later Lord, Birkett, gave the toast of cricket with that rare felicity of phrase and articulation which so many cricket diners-out soon came to know so well. This was replied to by H. S. Altham, whose great services to MCC and the game generally had scarcely then begun (apart from his authorship of *A History of Cricket* and his marvellous work as coach at Winchester). It would have been hard if not impossible for anyone to have followed these two speeches in a similar classic mould. But happily the next man in the order of going in was R. C. Robertson-Glasgow, whose oratorical style was as unique as it was uproariously funny. 'Crusoe' proposed the guests. But who to follow that? For the sixth and final speech – nowadays, of course, six speeches are at least two too many – I had recruited none other than 'Parson' – or to be exact the Rev. Canon – F. H. Gillingham, a batsman of note between the wars for Essex and the Gentlemen. He was widely known as an Anglican preacher, a large lantern-jawed fellow with, in repose, a face of unrelieved gloom. What the Australians thought was coming when this avenging prophet got up in his clerical rig goodness knows, but within a few seconds he was putting up a performance that would have fetched hundreds a week – in 1948 currency – at the Palladium. His dog-collar and that dead-pan expression naturally enhanced the effect. What he said I have no idea except that there was a story about some Australian so tough that he bound his bat with barbed wire – or perhaps it was that he used it to protect his knuckles. No matter. It was all a riot.

The occasion was calculated to bring the best out of any-one, but the luck was happening on such a selection of speakers and getting the batting order right. A good speech is always talked about, and followed by further invitations, and in two of these cases especially this night was the precursor of, literally, hundreds of others. Between 1948 and their deaths in 1962 and 1965 respectively, no cricket after-dinner speakers were in such demand as Norman Birkett and Harry Altham, and such was their love of the game and natural generosity that they went to the greatest trouble to accept if it was humanly possible. They gave the utmost pleasure to many thousands, and it is one of the things most agreeable to look back on that I was one of those who chanced to start them off.

At the end I quietly asked Prince Philip if he would like to round off the evening, though the understanding when he had accepted the invitation was that he would not speak. He said, 'They've had some wonderful speeches. Let's leave it at that.' I naturally could not press him, though one soon came to realize that he would have played an innings well worthy of the occasion. The date was 22 April, 1948, and as he had been married only five months in all probability was his first official cricket occasion. It might even have played some small part in persuading the Duke of Edinburgh to patronize the game to the extent he afterwards did.

It is a temptation to live again the events of each English season, but lo! is it not all written in *Wisden*, to say nothing of *A History of Cricket*, and many other places besides, and if this book is not to run to an indigestible length I must sub-edit my thoughts even more drastically than in this particular summer they had to be confined in the *Daily Telegraph*. The newsprint shortage was at its worst at this time. When Brad-man opened the tour with his usual hundred at Worcester – following his three successive double-hundreds there in the 'thirties he was satisfied this time with a mere 107 – the account had to be compressed into half-a-column. As to Compton's 184 in the Trent Bridge Test (one of the truly great innings, played in that strange and eerie yellow light), the report and scores could not be stretched beyond three-quarters. Single column headings were the rule, and the seven-point type seen today makes difficult reading. Even so Frank Coles, my sports editor, was able to take some shortish general pieces, which from the start of this summer were dignified by the 'strap-line' Cricket Commentary. This feature then, so far as I am concerned, has run now for twenty-five years.

I shouldn't have minded the lack of space perhaps seeing that in this and many subsequent years I was also a full member of the BBC running commentary team for every Test, either on sound or television. The writing, and around two hours of solid talk on the air, made for a concentrated day.

The Australians drew vast crowds everywhere, and the only disappointment was that their magnificent all-round side won the rubber rather too easily. Yet but for a succession of regrettable accidents the outcome would have been prolonged until the last Test at the Oval. The day that decided everything was the last at Leeds in the Fourth Test when on a dusty pitch, you may remember, Norman Yardley declared England's second innings and left Australia all day bar quarter of an hour to bat, with 404 runs between them and victory.

History records how, for once, Evans had a bad time behind the stumps, how half a dozen chances in all were missed, how a phenomenal stand of 301 between Bradman and Arthur Morris turned the tables, how Australia's captain decided quite early in his innings that the game might be no less easy to win than to draw, and how his side did so by seven wickets.

But here is a small item told me some years later by 'Fergie' (the famous scorer W. H. Ferguson) and not, I believe, recorded before. The Australians that year were travelling everywhere by coach. When it had deposited them at the ground on that last morning Bradman quietly told 'Fergie' to make sure the driver came back for them by mid-afternoon – and this although they had only a short journey to Derby in prospect. The Don cannot have thought they would have won by then : he can only have supposed that they might have lost. As they should have done. I expect the Aussies sang their way to Derby – I only remember driving down to play a match at Oxford sick with disappointment.

I am in no position to be dogmatic about the respective qualities of the Australians of 1921 and 1948. Armstrong's team was a magnificent instrument in the hands of a highly determined leader, but had it quite the depth of batting or the rich variety of bowling at the command of Bradman? Here is the side in batting order that played in the last Test of 1948, and remember that all save the captain were either in their prime or approaching it : A. R. Morris, S. G. Barnes, D. G. Bradman, A. L. Hassett, K. R. Miller, R. N. Harvey, S. J. E. Loxton, R. R. Lindwall, D. Tallon, D. T. Ring, W. A. Johnston. Note that W. A. Brown (despite an average of over 50) had been dropped for the nineteen-year-old Harvey who promptly celebrated at Leeds by making a hundred; also that Colin McCool did not get in for a single Test while Doug Ring played at the Oval only because Ernie Toshack had broken down, and in preference to Ian Johnson. Australia in fact were more than covered in every department.

One way and another English cricket had no very good conceit of itself when that same autumn, under a new captain untried in Tests, MCC sailed off for South Africa. Norman Yardley being unavailable – and for all his qualities there was much to be said, after the Australian defeats, for a new leader whether he was or not – the selectors plumped for F. G. Mann, who that summer, though unable to repeat Walter Robins's success of the previous year, led Middlesex to an honourable third place in the championship.

At the Oval in the last Test against Australia England had suffered the ultimate humiliation of being bowled out for 52. Morale was at rock bottom. On the first day of the South African tour the MCC bowling was hit by a not particularly distinguished Western Province side to the tune of 386 for four, and, reading the news, I recall wondering then whether even George Mann, for whose leadership gifts I had the highest regard, could re-enthuse our top cricketers, considering the limitations of his attack. (For the one and only time ever MCC were obliged to go abroad without a single bowler fast enough to necessitate the 'keeper standing back.)

I need not have worried. The very next day the captain was completing his hundred with a six, and from this beginning at the Cape his side advanced by leaps and bounds, becoming among other things the best fielding side I have seen under the flag of MCC. Having just taken on the job of Rugby football correspondent I was unfortunately only able to spend a month with the team, taking in the first three Tests, starting with the extraordinary First at Durban when England won by two wickets off the last ball thanks to a leg-bye. On the first Tuesday of December I had been at Twickenham recording Oxford's victory in the University Match. By the Friday I was watching MCC at Johannesburg. At the end the switch back from one game to the other was almost equally swift.

At the time I regretted the return, as I now do in retrospect, for in view of previous tours and of many more to come one would have relished both the reality and the memory of one tour at least where everything went absolutely right. As always

166

all centred round the leadership, and of Mann's performance R. J. Hayter, Reuter's correspondent with the team, wrote in *Wisden*: 'As a captain he was ideal, zealous to a degree, and considerate in all things at all times' – which, when you come to think of it, would make a pretty fair epitaph.

When seasoned professionals are obviously enjoying their cricket it is a sure bet that their play will be enjoyed and appreciated by the crowds, and just as this was the best MCC fielding side in my memory so also it was the most popular. Naturally one was proud to see an English side making such an impression, and gladly cabled home items that reflected the state of affairs. One gesture I remember was the sending back by a Johannesburg ladies' committee of a hundred food parcels to the home town of every member of the MCC team. In South Africa, as in Australia and the West Indies the previous two winters, the team was identified in people's hearts with the British war effort, and the shortages at home were very much in their minds.

Politically, by the way, the Nationalists had assumed office (on a minority of the votes cast) a few months before the MCC tour. They were in power, but they had scarcely yet pulled on the jack-boot. I found the atmosphere all too pleasantly reminiscent of the tour of ten years earlier. The bitterness and strife lay in the future.

When George Mann came home he told me that before going to South Africa he had been given two pieces of advice by his father, Frank, who had led the MCC team quarter of a century before. His father said he had made it a rule never to accept a private dinner invitation on tour. He thought his place was in the hotel dining-room with the team, irrespective of how many or how few happened to be there. They may not be many, but they were perhaps inclined to be the same ones who had either not been asked anywhere or had preferred to relax among their companions. It was one time and place when the captain could always be found.

This was undoubtedly a shrewd piece of psychology, as well as an impressive piece of self-denial considering the intense social activity that centred especially around the amateurs on MCC tours between the wars. It might be added that Frank Mann was given (unlike his son) just about the most difficult side to handle – full of contentious, unusual personalities, with a handful of wives thrown in – that any MCC captain has been saddled with, and that, by all accounts, he too came out with flying colours.

The second subject on which father Mann expressed strong views was the press. Steer well clear of them, he said. They were apparently (in 1922–3!) a dangerous lot. George, I believe, followed the parental precept in the first case – which perhaps is why he did not encounter his wife Margaret, from Johannesburg, until they met on the ship sailing home; but, of course, he did not commit himself to the second, and indeed established the smoothest of relations with the cricket-writers.

The manager and vice-captain must be given due credit for their share in the success of the operation – Brigadier M. A. Green and S. C. Griffith respectively. Mike Green, assisted by a South African manager who looked after the purely local chores, presided benignly over the proceedings discreetly fortified by gin and tonic. Billy Griffith, fulfilling a rather less exacting role than in the West Indies a year previously, distinguished himself by winning his place in the last two Tests as wicketkeeper in preference to Godfrey Evans. It may be forgotten today that in his prime (which perhaps extended from the 1945 Victory Tests until he joined *The Sunday Times* in 1950) the present Secretary of MCC was among the best two or three 'keepers in the game. Which reminds me that I've written about the West Indies tour without mentioning his remarkable effort in making a hundred, going in first in his first Test at Trinidad. Two things I recall about that day – which happened among other things to be my birthday. First, when he came in at tea the sweat had come through and was clearly to be seen on the front of his pads. I've never known that before or since. Also that night, the centre of an admiring circle, when he said 'The next is on me, boys,' and put his hand into his pocket he promptly slid off his chair on to the floor. There, amid much heartless hilarity, he lay rigid and helpless with cramp. All the salt pills he had swallowed (standard diet for English cricketers in hot countries) had not been enough.

Though it is a temptation, I must not linger too long over these first post-war years, but the 1949 summer cannot go unmentioned. In weather it was not far off the record vintage of 1947. The crowds were still very large, and Denis Compton was still the hero-in-chief. The story of his benefit illustrates both his good nature and his luck. He was due for a benefit in 1948, but seeing that Laurie Gray was a bowler readily agreed to his taking precedence. After all his records in 1947 and with the Australians here, he must in 1948 have had a wonderful response. As it was, Gray collected £6,000, which was – briefly – a Middlesex record. Came Whitsuntide 1949, when for Denis, naturally, the sun shone, 55,000 people watched the game between Middlesex and Sussex, the gates being closed on the Bank-holiday, the man of the moment flicked up 182, and his score in £.s.d. at the end of the season was £12,258.

The only cloud was the failure to get a result in any of the four Tests of three days each against Walter Hadlee's strong New Zealand side, the best they have ever sent here. Thereafter all home Tests became five days, and since the next thing was to ordain five of each every summer – six when the 'twin tour' system was started – the season's natural balance was ruined for ever. The surfeit of Test cricket has put the County Championship progressively deeper into the shade.

Prince Philip was nominated President of MCC at the AGM of the Club on the first Wednesday of May, 1949, and duly attended the Anniversary Dinner that followed. Of course, the appointment caused much surprise, and much delight. We dined then in the cosy old Members' Dining Room adjacent to the Tavern, now alas all gone, with its bar adjoining. After the party had broken up some twenty of us were lingering on enjoying a night-cap when to our great surprise in blew the new President and his equerry, Lt.-Commander 'Mike' Parker. It happened that I was the only member present known to either, and so it fell to me to introduce some of the rare characters of MCC who frequent these occasions. There followed a remarkably happy and relaxed hour or so which served to increase the admiration which I had formed for HRH at the Cricket Writers' Club dinner to the Australians. What had happened, so Mike Parker told me, was that Prince Philip, having driven home from Lord's almost to the Palace, suddenly thought it would be fun to return and see whether anything was still going on, and to meet a few members apart from the top brass among whom he had been sitting. We did our best to make his journey worth while.

At the end of the season the Duke made his one and only appearance against a county in the company of a side that apart from him were Test or first-class players. This was at Bournemouth in a match for the Silver Jubilee Appeal of the National Playing Fields Association, between Hampshire and the Duke of Edinburgh's XI. It was a sporting effort on his part to submit to so public an exposure of his skill even in a game contested in a comparatively carefree way, for his playing experience since captaining the XI at Gordonstoun – where cricket reputedly does not rank specially high among the school activities – can only have been an occasional appearance for a naval side and in a few Household games at Windsor.

But all went like a marriage bell. The sun shone, Dean Park was comfortably full, and HRH followed up a creditable piece of slow-medium bowling which earned him a wicket by going in No. 6 and making 12. Readers of the *Daily Telegraph* were informed that the Duke:

> wearing an I Zingari cap, came in at 191 for five and, beginning with a straight drive for two, brought the crowd to its feet with two fine, crisp drives for four past mid-off off the front foot, all along the ground. The common picture of him is of an ardent village cricketer, but these were strokes of a pedigree not normally seen on English greens. He stayed long enough to make it clear, as his bowling and zestful fielding had suggested, that he would always hold his own in the company of good cricketers if he could contrive the time to practise.

The NPFA (of which he had just become President) raked in £1,400 as a result of the day's activities.

The only abnormality about Prince Philip's cricket was that he wore dark glasses. When we were talking at the party afterwards he said, 'You know, I love this game. But of course I'd never have time to play it regularly. Besides, these' – pointing to his eyes – 'won't get any better.' He wore glasses in fact because he was short-sighted.

The pleasantest function that befell the MCC President in his year of office was to chair the Special General Meeting which approved the change of rule whereby the first batch of great professionals, 26 in all, were made honorary members of the Club. It was also in this year that MCC set up the Enquiry, from which emerged the whole broad national scheme of coaching called the MCC Youth Cricket Association. Harry Altham was the mainspring and chief motivator of the coaching scheme, though it was Gubby Allen who at a general committee meeting under 'Any Other Business' first suddenly asked, 'What has MCC ever done to help the boys of this country as a whole over their cricket?' The challenge was accepted, and everything moved from there.

It was Allen, too, who first thought up the honorary membership idea, which has since been extended to famous cricketers and administrators overseas. Prince Philip would not claim any personal credit for these things, but both must have won his warm approval and the fact is that they were inaugurated during his Presidency.

I flew out in the winter of 1949–50 to see a couple of Tests in the series between South Africa and Australia, the first of just a few I've watched in the luxury of neutral detachment. This tour, like MCC's a year earlier, passed off with exemplary smoothness under the control of Lindsay Hassett as captain and E. A. Dwyer as manager. No one could have had a better manner or presence for the job than 'Chappy' Dwyer, and I always hoped he would come as manager to England. The fact that he never did so was due to politics, for this particular plum is reserved for a member of the Australian Board of Control and to that august, but in those days long-in-the-tooth, body my candidate never quite aspired.

England's buffetings from the strongest Test sides were far from over, for in 1950 the West Indians came, saw and conquered and in the following winter MCC, though putting up a fight of a kind not quite reflected in the score-book, endured another fruitless tour to Australia. Perhaps fruitless is not quite the right word since they cheered all hearts, Australian as well as English, by winning the Fifth Test at Melbourne.

I suppose that one of the most significant moments in modern cricket history was when the West Indies won the Lord's Test of 1950. It was the first time they had beaten the full strength of England, they did it by a thumping margin, and it happened at headquarters itself. Small wonder that their countrymen paraded the field afterwards with impromptu steel band, the victory already immortalized in calypso, paying tribute to

> 'those little pals of mine,
> Ramadhin and Valentine.'

The only incongruous sight was a solid wall of Bobbies stretched across from the Tavern block to the top of the ground guarding the pavilion as though the very sanctuary of English cricket was being threatened. Someone should rather have set the President on the balcony to take the salute. He would have loved it, for by this time the Duke of Edinburgh had been succeeded by Sir Pelham Warner, who understood his countrymen and had a deep affection for them.

The great question of the summer was who should take MCC to Australia – and, of course, who should be sent with him. Norman Yardley, who had been restored to the England captaincy against the West Indies, had his backers, and so assuredly did George Mann though there were known to be doubts about his being able to go. Failing them the *Daily Telegraph* correspondent thought that consideration should be given to Freddie Brown and Tom Dollery whose leadership was working great things with, respectively, Northants and Warwickshire.

MCC left it until 10 July to announce that neither Mann nor Yardley was available – they had invited them in that order – despite which the selectors continued to pick Yardley against the West Indies. So there they were on 26 July with another overwhelming Test defeat to chew over, and committed to name captain and team before the end of Gentlemen v. Players starting next day.

When Cliff Gladwin had gone in to bat at the crisis of the Durban Test a year or two earlier he had remarked cheerfully to the nearest South African fielder, 'Coometh the hour, coometh the man.' When Brown came in to face the new ball shortly before tea at 194 for six in the Gentlemen's first innings he was no doubt thinking, or hoping, something rather similar. His batting was a classic of clean, old-fashioned straight hitting as one tail-ender after another came and went. When it was all over he had made 122 out of 131 while he was at the wicket, with no chances, in an hour and fifty minutes! There was a six into the pavilion and 16 fours, and as 17,000 stood and applauded him in, in the evening sunshine, there could have been none who doubted that the man they were saluting was the man for the job. It was the classic case of the exact psychological moment being seized.

If that was one classic, the method of choosing the rest was a classic of 'how not to'. With Brown's name came eleven more. The remaining five places were chosen by a selection committee of eleven (!) in three instalments. Last in was John Warr, whose progress I had followed with interest and approval since the beginning of the preceding summer, for this reason. In early May the Arabs at the last minute were short of an opening bowler for their two-day match against the Crusaders at Cambridge, and I therefore wired the University secretary asking if he could recruit one for me. When we arrived Hubert Doggart said: 'I've got you a chap I hope will do. He comes from Ealing County Grammar School, and we think he has possibilities – and he's a bit of a card.'

J. J. Warr duly showed up at the Magdalene ground, and had a modest success. More important, after dinner he sat at the feet of G. O. Allen and learned all about the grip for the outswinger and other mysteries of the bowling art. Within a week he was playing at Fenner's and taking six for 35 against Lancashire, from which point, as they say, he never looked back. After captaining Cambridge (with great success), and through the interest of R. H. Twining, then President of Middlesex, he joined the Union Discount Company, and made his mark both in the city and at Lord's, captaining Middlesex in the summer and, out of season, striding the environs of Cornhill in a silk hat. When John Warr exchanged county cricket for a column in *The Sunday Telegraph* a wider public than that which frequents club cricket dinners came to know him as 'a card' indeed. He is, to my mind, about the most consistently funny after-dinner speaker of his time. Now he is a director of Union Discount and among other things a racing steward. I'm not suggesting that in that Arab match we did more than give him a stepping-stone to success, for he would no doubt soon have come to light in any event. Yet it is a fact that ours was the first game of any consequence he played in. In a lean fast bowling period he was lucky to be chosen for Australia. He was at his best a little later, but by that time good bowlers of his type were as plentiful as before they had been rare.

I have always had secretarial help of one kind or another, but about now it seemed a good idea to find someone with ambitions to be a sporting journalist who might serve some sort of practical apprenticeship by helping me in a variety of ways. J. C. Woodcock, who as a freshman at Oxford in 1946 had joined what to him must have seemed a hoary Arab band on our tour to Rhine Army, abandoned the teaching career he had embarked on to try his hand with me, and as the summer of 1950 progressed I tried to think how I might finance his coming out to Australia with MCC.

Not long before we sailed out on the comfortable old *Stratheden* I interested Philip Dorté, the BBC Television Film Director, in the idea of Johnny Woodcock sending back some film of the Tests for Television News. Had he done much photography? I was non-committal as to this, the fact being that he had aspired to nothing much more complicated than a box Brownie. Anyway, it was arranged for him to report for a week's instruction to the Alexandra Palace studios. At the end of this he was declared fit to fire, and came staggering back with a Newman and Sinclair 35mm camera that looked and weighed something like a machine-gun. We had 20,000 feet of film, and a schedule was worked out to catch the BOAC flights. It was part of the contract that the ownership of the 'rushes', as the processed film is called, reverted to me.

So Johnny lugged his cumbersome camera all round Australia, sending back film and, of course, identifying captions, as prescribed, and it duly appeared on the TV screens of Britain some four or five days after being shot. The worst handicap of this very amateur film-cameraman was that he could never see a single foot of his work, despite which the photographic quality got better and better as each Test followed the last – as we saw for ourselves when we came to collect the rushes on our return to make our film of the tour.

It's really rather comical when one thinks of the millions spent today by the BBC on televised sport to look back on this pioneering effort which, patently, was all that Dorté's budget would run to in 1950. We were duly grateful to him for taking Woodcock on trust, and the BBC should have been to him for a brave effort. There was a rumour after it was over that there had been some trouble with the unions over the employ-ment of a non-union man!

Making a film out of the material we recovered from the BBC when we returned home was, of course, fresh ground for both of us, but early that summer all was done and the première of *Elusive Victory* took place in August 1951 at the British Council Theatre in Hanover Street. The narration was done by 'Crusoe', Rex Alston, Billy Griffith and myself, and it ran for an hour.

The chief credit naturally belonged to my young assistant, but I read afresh the review notices with some reflected pride. *The Times* thought that:

as a transposition of the printed word into terms of vision and sound it has an unquestioned educative and entertain-ment value. More than a mere pictorial impression . . . it brings one closer to the heart of an undertaking across the breadth of a continent. Here one can see and feel the game in Australia; the huge crowds, vast enclosures, and sense of urgency surrounding the Test Matches. One can sense too, the strain of such a tour with its exhausting travel, and its heat, brought into relief when the players are caught in their moments of relaxation.

The *News Chronicle* thought it 'an excellent film', while Peterborough in the *Daily Telegraph* as usual found something agreeable to say: '*Elusive Victory* may primarily be for cricketers old and, particularly, young, but everyone can enjoy this picture of the vitality of the Commonwealth, its cheering or groaning crowds, its great cricket grounds and, above all, its sunshine.'

The BBC wrote later that they had been 'most impressed', and booked the film for showing during the 1953 Australian visit. At the moment they could not 'say exactly what we can pay for the film but it will probably be in the region of £100 for two or three showings'. They weren't exactly throwing money about in the early 'fifties. However we were pleased enough. At rates varying from five to ten guineas a performance to clubs and schools, the film grossed £2,000 in the first six months, and had brought in £5,000 by the time it was laid finally to rest in 1966. Having seen it more often than anyone, Woodcock and I were aware well enough of its crudities. However it was the first-ever Test film. No one can take that away, and it is pleasant to think that one copy is still held at Lord's while another rests safe for posterity in the National Film Archive.

It showed me a profit in hundreds rather than thousands, but it had also paid for the exclusive and estimable services of the present *Times* correspondent both in Australia and during the following English summer, while he had drawn a modest salary in addition to picking up a valuable slice of experience which helped him through the doors first of the *Manchester Guardian* and shortly afterwards of *The Times*. He was only twenty-seven when he was made cricket correspondent of *The Times* by Donald Tyerman, the then Assistant Editor, in time for the season of 1954. That winter we were sailing once more for Australia – on equal terms.

I had given the film the same title as the book I did for Hodder and Stoughton which with my assistant's help was all written and despatched by air mail from New Zealand within a week or so of the Fifth Test ending, and was on sale at home in early June. The win in that last match was the 'elusive victory' for which everyone had waited so long. The book ran to 264 pages, and included forty-eight of the pictures that we sent back with the text. Looking back at the book after twenty years I find myself rather proud of it, as well as pleased to recall that it sold around 11,000 – which for any sporting book is good going, especially when the story to be told is one of failure.

The public apparently rated this a gallant and honourable failure, as indeed it was so far as the chief characters were concerned – Alec Bedser and Len Hutton, Trevor Bailey and Godfrey Evans, and in all ways, as captain and all-rounder, Freddie Brown himself. Once again, as at Leeds in 1948, England might have redeemed all – or at least set the stage for a great climax – by keeping Australia down once they had got them there. This time it was in the Second Test at Melbourne. Brown, Bedser, Bailey and Evans performed there like heroes, but they had too many passengers to carry. I've never known another Test between England and Australia when the home crowd almost to a man wanted the visitors to win. As Lindsay Hassett led his side in, victorious by 28 runs, the crowd just melted quietly away. I mention this because ever since Bodyline, perhaps before that, there have been those in England who see the average Australian spectator as a raucous, one-eyed fellow. Noisy, yes – fiercely partisan, yes at times – but he is a pretty good judge both of character and of a situation. I can't remember an English cricketer or an England performance not getting generous recognition down under.

The response was certainly enthusiastic enough when for the first time since the war England did at last beat Australia in a Test match. It was the Fifth Test of this series, also at Melbourne, and thanks chiefly to Reg Simpson's commanding innings it was – in the end – conclusive enough. But what a wait – the longest in history! If Denis Compton had not suffered the one complete and extraordinary eclipse of his career – Test average against Australia 7, for the other games of the tour 74 – England might well even have won this series, despite the weather, as had happened four years earlier, deciding the issue against us at Brisbane. However, the spell had been broken.

That summer of 1951 a successful series against South Africa under Freddie Brown kept spirits high. Two other significant things happened. Another and rather more roughly-hewn Freddie, Trueman by name, at the age of twenty was winning his cap for Yorkshire, while a certain P. B. H. May, only a year and a bit older, was stalking out, slim, tall, and just a bit stiff-legged, to play his first innings for England at Headingley and making 138 of the best runs imaginable.

10

Years of Victory

The decade beginning with the English summer of 1951 and ending with that of 1960 made up a span wherein, with one resounding exception, England mostly won or at worst were not beaten – and how refreshing it was to write and broadcast on a victorious note instead of recording misfortune and defeat. In this time they drew series in the West Indies, in India (with a weak side), in South Africa, and of all things at home against Pakistan in the wettest summer of history, 1954. But they also won three successive rubbers each against Australia and South Africa, two each against the West Indies and India, and one against New Zealand. After those first five post-war years it was a welcome change to be the bringer of good news instead of recording misfortune and defeat. The one blot on the picture was the MCC Australian tour of 1958/9.

The post-war generation, of course, was thrusting to the top headed by Peter May, with such men at Tom Graveney, Colin Cowdrey, David Sheppard, Willie Watson, Tony Lock, Fred Trueman, Brian Statham, Johnny Wardle, Trevor Bailey and Frank Tyson to join the earlier trio of Alec Bedser, Godfrey Evans and Jim Laker. Above all where there had been a complete dearth of English fast bowling now there were four or five jostling one another for places.

Trueman was the first of them, and if not quite the fastest certainly the most ferocious. After watching Lindwall and Miller operating for Test after Test while England had no armament of remotely equal calibre to fire back, there was a certain sadistic fun to be had in watching the poor Indians in 1952 being harried and chased by 'Furious Fred'. Tyson, briefly – to be exact from December 1954 to the end of May 1956 – could by sheer strength and courage work up a higher speed than I have seen in any bowler before or since, while Statham made a marvellously reliable partner for each in turn. Remember that Alec Bedser reached his peak in the early 'fifties – 30 wickets in 1950–51, 39 in 1953 – that Bailey took most of his 132 Test wickets within those eight years, and that Laker, Wardle and Lock were also in their prime, and think when the England bowling was ever as strong either before or since.

When England failed it was the batting that was the cause, and except when one of the top-classers was in spate much of it was pedestrian stuff by Test standards. Even May and Graveney, a little later joined by Ted Dexter, could not found a new Age of Elegance on their own. Style in batting was running a poor second to utility. But I must not indulge in weighty generalizations about the state of English cricket or in quantity at least I shall far exceed my target. Anyway, is it not all written in *Wisden* and *A History of Cricket*, and a host of books besides? This game is nothing if not well documented.

Let me concentrate on a few of the essential themes and figures: for instance Hutton, who in 1952 succeeded Brown in the England captaincy. For three years Len, without any county experience in the job, for Norman Yardley was still leading Yorkshire, bore the stresses of captaincy: a highly eventful time and, with some necessary qualifications, a successful one. Having swamped India, and guided Trueman in his four Tests to the capture of 29 wickets, he faced and overcame the challenge from Australia the following summer. There was the Coronation, and the British conquest of Everest, and finally at the Oval the regaining of the Ashes, and however incongruous it may seem to link the three events they *were* linked, and the Kennington rejoicings echoed over England to 'crown the year' in Jack Fingleton's happy phrase.

Lindsay Hassett accepted defeat with the grace that any who knew him would expect, and it was with a grin on his face that the following exchange took place directly after he had addressed over the loudspeakers the thousands massed round the Oval pavilion:

Robins: 'Well done, Lindsay, you couldn't have said it better.'

Hassett: 'Yes, not bad, I thought myself, considering Lockie threw us out.'

Now Tony Lock's fast ball had been no-balled three times in the Surrey v. Indians match the year before, and all that had happened was that Fred Price, the umpire, had been abused by the Oval crowd and members, while Lock had been chosen for another Test match a week or two later. Everyone thought that he threw his faster ones, but officially there was something of a conspiracy of silence. After all, there had been no throwing in English cricket since the turn of the century when in their respective spheres Lord Harris and Sydney Pardon had been foremost in stamping it out.

Possibly the throwing crisis might have been dealt with more rapidly, and with less fuss, if Surrey had acted, or if the England selectors had done so. Somehow a slow – or at any rate not a fast – bowler 'got by' in people's minds where a fast one would not have. I can see Doug Insole being to all appearances thrown out by Lock in a Champion County v. Rest match at the Oval and saying to the umpire, as one afterwards heard, 'How was that – run out?' I blame myself for not saying something forceful earlier than I did.

On this occasion Hassett, if I remember, was much less indignant about Lock's action than about Trevor Bailey, when England were likely to lose the Headingley Test, having taken an inordinate time to bowl an over. Time-wasting was due to be another thorn in the flesh in the years ahead. As to Lock his action was to be one of Hutton's sources of trouble the following winter in the West Indies – one of them, but not the worst.

The great thing that the regaining of the Ashes did was to give a fillip to English cricket which sustained the post-war boom in gates and helped to keep healthy not only the county coffers but those of the Australians who left for home richer by £100,000. (This was, and still is, the record tour profit.) As for the *Daily Telegraph*, the effect was to bring out a book comprising my Test reports scintillatingly embellished with prologue and epilogue by C. B. Fry. This was a notable rushed effort on the part of Harold Fish, the publicity manager, and all concerned, for the first copies were on sale inside a fortnight after the end of the series.

Celebrities such as Charles Fry, 'Plum' Warner and Jack Hobbs were quoted in praise of the book, which went into five impressions within a few weeks. It sold nearly 60,000 copies at what seems today to be the laughable price of two shillings, and the author was not too blasé to be otherwise than thrilled to read Sir Jack Hobbs's tribute: 'Mr Swanton is a master of his art. Everything he writes I read with interest . . .' It was characteristically kind of him to write so generously, even if all appreciated that the only 'master' recognized in the world of cricket was himself. The *Telegraph* made a few leather-bound copies, one of which in my possession is inscribed 'Warm congratulations, Camrose'. In modern times we have always given more space to cricket, and carried more signed reports, than any other paper, and it must have been the abundant evidence of series such as this on which the policy has been based.

I've told the stormy story of the 1953–54 MCC tour to the West Indies in *West Indian Adventure*, and this is not the place to hash up the whole matter again. But there is one important piece of first-hand evidence in which I have hitherto respected the confidence of one of the principal figures, the late H. S. Altham, and I hope that after twenty years, in the interest of history and out of fairness to Len Hutton (belated though it is), I may be absolved for breaking silence.

Before I went up to Sheffield to see the Roses' Match at the August Bank-holiday I happened to be watching Rugby and Marlborough at Lord's with Harry Altham, the Treasurer of MCC. Our thoughts turned from the Test at Headingley just over, in which England had escaped by the skin of their teeth to the winter tour of the West Indies for which Hutton had already been offered the captaincy. The manager, contrary to the usual practice, had not then been announced and had clearly not yet been picked, for the Treasurer (Altham) asked me if I could have a quiet word with Len, to see whom he had in mind as manager, if anyone, or who would be acceptable to him.

So on 1 August at Bramall-Lane I sought out England's captain, and we found the players' luncheon room empty and had our talk there. When I passed on Harry's message Len paused a moment, and then simply said: 'I should like the colonel.'

'The colonel' was the name by which Billy Griffith, who had commanded a wing of the Glider Pilot Regiment, had often been known on the last tours to the West Indies and South Africa, both of which the two of them had been on together. Billy, remember, had been player-manager to Gubby Allen on one trip and vice-captain to George Mann on the other, so Len had had ample chance to know him and judge his capabilities. When I told Len that I thought he had named the best possible man it scarcely occurred to me that MCC would decide differently.

When Ronny Aird had moved up from assistant-secretary to Secretary of MCC on the retirement of Colonel R. S. Rait Kerr in the previous autumn Billy Griffith had left his post on the sports staff of the *Sunday Times* to take his place. Griffith's job, as Aird's had been, was the cricket side of the administration while J. G. Dunbar, the other assistant-secretary, devoted himself more to the property and business part of the organization of the great Club.

So Griffith was at the disposal of the Committee, several of whom, it was strongly suspected, may not have been completely happy at the fact that for the first time a professional was about to lead MCC abroad. To be frank they had no choice, for Hutton (L.) was the reigning England captain, and after the West Indies' triumphs in 1950 it was clear that only the best side would do. If the majority of the Committee had been convinced that it would have been wiser, on so strenuous and taxing a tour to colonial countries on the verge of independence, to take some of the burden off England's leading batsman and had therefore invited someone else to captain their side, a public outcry would have been provoked at the very moment when the Ashes hung in suspense. To have snubbed Hutton (as nine people out of ten would have considered it) at such a time was unthinkable. In short if he wanted the job it was his – and now he had said he did want it.

How much the more incumbent on the Committee was it, in all the circumstances, to choose the best man as manager, especially since they knew that he was the nomination of the captain himself. If ever there was 'a natural' for the managership it was Griffith. Yet the Committee decided otherwise, on the ground – so I was told – that the assistant-secretary could not be spared from Lord's. It was unfair on the new Secretary, it was argued, to deprive him of Griffith's services for three and a half months. There was no doubt some substance in this to the extent of its being in some respects inconvenient, but what had to be judged was a matter of priorities.

So what then? The answer was perhaps the most extraordinary part of the business, for the decision arrived at was not to provide Hutton with a manager at all, but to appoint C. H. Palmer as player-manager. Charlie Palmer, captain of Leicestershire, was a pleasant and highly popular fellow. He did not know the West Indies, and had not played in a Test match though he had gone with MCC to South Africa. He was to be put in the contradictory situation of being under the jurisdiction of Hutton on the field, yet otherwise responsible to MCC for the administration and discipline of the team, presumably including even the captain. To cap the performance MCC, for the only time in my memory, failed to provide Hutton with a nominated vice-captain, though in practice when the captain did not play Trevor Bailey took over (Hutton, Bailey, Palmer and Compton formed the tour committee).

Even with the full status of manager Palmer, for all his personal virtues, would have been no one's pick as a disciplinarian, and in the potentially volatile atmosphere of the West Indies, with several potentially volatile English cricketers involved, a firm hand was the first requisite. Hutton by training was first and foremost a superb technician. He had plenty of instinctive dignity but was by nature inclined to be shy, withdrawn, introspective, not the sort to wear authority easily. Nor was he physically robust as he approached his fourteenth, and most difficult, Test series inside eight years.

As I say, my own account of the tour appeared the best part of twenty years ago. If anyone needs a judicial précis of it they can safely read R. J. Hayter's account in the 1955 *Wisden*. There is a modern appraisal, too, of one important aspect of the tour, the clash of temperament between the captain and his brash young Yorkshire colt which John Arlott brings out with sympathetic insight in his excellent biography *Fred*. This culminated in Trueman's tour bonus alone being withheld, and was at least a substantial factor in his being passed over both for the MCC tour to Australia the next year and that to South Africa following. Poor Fred had to wait six winters before he toured with a manager who understood and got the best out of him – until, in fact, MCC returned to the West Indies in charge of Walter Robins.

But, of course, the chief damage that the tour did was to British sporting repute and to the name of cricket generally, and the blame must rest fairly and squarely on MCC's shoulders. As a matter of fact the MCC Committee of 1953 looks on paper a notably good one, a dozen of whom are still alive as I write. How they reached their conclusion on the managership I cannot understand. It can only have been a case of several good men and true having a completely off day all together. In my experience it is just about the worst decision ever to have come out of Lord's.

Just one episode of the many that come to mind may give an idea of the atmosphere surrounding the team. Charlie Palmer one Sunday in Barbados rang me and asked whether I could join Len and him for a drink that evening. When he gave me the background to the latest spot of trouble which he was engaged in straightening out I thought I should give what moral support I could – though, as it turned out, I scarcely got a word in. Apparently two guests at the Marine Hotel where we all stayed had complained of the behaviour of two of the team in the lift the night before. The team 'club' always met on Saturday nights, and with an idle Sunday intervening the beer – and in this case no doubt the rum – was inclined to flow pretty free. It was not difficult to put two and two together and deduce a certain robustness of phrase offending delicate ears when the party broke up.

I arrived on the Marine balcony to find captain, manager, Messrs Trueman and Lock, all sitting nervously on the edge of their chairs, and two English ladies, the larger of whom, whose rank in the ATS could not possibly have been lower than brigadier, holding forth rather in the manner of Bertie Wooster's Aunt Agatha. The theme, of course, was what was expected of English teams abroad in the way of behaviour and example, and I found myself applauding the lady's admirable sentiments, expressed, as I recall, in a fine, manly baritone, more in sorrow than in anger, and at the same time feeling intensely sorry for poor Len.

Arlott relating this incident mentions that the Saturday was Trueman's birthday, which it was. He also says that Fred told the captain 'it weren't us'. As to this all I remember is that at the time Fred was working on the principle of discretion being the better part of valour. For that matter so were we all.

This, of course, was a relatively minor affair compared with the indiscipline on the field, the complaints of umpires, and the hostile reaction of the crowds to the team's attitude, much of which found its way back through Government Houses to the Colonial Office. The culminating wonder was that after ignominious defeats in the first two Tests it was the captain's own batting which rose so marvellously to the challenge (169, 44, 30 not out, and 205 were Hutton's scores in the last three) that the rubber was halved.

One could see the reflections of that 1953–54 West Indies tour in the England cricket of the following years, especially on tour. The leading players not unnaturally resented some of the criticisms levelled against them, and the conviction grew among them that this Test cricket was a desperately tough, grim affair in which, if you wanted to win, the opposition had to be kept well at arm's length. The team tended to withdraw into their own tight circle. There was little warmth left over for would-be friends and hosts, not only in the West Indies but also, for the remainder of the 'fifties, in Australia and South Africa.

It was in Australia that Alec Bedser, a genial, sociable chap, popular wherever he played, was taken aside by Len Hutton and asked not to fraternize with the enemy. Alec's answer was that, so far as he was concerned, hostility ended when stumps were drawn for the day. He added: 'You know I've got 69 wickets against Australia in the last two series – now you wouldn't call that very friendly, would you?' And he, if no one else, continued his habit of taking a glass of beer in the Australian dressing-room at close of play.

The philosophy in the West Indies seemed to be: 'These black beggars don't like us.' In Australia the 'black' was omitted. And after a while it tended to become true, because warm, spontaneous people like West Indians and Australians, who want visitors to enjoy their hospitality and their country, easily become hurt if approaches are coolly received, or if they suspect invisible barriers.

Being with touring teams but not of them, and having from past visits so many friends wherever we went, one was sensitive to the local reactions. It was misery to hear how in Sydney for a boat picnic, or some such amusement, for which elaborate preparations had been made, two or three only of the team would turn up: or that on the Wanderers' ground in Johannesburg, where the home and visitors' dressing-rooms adjoined, the connecting door had been locked on the MCC side.

It was easy to see how with so much attaching to the result, and with the greater publicity, and a heightening possibly of patriotic feeling (though I doubt whether this was the case in Australia), touring players needed to keep their own *esprit* high by sticking together. But there was a balance to be maintained that needed considerable managerial skill with, if possible, previous experience of the country. It was not until 1959–60 that MCC seemed fully to realize that nothing they did was more important than the filling of the manager's post for tours abroad. From Walter Robins's appointment onwards for the next decade things went much better on MCC tours. I exclude the most recent tour to Australia when manager and captain were chosen by the TCCB without reference to the Club.

Things worked as well for MCC in 1954/5 as they had done for Australia on the two previous visits. In particular it suited us that the notorious watering of the Melbourne pitch over the New Year week-end happened when it did, for England were given a temporarily restored surface to bat on a second time. Again Australia were unlucky in having to play the second tight-fought Test at Sydney without Keith Miller, as well as Ian Johnson, the captain, on a pitch made for fast bowling. The worst handicap, perhaps, though, under which Australia laboured during the series was the deep division as regards the captaincy, with the New South Welshmen, and a large slice of the press, clamouring for Miller, while the selectors and his home state of Victoria supported Ian Johnson. Into such a scene Hutton – at last – could call on speed of a degree greater than Australia could now muster : Tyson was the ideal instrument for his purpose. 'Typhoon Tyson' they called him and typhoon was right. For just six weeks it blew full blast, and in that time the series was decided. (England had made the least auspicious of all beginnings, Australia making 601 after being put in and winning the First Test by an innings and plenty.)

The story of the next two Tests is indeed windy in a double sense, for there was a high physical wind to aid 'The Typhoon'. The sight of Tyson tearing in with a gale behind him from the Hill or Randwick – or Botany Bay – end at Sydney is one that no one who saw it will forget – nor, surely, of Brian Statham toiling up into it from the other till even he was almost fit to drop. The Melbourne Test is memorable for the youthful Cowdrey's classic 102 out of 191 all out in the first innings, despite Miller's historic spell on the first morning (8–5–9–3), and finally and chiefly for the way that Tyson demolished the Australians on the last morning when at the start they had looked to have an even chance of winning.

Wind is not normally a crucial factor in Australian cricket but it was so now in Melbourne as it had been at Sydney. I spent the week-end at Frankston with the Norman Brookes's, and we woke up on the Sunday morning to the sound and suffocating heat of the dreaded north wind which occasionally and with little warning sweeps down the length of the continent to the southern coastline of Victoria. Since, according to the players, the pitch had been terribly brittle and parched the previous evening my first thought was that this had probably put paid to England's chances.

Incidentally, to the dismay of John Langley, the famous Walker Cup player, and Hersey, his wife, Norman's son-in-law and daughter, and of myself, the old man, then nearer eighty than seventy, insisted on our playing golf at Peninsula, and we duly did so, the only madmen on the course that scorching day. The shade temperature was 105, and it turned out to have been the hottest night (96) in Melbourne's history. I never knew anyone in whom the competitive spirit burned more fiercely than in Norman Brookes.

Anyway, the following morning, when England went out to

field (there were two Australian first innings wickets standing) they were staggered to find that whereas before the wind came it had sprouted dust the pitch was now so damp that their boot-sprigs sliced easily through the turf. There was, of course, a great outcry when in *The Age* next day Percy Beames categorically said that the pitch had been watered. This was promptly denied by the Melbourne Cricket Club, while the curator issued a statement that the wicket had 'sweated'. A learned university professor wrote, if I recall aright, that in the extraordinary atmospheric conditions, he would expect a last residue of moisture to be drawn up from deep down. But though an official enquiry revealed nothing *The Age* was on sure ground, and no legal action was taken against it.

What would have happened had England lost is hard to say, except that there would certainly have been bitter press recriminations. The Australian Board was said to be considering whether if their side won they should offer to play the match again, when the final rattle of stumps settled the matter. Tyson's seven for 17, by the way, is the best performance on paper I have ever seen by a fast bowler in nearly 240 Test matches.

At Adelaide the Ashes were safely retained, and there for the third time running the scales had seemed evenly balanced on the last morning. The central figure on this final day was Keith Miller. He was not out overnight, and Australian hopes rested heavily on his batting. Someone said:

'Did you have an early night, Keith?'

'Yes, rather. In bed by three.'

In the same over Statham clean bowls him. He summons a wry grin as he climbs the steps to the dressing-room. 'Reckon I must have missed it.' So in the end, after another Australian collapse, England need to make only 94 to win – a handful.

But Miller is driven to a supreme effort by the spectre of defeat. In a magnificent spell he bowls Edrich for 0, has Hutton caught in the slips for 5, Cowdrey for 4. England are 18 for 3. A handful? There then occurs, according to eye-witnesses, the sort of exchange that is retrospectively funny and is likewise a sidelight on how strangely on these tense occasions the minds of the principal characters can react. As Cowdrey is out the captain turns to his neighbour and says with deep feeling:

'The beggars have done us.'

To which Denis Compton, pulling on his gloves, says:

'Steady on, Len, I haven't been in yet.'

As it turned out Denis and Peter May weathered Miller's

storm, while Len Hutton, emotionally and physically exhausted, refreshed himself behind the scenes, not watching a single ball. By the time of the winning hit he was changed, composed again, and ready for the press and radio interviews, the television and newsreel appearances, and the whole modern palaver.

But 'the media' were to see little more of the hero of the hour. On his return to England the selectors paid him the then highly unusual compliment of appointing him captain for the whole five-match series against South Africa – Charles Fry was the last man to be so honoured in 1912. But he could find nothing like true form for Yorkshire, dropped out of the first Test, and then resigned the job altogether in favour of Peter May.

He did appear once at Lord's in 1955, leading MCC against the South Africans, and when he went in on the Saturday evening was saluted by the crowd all the way from the pavilion door to the wicket. But over the week-end he was hit by lumbago, and that was the last Lord's saw of him. The one flash of the real Hutton was seen at Trent Bridge at the end of June, when he made a chanceless 194, the last 94 of them in 65 minutes!

The Australians were signalled to come to England the following summer, but in January Len ended all speculation by announcing his retirement from first-class cricket. Though still just on the sunny side of forty he 'left first-class cricket with a feeling of relief rather than regret. He had completed an exhausting journey.' That is the summing-up of J. M. Kilburn, who knew him almost better than anyone, in *A History of Yorkshire Cricket*.

It would be dishonest to conclude that Len Hutton's influence on English cricket was unreservedly admirable. Apart from his attitude to the opposition – which derived partly at least, I believe, from a patriotic reaction against the failures of the early post-war years in Australia and the West Indies – he must have either originated or connived at the slowing-down of the over-rate as a tactical ploy. I blush now to recall the prolonged booing of the New Year's Day crowd of 65,000 at Melbourne as England spent the whole five hours getting through 54 overs. Neil Harvey was the chief threat to England in that 1954–5 series, and he was palpably irked if the natural tempo of the game was reduced.

Yet what man who has achieved anything can look back on his life without regrets? I do not doubt that Hutton, like the rest of us, if he had his time again, would have ordered some things differently.

But what has he not got to show on the credit side? He brought England back to the forefront of world cricket, and showed to his fellow-players a perfection of technique and a dedicated example that were faithfully followed by his young disciples, Peter May and Colin Cowdrey. Both of them likewise saw in their first touring captain, and followed in their turn, the dignity and reticence he brought to the job. These attributes did not desert him when after retirement came the blandishments of newspapers and publishers to 'reveal all'. Len felt the lure of t'brass keenly enough, but unlike most of his professional contemporaries he never yielded to the temptation to depict his career and times in the sort of language that the 10% agents could have made a small fortune from.

May for Hutton was the obvious succession in the England captaincy, and it is extraordinary how similar was their approach in so many respects. Both were serious, reserved, difficult to penetrate – and both in turn had the added burden of carrying the England batting on their shoulders. The parallel can be carried further in that May, like Hutton, suffered a breakdown in health, and bowed out quietly when still full of cricket. That the former did so at thirty-three was due to the different circumstances of his being an amateur faced with the need to provide for a family by making his way in business.

But with Peter I am starting at the wrong end. The years of his prime were now at hand, coinciding almost exactly with Len's retirement. With Denis Compton struggling bravely on despite persistent knee trouble and the eventual loss of a knee-cap, but scarcely half the cricketer he was in those golden years before it beset him, May was unarguably the best English batsman of the middle and late 'fifties. Moreover, looking back now with a quarter of a century's play and more since the game was resumed, he stands out surely as the best English post-war product, fulfilling all that George Geary quietly predicted for him when I went down first to Charterhouse in 1946 to play for MCC against the boys. (It's a vain but rather pleasant thought that I somehow contrived to have him caught at slip. Could I have turned one an inch or two on that perfect wicket?)

Under May England on their own wickets beat South Africa, Australia, the West Indies, New Zealand, and India in successive summers and in every series the captain was the dominant batsman. On tour he was less successful, for a variety of reasons, some of them outside his control. The MCC tour of South Africa contained the dullest cricket – and some of the worst – I ever saw in a Test series, while the Australian tour following (1958–59) was bedevilled and ruined by the row over throwing.

That (for me) last South African visit was the only one of all the many I've made abroad that I failed to enjoy. There was not only no savour to the cricket as each side aimed to grind the other down, but one had the oppressive, helpless feeling of being in a lovely country divided and rent in spirit by the various racial frictions. No doubt increasing contact with the West Indies where black and white, each enjoying equal rights, lived alongside one another on terms, generally speaking, of mutual amity and respect made one more sensitive than before to the injustices that pressed on the non-Europeans of whatever sort in South Africa. One's friends of English stock had no love for – and little contact with – the Afrikaners whose politicians, while busy in parliament sharpening the asperities and in-humanities of apartheid, seemed at the same time to be going out of their way in their public utterances to say demeaning, contemptuous things about the native population: literally indeed adding insult to injury.

One saw all too little of the black African: enough though to assure oneself that he had far better natural manners and a warmer sense of humour than his Afrikaner master. I watched with the Rudd brothers, Robin and John, a non-European athletics meeting of rather moderate standard on the outskirts of Johannesburg, but to my great regret missed at the Cape the chance of seeing some Coloured cricket.

At home England's notable run of success naturally was a joy to write about and to describe to the ever-widening audience on television: especially, need I say, the third successive Ashes victory over Australia in '56. It mars the picture, even at such long range, that the pitches at Headingley and Old Trafford were poorly prepared, which gave England, with Laker and Lock in their prime, a formidable advantage. Yet taking the series over-all it looks now, as it did then, that the right side finished on top. For the third successive time the *Daily Telegraph* reprinted my Test reports, and with Charles Fry on his death-bed Sir Norman Birkett this time wrote an Introduction which seems to me (apart from the too-generous references to my reports) a classic of cricket writing, and in particular a valuable setting down of the functions of the critic.

I must content myself here with a mere glimpse or two: the

royal greeting that Keith Miller had from the pent-up crowd as he marched in to bat on the Saturday afternoon at Lord's in what by the end had become 'Miller's Match'; Richie Benaud, also at Lord's, breaking free of his shackles at last after a long, long Test apprenticeship with a brilliant innings; Cyril Washbrook, recalled not a little reluctantly to Test duty after five years' absence, going in to face the music at Headingley with 18 for three on the board, his chest pushed out, as someone wrote, like a pouter-pigeon, and coming proudly home at close of play not out 90; above all Jim Laker strolling nonchalantly back to the Old Trafford pavilion, sweater on shoulder, for all the world as though returning from the nets, having taken all ten Australian wickets and in the match 19 for 90!

The cuttings-book reminds me, too, of some appallingly characteristic letters in the paper on the subject of the Test pitches and alleged Australian 'squealing' which called forth from me a sizeable screed in their defence. For Ian Johnson and his manager W. J. ('Bill') Dowling had borne the slings and arrows with admirable reticence. Truculent public reaction to English successes has often surprised me. Might it be just a little way towards the truth if it were said of the English, as it was by Churchill of his very famous general, that while we are 'in defeat indomitable' we may sometimes appear 'in victory intolerable'?

Charles Fry, who died in the September of that year at the age of eighty-four, had been an unfailing friend to me for more than twenty years – since, in fact, we had travelled the country together watching the 1934 Australians on behalf of the *Evening Standard*, I doing the straight reporting, he contributing a daily column – or two, or three – called *C. B. Fry Says* which made a sensation as it burst upon the world when the Australians as usual began the tour at Worcester.

The title was embellished by a characteristic picture of the author wearing a monocle and looking out at the reader with a bland, patrician gaze. I have no clearer memory of him than the first morning of that game at Worcester. The press-box then was in the little stand behind the bowler's arm at the New Road end, and here we were installed with Brooks, the chauffeur, stationed just below, at ground-level and within reach, handy for the dispensing of champagne from the large hamper in his charge. Everything about Charles was highly individual and arresting, his looks, his dress, his voice, and above all his talk. He wore, for instance, his own version of a Norfolk jacket with a belt and specially large pockets, and trousers, to conform to some pet theory *buttoned* above the ankle. The brim of his hat was broad, as was the ribbon that carried his monocle. Nothing was undersize about Charles, least of all his kindness to the young.

That spring morning, seeing Bradman and the Australians for the first time, writing away ceaselessly in a large script on endless octavo sheets, conversing amusingly the while, refreshing himself modestly from time to time and offering hospitality to all and sundry, he was in wonderful fettle. By lunch he had concocted nearer two thousand words than one of crisp, staccato stuff, epigrammatic and brilliant, and as it went on cascading over the wire caused the office to cry out for mercy. They already had more than they could carry! He was the only man I ever knew who could write and talk simultaneously on two different subjects.

He had been, of course, not only an incomparable all-round sportsman but a top-rate scholar, and some of his references were way above the heads of every *Evening Standard* reader. Yet they gave him his head – only jibbing, I seem to recall, at the Greek quotations – and the thing went like hot cakes. To a young man in his twenties who knew Charles Fry's astonishing background of achievement as sportsman, scholar, and incidentally trainer of youth for the Merchant Service for over forty years on his ship *Mercury*, his company was a permanent fascination.

I only once heard of his being ruffled in his time as a cricket-writer – at Brisbane where the old press arrangements would have tried the patience of a saint. Though he had captained England against Australia he was brusquely denied access to pavilion and stands and confined rigidly to the press-box which itself, in my day, was literally marked off from the public seats by barbed wire. Brisbane before the present very different régime did strange things to journalists, and to Charles it had the stunning effect of causing him to throw the typewriter of poor, unoffending Bruce Harris off his desk and, reputedly, out of the box!

C. B. Fry in his younger days was, I'm sure, too much of a good thing for some tastes. He did not suffer fools gladly maybe and always spoke his mind – as to which he used to tell how he once had something of an up-and-downer with Kent in the Canterbury Week. In the last over of the day he complained that he could not see Blythe's bowling as he was throwing the ball up into the sun. Getting no response from the captain E. W. Dillon, he said:

'Right! I appeal on two grounds – against the light, and for unfair play.'

The umpires duly took the bails off, the crowd were annoyed, and he was jostled on his way in. Whereupon he harangued them from the pavilion gate, saying:

'Very well. I shall now bat all day tomorrow.'

He didn't exactly do that, but by making 112 to add to his 123 in the first innings he certainly saved the match, and so, as it turned out, prevented Kent winning three championships in a row. Fry was resentful because he thought he should have had some protection from the Kent amateurs. Speaking as a Man of Kent I imagine if his approach had been couched in a rather different vein the matter might have been resolved without friction. But that is a mere supposition – after all, I was only four at the time, and never heard any other version than his.

My final recollection of the great man is of his proposing the health of 'Plum' Warner at Lord's on the latter's 80th birthday – the first dinner, I think, ever to be held in the Long Room. Charles, himself at the time a mere eighty-one, began brilliantly and held the company captive. If he had sat down after ten minutes it would have been perfect, but he tired and his voice weakened and the end was anti-climax.

A passing thought: 'Plum' Warner had to wait until he was seventy-six before he was nominated President of MCC by his predecessor, the Duke of Edinburgh. He was luckier than Fry, who for all his gifts and qualities was never President nor even on the Committee. In his mellow years who could have made so splendid and effective a figure-head? Shall we let his contemporaries down lightly and say perhaps that if the Presidency had changed during the war years instead of remaining in the same hands – those of Stanley Christopherson – one of them might have nominated him?

The pride in the string of English successes was reflected, when England next set sail for Australia, in a dangerous mood of over-confidence in many 'sections of the press' which announced that this was the most powerful side ever to leave these shores. Such an assessment was, frankly, poppycock, but when the string of failures came the original estimate had to be justified and excuses found. There was a thoroughly valid one in the throwing, but others were sought, including criticism of the captain for allegedly neglecting his team off the field because of the presence, for part of the tour, of his fiancée, Virginia, daughter of Mr and Mrs Harold Gilligan with whom she was travelling. Peter May had never been 'one of the boys', and was no worse a captain for that. There was no substance in the reports, needless to say, for he is a highly conscientious person, but the fact the allegations had been made added nothing to the harmony of the English party.

But what most greatly worried them was the conviction that several of the Australian bowlers they met, including three who played in the Tests, threw. First on the way round there was Slater at Perth, then Meckiff at Melbourne, and finally Rorke at Sydney. When on the second circuit Adelaide produced an opening pair called Hitchcox and Trethewey (the jokers inserted an 'r' before the second syllable) the players felt that Queensland was the only state without 'a chucker'. Indeed Ray Lindwall up at Brisbane re-introduced himself to them as the last of the straight-arm bowlers.

In what looked to English critics beyond the boundary much the most blatant case, that of Meckiff, MCC probably made a tactical error by not registering their doubts privately with the Australian powers-that-be the first time they met him in the Victorian match. They said they thought he threw, but didn't think he did it very well, and they preferred to say nothing. When a couple of months later he was taking nine wickets in a Test match, bowling out England for 87 on a plumb wicket, and more or less clinching the rubber in an afternoon, England could only grin and bear it – or at least bear it. They weren't exactly beaming.

The second innings collapse in the vast Melbourne bowl, with Meckiff firing away full-split, the roar of his home crowd behind him, comes back to me with sickening clarity. I was watching alone at the top of the huge Melbourne pavilion in direct prolongation of the bowler's arm when I saw Raman Subba Row (who was nursing a broken thumb), and went to join him. I said :

'Raman, this is terrible. I can't bear to watch it.' Whereupon Sam Loxton, now a Test selector but then one of the broadcasting team, whom I hadn't noticed on the other side of Subba Row, chipped in :

'Now then, Jim, you can't say that. The New South Welshmen thought he threw, and we had a film taken which proves he doesn't.'

I hadn't intended to be caught in an argument but couldn't let that go by. So I merely said :

'Sam, I'm not concerned with whether he threw against New South Wales. All I'm saying is he's chucking away there now.'

Apart from Griffin, the young South African who came to England with a grotesque action the following year, Meckiff's bowling that fatal afternoon at Melbourne was the most blatant thing I've ever seen. Yet fifty thousand or so Australians roaring away round the ring appeared to have no scruples about it. Hence, perhaps, the phrase 'blind patriotism'.

But neither side could claim a monopoly of virtue. Though, as it happened, he took no significant part in the series, we had Tony Lock – whose conversion to orthodoxy was just round the corner. It is a perfectly true story how when MCC went on to New Zealand Lock saw a film taken by one of the New Zealand team showing him bowling in England the previous year, and was shattered by the sight of his own action. To his infinite credit he altered his method forthwith, reverting to the much slower style of his youth.

'Drag' was also a pressing problem at this time, and when it was combined, in the case of Rorke, with what May's side to a man regarded as a throw the result could be shattering. I never myself batted against a chucker but all who have agree that the significant, crucial difference is that one picks up the flight of the ball from the hand that little bit later. When a man of Rorke's speed drags so far you think he's never going to let the ball go and on his delivering at last from about eighteen yards' range you then get a delayed sight of it, the scales are weighted against the batsman, to say the least.

There were a lot of English injuries on this 1958–59 tour and replacements had to be sent for. The joke that went the rounds was of the two old clubmen discussing MCC's problem:

'I hear they've sent for Mortimore.'

'What! Forty more?'

Neither John Mortimore nor Ted Dexter when he was pulled over in late November from his job in Paris could shift the side's fortunes, and the most decisive defeat in Australia since 1920–21 was the outcome. To say that the tour was in all respects ill-starred probably just about sums it up.

The MCC visit to the West Indies the following winter marked the start of a happier decade altogether so far as English sides abroad were concerned. There were troubles certainly – bottle-throwing in Trinidad, for instance, on a scale rather more serious than had occurred in BG on Hutton's tour. But the disorder was in no way provoked by MCC who under May once more, and with Robins as manager, came through the tour successfully and with the utmost credit all round. The only thing that marred the picture was that the captain was far from well, and after disguising the fact for upwards of a month succumbed and handed over the captaincy for the last two Tests to Cowdrey.

Peter May's state of health was probably responsible for the one discordant happening of the tour which might have had disastrous results if the atmosphere surrounding him and his team had been less cordial. On the last evening of the Jamaica Test when the West Indies were trying to win the match against time Rohan Kanhai, batting brilliantly, was struck by cramp and asked for a runner. After some parley involving May, the umpires, and Gerry Alexander, the West Indian captain, who was batting with him, the request was refused, play continued and Kanhai limped singles where ordinarily he would have had easy twos. Then he was bowled, and the game ended quietly. At the time of the request however the West Indies were in with a chance, and according to Law 2 Kanhai was definitely entitled to a runner without the need for an approach to the opposing captain, though this is always made as a matter of courtesy.

May's attitude in fact was quite wrong, and the umpires should have over-ruled him (it turned out afterwards that one wanted to do so, the other not). What would the press reaction be? If it were strongly critical the writers would be on sure ground. Everything depended on the English explanation which after the game Robins came over to the press-box to give. He said that May realized on coming off the field that his interpretation of the law was at fault and that he had since apologized both to Kanhai and to Alexander.

The doyen of the West Indian writers was Strebor Roberts, of the *Jamaica Gleaner*, a forthright critic who had had specially stern things to say on some aspects of Hutton's tour. The other members of the box looked instinctively for Roberts's reaction. To my intense relief – and still more to Robins's – he thanked the MCC manager for his statement and added, 'It was a natural mistake in the heat of the moment – it is a small matter.'

In the result the West Indian and English press both played the thing down, and there was no loss of goodwill. The point was that from the start of the tour Walter Robins had gone to the utmost trouble to know and to help the press generally. They therefore trusted him and accepted that an honest mistake had been made. This is the best example I can think of to illustrate the fruits of good management and public relations. If the same thing had happened under different auspices – for instance on Hutton's tour or on certain occasions in Australia or South Africa – there would have been an unholy uproar.

Unfortunately English tactics on the field, under Cowdrey's leadership as well as May's, were too defensive for the manager's taste, and he was never one to mince his words. It would be wrong to say that he was *en rapport* with all the senior members of the side. This hurt him, but despite it he performed an invaluable service, enforcing the strictest discipline in his own party, and establishing the friendliest relations with the West Indians. Not least he found a way to Fred Trueman's heart, and it was his bowling on those adamantine pitches that was the biggest factor in England's success in the rubber.

What made this tour all the more enjoyable for me – the happiest perhaps of them all – was that my wife was seeing the West Indies for the first time and so falling in love with the islands that at the moment of writing she has not missed a visit in any winter since.

There seems little point in sketching at any length the several things which made the 1960 summer in England such a tense and unhappy one. The South Africans were incredibly foolish to send over young Griffin, who had been twice no-balled for throwing at home, and had an action which might have been specially designed to show how not to bowl. There was the embarrassment of Geoff Griffin being picked for the Lord's Test although six first-class umpires had already called him for throwing. At Lord's, D. J. McGlew, South Africa's captain, shielded Griffin from the scrutiny of Syd Buller at square-leg, only to see Frank Lee, the other umpire, no-ball him eleven times. As if this were not conclusive McGlew at last allowed Buller to see him from square-leg in a limited over exhibition game staged because the Test had ended on the Saturday at lunch-time. In this unreal atmosphere – and, to bring the thing to the ultimate in bathos, in the presence of the Queen – Buller did his inevitable duty, and for his pains was removed from the Test umpires' panel for the series on the South Africans' objection. The row did no good whatever, needless to say, to the morale of the South African team which was comprehensively beaten in the rubber.

The real confrontation on the throwing issue occurred with the arrival of 'Bill' Dowling, the chairman of the Australian Board, and Sir Donald Bradman to what was still in those days called The Imperial Cricket Conference. The 1960 Conference agreed on a new experimental definition of a throw which, as it happens, has not stood the test of time. However all cricketers know, in theory at least, what is or is not a throw. The point about this meeting was that the threat to friendly relations was freely acknowledged, and in the light of this each country promised to do everything possible to eliminate throwing.

To accommodate the Australians – who in turn had to consider the reactions of their own public, always sensitive to any suggestion of dictation from Lord's – England agreed to a moratorium for suspect actions for the first five weeks of the Australian tour to England in 1961, and a special system of reporting by umpires was agreed. In practice, though, Australia, at Don Bradman's instigation, conducted their own purge throughout the states, the suspect bowlers were not picked, and they brought no one over whose delivery could be faulted in any way. In England the umpires were finally persuaded where their duty lay, and the whole rumpus subsided. But it had done much harm to the image of cricket, as also did other sources of friction around this period.

One was the publication of Jim Laker's ghosted book *Over to Me*, which led to his honorary membership of MCC and Surrey being suspended, and another the dispute between Gloucestershire and Tom Graveney over the county captaincy. The Laker affair has been long since resolved by his retraction and apology, and he has won a position of much respect in cricket by his sympathetic interpretation of the game and laconic asides as a television commentator. But it caused much bitterness at the time, and one way and another the feeling that the cricket world was so much at odds with itself had an unfortunate reaction in terms of public support. The South African tour of 1960 actually made a loss – an unprecedented state of affairs for a major Test series.

When in the autumn of 1960 I heard of the troubles in Gloucestershire, with young Tom Pugh appointed captain instead of Graveney and the latter resigning in protest at the way the matter had been handled, my thoughts went back to the annual dinner of Gloucestershire two seasons before at which I had proposed the county's health and naturally wished Tom, the new leader, all good luck. A friend who was then in one of the seats of power told me after the dinner that if things didn't go well they had in Pugh a good man whom they were grooming for the job. When I said I didn't think a man of Graveney's reputation and character might much care to be superseded by an amateur ten years his junior, the answer came:

'Oh, I don't think there would be any trouble. The pros don't like the responsibility very much, you know, they're happier without it.'

My comment that this point of view seemed to me a good deal out-of-date was not particularly well received. It is worth recalling this snatch of talk perhaps as some slight evidence of the attitude that existed then in some county committees with regard to captaincy. The problem of leadership is with us perhaps today in a more acute form than then since there are no longer any amateurs, who could be sacked, or asked to resign, without much fear of friction, and the counties are therefore regularly exposed to the risk of picking one of the senior men whose performance may turn out not to satisfy his exacting contemporaries. And then what? It is a delicate business making a change where a man's professional status is affected. Yet it is seldom easy to anticipate the reaction to responsibility. Cricket depends more almost than any game on the quality of leadership, and the difficulty today of happening on the right man where several probably are of similar seniority and background is one of its most pressing problems. Indeed one finds great professionals of the last generation, such as Sir Leonard Hutton and Denis Compton, candidly sighing for the return of the amateur. However, these are weighty issues which must not obtrude too violently into a personal story.

Let me end the chapter on a happy note, even though it is dragged in second-hand. At the very end of the 1951–1960 decade Australia and the West Indies, up at Brisbane, contested what those who were present declare must be, from start to finish, the greatest match ever played. I mean, of course, the tied Test Match with its last over to beat all last overs. When Wes Hall began it Australia needed six runs to win and had three wickets standing. Seven balls – or half a lifetime – later the third of those wickets had fallen to a run out from a throw by Joe Solomon, who from square-leg hit the stumps with only one to aim at, with Meckiff and Kline going through for what would have been the winning run. How one envied from the cold and gloom of an English winter those who saw not only this incredible game but the rest of that matchless series, fought so bravely and chivalrously by Richie Benaud and Frank Worrell. Ninety-thousand in a day at the Fifth and deciding Test at Melbourne (won by Australia by two wickets!). Quarter of a million, was it, lining the Melbourne streets to bid the West Indians farewell?

But I was still Rugby football correspondent of the *Daily Telegraph*, and so was busy at home recording the season generally and in particular the progress of the South African tour. The Springboks were managed by a tough Afrikaner called 'Ferdie' Bergh, with whom I happened to be in conversation directly after the tied Test. As he seemed interested – and, I must confess, with some malice aforethought – I tried to describe to him what I had gathered of the final scene, culminating, of course, in the brilliant run-outs effected by Hunte and Solomon. I must have told the story rather poorly for he got exactly the wrong end of the stick.

'Ah!' he cried approvingly, 'that's vot ve always say and you fellows over here often don't realize. When it comes to the point these fellows get excited and always lose their 'eads.'

'You haven't quite got it right,' I said. 'The point was that at the crisis the West Indians kept their heads marvellously.'

'Oh,' he said dejectedly. 'Oh!' I might have been almost sorry to disappoint him had the Sharpeville massacre not been still hatefully fresh in one's mind.

11

Cricket in Distress

Distance lends perspective, and I daresay we are too close to the momentous happenings of this last period of my cricket story to see them altogether truly in the context of the game's history. Maybe, but there can be little doubt that the years that began with the throwing crisis in Australia in 1958/59 and extended at least to the performances of the England XI which drew a rebuke from the Cricket Council in 1971 will be regarded in future as the most distressing and deplorable since cricket became a great national sport. In England especially, almost everything has gone wrong that could go wrong, and there can be no telling whether the malign cycle has reached its end – or, to change the metaphor, whether the cyclone that has turned everything upside down, knocked legislators and administrators off their balance, and contorted players into strange and ugly attitudes, is blowing itself out. One can only hope so.

Meanwhile I trust the reader can brace him or herself for shocks. We have to ride together various sinful decisions affecting English domestic cricket. We must note the abolition of the amateur. We will follow the steps which have led to the breach of playing relations with South Africa. We shall be shocked by an ugly echo of the throwing difficulty in the challenging of Charlie Griffith's action by Richie Benaud. There was the sad circumstance whereby Brian Close in effect deprived himself of the England captaincy. There was the riot at Kingston, Jamaica, and then, overshadowing all else, the succession of sorry events that are expressed in the phrase 'the D'Oliveira Affair'. Lastly, and most starkly clear in mind, came the rumpus at the Sydney Test last year with Ray Illingworth in open conflict with an umpire before taking his team from the field, and so souring what should have been the joyous occasion of England at long last recapturing the Ashes.

If this catalogue seems altogether too gloomy to be faced I hasten to add that there is some brave, skilful, chivalrous cricket to lighten the picture and fine players moving over the scene, headed by Gary Sobers, in my estimation the greatest of all. Add to him such men as these, all of them in their prime in some part of, if not all, the 'sixties, and it will be evident that nature has played her refreshing part: Bob Barber, Ken Barrington, Richie Benaud, Geoff Boycott, Colin Cowdrey, Alan Davidson, Ted Dexter, Basil D'Oliveira, John Edrich, Tom Graveney, Wes Hall, Rohan Kanhai, Alan Knott, Bill Lawry, Clive Lloyd, Graham McKenzie, Colin Milburn, Norman O'Neill, the Nawab of Pataudi, Graeme Pollock, Mike Procter, Barry Richards, Bobby Simpson, Mike Smith, Brian Statham, Fred Trueman, Derek Underwood. This is a selection only, not a classified list, and excludes many other admirable cricketers from several countries. The ills that have of late been afflicting the game are in some degree economic, in some political, while a certain maladroitness by its rulers in ordering its affairs cannot be left out of account.

Around half of those named above took part in the England-Australia series of 1961. Looking back at the reports of that rubber one cannot honestly say that England were manifestly the stronger side, but as things turned out we threw away a gilt-edged chance of snatching the Ashes back again at the first time of asking. It was an infuriating aspect of the 'sixties from the English angle how somehow, by the skin of their teeth, Australia managed, time after time, to cling to the Ashes.

Twice rubbers were won by the margin of one match, three times they were halved. Several times the weather befriended the enemy. But at Old Trafford in the Fourth Test of 1961, conditions were equal, and when the last day started (each side having previously won once) England had the edge. Australia had fought back marvellously from arrears on first innings of 177, but in their second they were still only 154 runs on with the first six out. In the first quarter of an hour of the fifth morning David Allen, on a good wicket slightly dusting, took three of the four wickets needed: 334 for nine with McKenzie joining Davidson. It was a significant moment, with England all but sure to win if McKenzie failed to stay.

Spin held the key, and Davidson kept to himself Allen from whose first nine overs, in addition to the three wickets, only two runs had come. When Davidson at last launched forth at Allen and in one over took two sixes and two fours May promptly withdrew his best bowler and the moral advantage shifted automatically to Australia. That last wicket in the end yielded 98, and when England went in shortly before lunch it was to make the formidable score of 256 or to bat out just under four hours with a long tail.

At lunch John Woodcock said with startling, if gloomy prescience, 'I have an idea that Ted is going to play "a blinder" which will put us in a possible position to win – and then we'll make a mess of it.' This is exactly what happened. Dexter made a superb 76 in 85 minutes, putting on 110 with Subba Row. At 150 for one with an hour and three-quarters to go England had scarcely a care in the world. Then Benaud, with two of his bowlers semi-crocks, tried his last ploy, bowling his leg-breaks round the wicket. The difference in the angle deceived Dexter, May was bowled off the rough behind his legs, Close played like a man demented for a few minutes, and Subba Row was bowled: all victims of Benaud. England at tea were 163 for five with the weak tail exposed. We lost in the end by 20 minutes, having played at the crisis, I thought, 'in a tactical vacuum'.

As for Richie, he had pulled off a gigantic confidence trick. When I wryly told him as much on our next meeting he said, 'Neil and I just sat there afterwards in the dressing-room having a few beers, and whenever we caught each other's eye we just roared with laughter.' They could scarcely believe their luck, and no wonder.

I've told the story of the climax of this famous match at some length because it cast its shadow over much of the Anglo-Australian cricket of the 'sixties. Benaud had taken a long time to make good in Test matches, so that Len Hutton was inclined on his arrival at the wicket to say 'Here comes Festival cricketer', the reference being to a wonderful piece of hitting in the relaxed atmosphere of Scarborough. Benaud had to wait until Hutton's retirement before he did so but he returned the jibe with interest in the end. He played his last two Test series against England with an ailing shoulder, but with a mixture of bluff and cunning, justified his place as a player, at the same time confirming his reputation as a great captain.

This was the end of Peter May's seven-year reign (interrupted only by his illness) as England's captain and of Gubby Allen's corresponding stretch as Chairman of Selectors. It had been a happy and profitable collaboration in all respects with every home rubber won – until this one. Peter led Surrey for another year, then at the age of thirty-two announced his retirement from first-class cricket, and despite many appeals to return has stuck to it. That was his nature: he gave either all or nothing. The editor of *Wisden*, taking due time before acknowledging the inevitable, delayed the full-scale tribute that his career commanded until last year. It is there in the 1971 edition for all to see, with a detail of figures which supports the opinion of every man who ever played with him – that of those who have come into English cricket since the end of the war, technically, temperamentally, he is the best.

It was in 1961 that South Africa left the Commonwealth and so automatically excommunicated her cricketers from the ICC – which stood for Imperial Cricket Conference until 1965 when the I became International and the rules were changed to embrace any cricket-playing country whether in the Commonwealth or outside it. Each year the ICC considered South Africa's position and deferred a decision, and each year in the early 'sixties before opinions grew hopelessly rigid one had the feeling that if the SA Cricket Association had taken a bold initiative they might have been allowed back. In this first year their President, Foster Bowley, was asked to attend the ICC as an observer, and on the day of the meeting in a letter to the *Daily Telegraph* Clive Van Ryneveld, the great South African all-round sportsman, appealed for the readmission of his country. He said:

Writing about the meeting of the Conference Mr E. W. Swanton has suggested that the South African Cricket Association should declare itself in favour of including non-white cricketers in national teams on merit and of matches against non-white countries.

From many points of view I would welcome such a statement, and it would certainly assist the Conference in its decision. I believe it would also represent the view of very many white cricketers in South Africa, possibly the majority.

There is, however, a danger that such a declaration would have the effect of inviting Government action to stop the inter-racial sport which is quietly developing.

The following day when the ICC had decided to leave a decision until next year I pleaded for 'a show of earnestness by the South African cricket authorities on these lines', and my instinct at the time was that if Foster Bowley had his way all might be well. He was a liberal-minded man, and responded very readily to my invitation to meet Basil D'Oliveira who was playing for me in the annual match in which for many years my side played Didsbury on the Sunday of the Old Trafford Test for successive Lancashire beneficiaries. There were a dozen or more of them altogether, and I write as a proud vice-president of that keen and friendly stronghold of cricket.

Clive Van Ryneveld at this time sat for East London in the

South African parliament as a Progressive. This multi-racial party has had some appeal to intelligent young South Africans but Clive subsequently lost his seat and turned to law. Mrs Helen Suzman now alone stands for coloured and native interests in Parliament, representing ironically enough the electors of Houghton, Johannesburg, an affluent constituency corresponding very roughly perhaps to London's Belgravia.

It was John Arlott who had arranged for D'Oliveira to come from the Cape to Middleton in the Central Lancashire League, and it was another much-travelled cricket-writer who in the few years remaining to him made an astonishing personal contribution to the cause of multi-racialism in cricket. Early in the 'fifties a young west-country journalist unknown to me sought my advice about going on tour as a free-lance. This was R. A. Roberts. I gave what help and encouragement I could, and Ron began his globe-trotting with the South Africans in Australia in 1952/3.

In the next twelve years he undoubtedly travelled farther and saw more cricket than any man in any comparable period. In addition to his professional work he took International sides to a dozen countries, and in the 1961/2 winter brought off perhaps the most ambitious of his expeditions when he managed a side including more than a dozen world-famous players on a tour embracing Rhodesia, Pakistan, Hong Kong, New Zealand and India. He took Everton Weekes (as captain), Sonny Ramadhin, Hanif Mohammed, Saeed Ahmed and Basil D'Oliveira to play a mixed South African and Rhodesian XI in Rhodesia, after which Roy McLean, Neil Adcock and Colin Bland joined the party. Unfortunately McLean and Adcock were not permitted to play in India or Pakistan, but this political bar was the only discordant decision in a trip that was from all aspects a marvellous success. They travelled 40,000 miles in eight weeks under three captains, Weekes, Lindwall and Benaud, and Roberts, single-handed, looked after twenty-five players in all, since several came for a portion only. Having done a bit of this sort of thing in a small way – and always provided myself with John Haslewood as treasurer – I find this project of Ron Roberts's even more extraordinary to look back upon than it seemed at the time. Ron's impact on cricket was wholly admirable and pathetically brief for within four years of this undertaking, aged only thirty-eight, he died of cancer.

Walter Robins took over the chairmanship of selectors from his friend Gubby Allen in 1962. There was one of the periodic drives towards more attractive cricket at this time, and no one could better express and translate the current mood than Walter. The players did not always enjoy his caustic tongue, and tact was not his strongest suit. But in his time as chairman (1962–64) all knew he would not tolerate slow or selfish cricket, and the play of our Test teams was the better for his sharp eye on the scene.

Unfortunately the Advisory County Cricket Committee in their frantic search for aphrodisiacs tried out various futilities, such as a maximum 75 yard boundary because they thought people wanted to see more fours, and a suspension of the follow-on to prevent games ending early. Of course these artificial things soon died a natural death, as did a later notion to restrict the first innings of a three-day match to 65 overs. But the general effect was to persuade everyone, players and spectators alike, that the game was in a critical, neurotic state. I came to dread each meeting of 'the Advisory', fearful of what stunt it would think up next.

Later that same year it produced its most far-reaching decision – and, in the nature of things, an unalterable one – abolishing the amateur. This was announced, as it happened, while MCC were at Brisbane preparing for the First Test of a new series, and some Australian friends, considering me a prime supporter of the system of differentiation which in their country they have never had, planted a wreath and a droll cartoon or two on my desk in the press-box.

I wrote regretting that MCC accepted the verdict of 'the Advisory', which they were not bound to do. It had been reached only by ten county votes against seven, and I thought that a change so fundamental should have been referred to the members of MCC and of the counties (some 100,000 of us) who, broadly speaking, paid the bill for first-class cricket. I deplored the loss of the independent player and reminded my readers that 'the evolution of the game has been stimulated from its beginnings by the fusion of the two strains, each of which had drawn strength and inspiration from the other. English cricket has been at its best when there has been a reasonably even balance . . .'

However, we are back in Australia, and I must say a little about the MCC visit of 1962/3 if only because although the *Daily Telegraph* made another book of my writings on the tour, which we called *The Ashes In Suspense*, it has never had its full due in print. This was chiefly because the last Test on which the Ashes depended was for various reasons such an anti-climax. Taking the tour and series as a whole however there was some extremely good, attractive cricket, and Ted Dexter's side contributed more than a half-share thereto. Ken Barrington had a great tour, and the England batting with Dexter, Cowdrey, Sheppard, Graveney, in support was mostly set in an attractive key. Our runs were scored faster than by England in any Test series in Australia since 1924/5, and though the out-cricket was not so satisfactory, Trueman had great days, Statham was the wonderful trier he has always been, while Titmus I described as 'the find of the tour' as an all-rounder.

At Melbourne Dexter's innings against the Australian XI was 'one of the finest pieces of forcing batsmanship I have ever seen' (102 in an hour and 50 minutes) and MCC made 458 for five on the first day! After the 1958/9 tour it was imperative for this side to show positive cricket from the start, and their success may be judged from the fact of their drawing more than a million spectators and bringing home a profit of £30,000. Unhappily when with one win apiece in the rubber the Ashes depended on the last Test at Sydney neither side could over-come the handicap of a deadly slow pitch, and what was just as crucial, an infield so sluggish that the fiercest hitters had much difficulty in piercing it. England with the Ashes to get back and having won the toss should have been the aggressors, but started slowly on the inaccurate assumption that the pitch would not last. Thereafter they strove to make up time, but were the prisoners of circumstance. One cannot often fault Australian groundsmanship, but this Sydney pitch and soft, sandy infield were horribly inadequate, and were chiefly responsible for the tour ending in slow hand-claps and press recriminations. This was one of many occasions, incidentally, when a Test would have been far better played to a finish.

Scarcely any of this criticism was personal. Indeed this was one of the most popular MCC sides I have travelled with. It was unusually but admirably managed by the Duke of Norfolk with Alec Bedser as his assistant and Billy Griffith deputizing for the Duke when affairs of state brought him home for a month in the middle. Australians were vastly intrigued by the presence in their midst of the Earl Marshal and premier duke, as for that matter at first were the team and the press. All concerned however (or, to be perfectly accurate, all with one characteristic press exception) soon recognized the manager for the extremely conscientious, friendly, and amusing person he is, while Alec, always popular in Australia, resumed many friendships and with David Sheppard and Colin Cowdrey drew generously on his spare time visiting schools and giving talks and practical instruction. If there was a weakness in the set-up it lay in the assistant manager's reluctance to offer guidance on the playing side. He would answer maybe that with three experienced Test captains in the side in Dexter, Cowdrey and Sheppard, no word was needed from him. My own view however is that the performance of modern England teams would always be the better if there were a wise watcher outside the heat of battle for the captain to turn to, and I would also add that Dexter – contrary perhaps to popular belief – was more amenable to advice and constructive comment than most of his contemporaries.

A note here in parenthesis about the captaincy in Australia which underlines the ill-luck that has pursued Colin Cowdrey. MCC were due to announce their tour captain during the 1962 Gentlemen and Players – the last ever played, as it turned out. Colin had led England in the Test immediately preceding, and he was then chosen as captain of the Gentlemen. The 'race', as some of the press portrayed it, was going to him at the expense of Dexter when he was taken suddenly ill during a Kent game just before 'G & P', was packed off to hospital, and played no cricket for three weeks. So Dexter led the Gentlemen and got the job after all.

David Sheppard, by the way, was in the unique position of an ordained priest of seven years' standing enjoying a Sabbatical leave from his wardenship of the Mayflower mission centre in the East End. He preached to big congregations on Sundays while fulfilling every team demand, and with a hundred in the second innings had a major share in the great Test victory at Melbourne. The tour was for him a success in the fullest sense.

The fact is that though Dexter and Cowdrey were as different as could be in style and disposition, and though the manner of their leadership reflected these differences, in effect their respective merits added up to a similar result. Cowdrey's strength was a thoughtful approach coupled with the utmost consideration for every member of his side. Dexter was the more inclined to grasp an initiative and to rally his side by his own vivid example.

These were times packed with Test cricket of the major rather than the minor sort: Frank Worrell's West Indians in England in 1963, and the Australians, now under Bobby Simpson with Benaud in the press-box, following in 1964. England lost to the strongest as well as the best-led of all West

Indian teams, 3–1, and, with the worst of the luck with the weather, to Australia 1–0, with four draws. Dexter was still at the helm, with Cowdrey when fit his right-hand man.

I must not venture closely into the cricket in these series but the 1963 Lord's Test against the West Indies, and in particular the captain's great innings, were classics that command some notice. It was a tremendous match right through, full of brave and challenging play. Trueman with eleven wickets was at his best for England while Barrington and Close played important parts as batsmen. Butcher and Kanhai batted with distinction for the West Indies. Hall and Griffith bowled with ferocious speed, and Worrell directed his side with the cool aplomb of a great general. There were several subsidiary heroes, too – it was the kind of occasion when almost everyone plays above his normal self.

The moments that stand out, though, apart from the drama of the finish, were those of Dexter's confrontation of the fast bowling. He went in number three after Edrich had been out first ball, and with Hall and Griffith in full career on a true fast wicket. Stewart endured awhile but his lack of inches put him at a serious disadvantage against the rising ball. When he left, Barrington for a while could only spar unhappily. Dexter however stood up to his full height, fending off the shorter stuff safely and profitably, and driving the ball of good length and above with powerful, classic strokes and an air of rare disdain. In cold figures he made 73 in 80 minutes off 75 balls, which may give some sort of picture of his dominance, but it was an epic response to challenge that one had to see to appreciate fully. I wrote next morning: 'It was one of those occasions when men bask in the reflected virtue of great deeds. We will talk of this batting for weeks, and many years on cricketers will say to one another: "But did you see Dexter that day at Lord's?"'

People are indeed still saying it.

The climax on the last evening was the most exciting thing I remember on the cricket field, with a monumental effort by Hall, supported as ever by Griffith, standing between England and victory. Hall bowled unchanged apart from the tea interval at his utmost speed for 24 overs, starting at 2.20 and ending with the final over at six o'clock. Shades of Tom Richardson at Old Trafford in 1896! Close, showing all the courage in the world, took a fearful battering, indeed invited it by *coming down the pitch* to Hall and at times by deliberately taking the ball on the body rather than risk giving a catch from a defensive stroke. There were only 15 runs needed in 20 minutes with two good wickets left plus Cowdrey, a broken left arm in plaster, who was prepared to defend with one hand. Then alas! Close adventured once too often. By the start of the last over 8 were required with Allen and Shackleton batting, Cowdrey waiting in the wings. Two came, then the run-out of Shackleton, leaving Allen at the batting end, with nine wickets now down, needing 6 runs off the last two balls, the field, of course, far spread. Allen decided against chancing his arm and at the same time risking Cowdrey having to face the last ball, and played them both safely. 'What palpitations! What a pulling at the heart-strings! And at the close the best sight ever to be seen on a cricket field, the crowd besieging the pavilion and its heroes coming out, tired but happy, to make their bows.'

The West Indies of 1963 made a universal appeal, but it was pointed out with some dismay that as the programme of future tours stood they were not due to return to England until 1971. Australia and South Africa with two visits each and New Zealand, India, and Pakistan with one, took up the seven years intervening. During this Test I was hurrying up to the top of the pavilion to do a broadcast when T. J. R. Dashwood, an excellent all-round games-player and fellow-member of several cricket clubs, stopped me and pointed out that they could return sooner if the programme could be rearranged to provide for 'twin tours'. I asked him to write a letter to the *Daily Telegraph* and this duly appeared the day after the Test ended, putting forward a novel and clearly sensible idea.

The annual ICC Meeting, whereat the dates of Test tours were settled even if as a rule not much else was, was only a few weeks ahead, and I decided to push Jack Dashwood's scheme all I could. I therefore persuaded my editor to accept a leader page article entitled Diplomatic Cricket, and as there was an MCC Committee coming up, at which the English line at the ICC would be decided, I did some lobbying, sending advance copies of the article to Lord Nugent, the president, and to some other friends who I thought would be sympathetic.

They were, and when John Dare, the West Indies president, pleaded at the ICC for an earlier return to England he was backed by MCC and the dual tour duly came to pass, to the great benefit of all concerned. No doubt it would have happened eventually in any case, but only the luck of my chance meeting with Jack Dashwood enabled us to strike while the iron was hot, and muster opinion so quickly.

The West Indies were on top of the cricket world, and when the Australians paid their return visit in early 1965, I determined, having now been released from my rugger duties, to be there. The Barbados house my wife had designed was completed in January, so the dates fitted in very well. Since the epic Australia–West Indies series of four years earlier both captains had retired, but both were still on the scene, Benaud, the professional journalist in the press-box, Worrell (now Sir Frank) as manager of the West Indies team, which was to be captained by Gary Sobers.

The series produced much stirring cricket watched by crowds as large as could be crammed in, and they saw their heroes gain the success of which they had been unluckily deprived in Australia. So far so good, but unhappily the spirit of chivalry and mutual respect with which the previous rubber had been fought was destroyed in the first Test in Jamaica when Benaud, writing both for West Indian, Australian and English papers, accused Griffith of throwing. He did so before the last day's play when Australia had just come in a second time, thus risking the counter accusation, which was quickly made, that he was attempting to influence the course of the play.

Richie, I'm sure, had absolutely no short-term tactical advantage in mind. The fact was that the throwing crisis with him had left a cruelly deep mark. As a young man he had seen Lock's method winked at, to the confusion of Australia. When on his unexpected promotion to the Test captaincy he had won back the Ashes in 1958/9 the throwing accusations had taken much of the glamour from the victory. He had been behind Sir Donald Bradman, when the latter, following the momentous ICC meeting of 1960 which he had attended, had almost completely purged Australia of throwing in a single season, with the co-operation of the state captains.

Since then Benaud had seen Griffith in England in 1963, and privately questioned his action, as had some leading English players. Then he had returned to Australia, found himself captaining Meckiff in the First Test against South Africa at Brisbane and seen his opening bowler in his first over called for throwing by Umpire Egar and effectively no-balled out of the match and out of cricket.

That experience – traumatic is the over-used but appropriate word – had so affected him that he was determined no one else should get away with it if he could help it. When during the Kingston Test we talked over the implications of what he was intending to write Richie said with deep feeling, 'I'm sorry, but after Brisbane if I could prove my own brother threw I'd expose him.'

I did my best, as a close friend with whom I had spent several tours and many, many hours in press and broadcasting boxes, to dissuade Richie Benaud from making his evidence public, at any rate at this stage. I said he had been welcomed as a hero in the West Indies. His prestige was enormous. If with Bob Parish, the Australian manager, he would seek a private meeting with the West Indians, showing them the pictures he had taken from the press-box behind the bowler's arm, there was at least a likelihood that they would have acted, difficult though it would have been in the light of public opinion (crowds generally take the bowler's side, as had been the case with Meckiff at Brisbane, and even Griffin at Lord's). I said that if he made the accusation in print it would unite the whole West Indies behind Griffith. As it was, Griffith seemed to me, with Sobers's help on the field, and Worrell's from the pavilion, to be making a real effort to keep close to the stumps with the left shoulder pointing to the bowler. Admittedly some of the pictures looked highly dubious, but on a fast bowler's pitch it was Hall who had been far the more dangerous, both physically and otherwise. I pointed out as evidence of the West Indies being themselves much concerned for Griffith to bowl fairly that Sobers, who invariably fielded in the slips or at short-leg, had stood at mid-off or mid-on for every over Griffith had bowled, watching and advising.

But Richie was determined to 'publish and be damned'. He was now purely a journalist, he said, with a first duty to his newspapers. No one could deny this, nor withhold from him the admiration due to a man with the moral courage to take, with his eyes open, a course of action that he knew must make him highly unpopular. Far be it from me to blame him.

The predictable outcome was that Sobers went back to his usual close catching positions, and the Australian side developed a sense of injustice as regards Griffith's bowling similar to that which had affected May's side in Australia. After the tour Norman O'Neill expressed their feelings when articles appeared under his name which elicited a protest from the West Indian Board to that of Australia.

About several of the cricket contretemps of this decade there is the kind of gloomy inevitability associated with Greek tragedy. This was one of them. Looking back, it seems to me that the one person the West Indies would have listened to, and whose diplomacy might have availed if Benaud had attempted a solution in consultation, was Frank Worrell. It is a fact, though I am not sure it has appeared in print, that Frank had had such doubts about Griffith's action he had not wanted to bring him to England in 1963. The West Indies selectors picked him in spite of the captain's opinion.

Charlie Griffith's situation was akin to others whose action for the most part was pure – in his case it was even classical – except when he attempted to achieve either extra pace or extra length (i.e. the yorker, of which he was a master). I dare say that in a moment of self-revelation Griffith might declare, as Peter Loader – who was suspected but never called – once did, 'I've never intended to throw, but I've always known when I've done it.'

Having beaten England and Australia within two years the West Indies could now in 1965 consider themselves cock of the roost. Their brilliant but unpredictable talents had been unified by Frank Worrell, first as captain and latterly as manager. But South Africa, halving one series in Australia, and losing to England at home by the only one of five Tests finished, were also coming up with a new and highly talented generation headed by the Pollock brothers, Graeme and Peter, Eddie Barlow and Colin Bland. It was one of the ironies and frustrations of the 'sixties that as the quality and character of their play rose to new heights – Barry Richards and Mike Procter, two cricketers of world class by any estimation, were due to emerge on the Test scene in a year or two – so the policies of the South African Government forced them into isolation.

In the second half of the English summer of 1965 we had a short glimpse of the new South African spirit in an evenly-contested three-Test series which they managed to win by dint of the one Test finished. This was at Trent Bridge in a game made memorable by Graeme Pollock's hundred. It was an innings 'which in point of style and power, of ease and beauty of execution is fit to rank with anything in the annals of the game', wrote the *Daily Telegraph* correspondent, and I don't think he was unduly carried away. This tall left-handed twenty-one-year-old made batting look supremely easy while everyone else either failed or struggled. The comparison with Frank Woolley was inevitable – and that is the ultimate accolade.

At the end of 1965 there came to fruition an enterprise on which I had been engaged for more than three years. Originally

I had been approached to act as editor of a work on cricket which was to be published as a set of four volumes and sold on the house-to-house never-never system by a firm specializing in this sort of thing which similarly sold bibles and encyclopaedias. With Michael Melford as my Associate Editor and Irving Rosenwater and Antony Winlaw as my assistant editors we planned the book on a broad, comprehensive basis and ordered from all the best writers wherever cricket was played articles and other material adding up to about a million words. When all was well in train circumstances caused these publishers to pull out, which put me in a rare spot, though of course they compensated authors for work already done.

It was now that Ron Roberts came to my rescue, suggesting that there was no better man at handling publishers than George Greenfield. His agent thereupon also became mine (and, I am glad to say, still is) and after other publishers had said, not unreasonably, they would be interested only in a much smaller book Peter Hebdon, managing director of Michael Joseph, agreed to swallow the whole thing – and in one vast volume.

Hence *The World of Cricket*, with its 1,100-odd pages and 123 contributors, in a quarto-sized format, a big production if nothing else, weighing 5½ pounds. Rosenwater's Who's Who of Contributors alone ran to ten thousand words, and I calculate its content is about seven times that of this one. The book was its own index, beginning with a sketch of Abel (R) and ending with a piece about the game in Zanzibar. I can't remember how many entries it contains, but we aimed at an encyclopaedia, and the reviewers seemed to think we achieved it, even though one pundit, who dabbled in the more esoteric side of cricket history, in advance of publication urged his readers against buying the book, saying it would soon be on sale at a knock-down price.

I'm glad to say this amiable prognostication proved inaccurate. Hebdon aimed at an edition of 10,000 to sell at six guineas, with a guinea discount in advance of publication. In the event someone under-estimated the paper required, and there was enough for around 9,000 copies only. More than 3,000 were ordered before publication, and the whole edition has long since been sold out, even though by another grievous miscalculation the whole of the Christmas 1965 sale was missed. Invitations had been printed for a ceremonial launching in the Long Room at Lord's before word of a delay at the printing end came through. Inevitably in a book of this scale there are things that one would do differently another time, and we made one tiresome, inexplicable omission of Rhodesia (nothing to do with UDI!). But on the whole it is a book that all concerned look back on, I think, as something of an achievement. Whether the economics of publishing would allow a second edition bringing the story up to date I would not know, but if it did Peter Hebdon unfortunately is no longer at hand to guide it. He was in Melbourne for our Australian launching – kindly done with his usual humour and panache, and to our great pride, by Sir Robert Menzies, then still Prime Minister – but has since died with tragic suddenness at a Scandinavian airport.

The MCC Australian tour of 1965/6, with M. J. K. Smith as captain and S. C. Griffith as manager, had several parallels with the one three years earlier. Both were well-conducted affairs wherein England more often than not held the initiative, but after taking the lead were again pulled back.

England, it could perhaps be said, just about won the series 'on points', but they had not the quality or variety in attack to back their powerful batting. In particular they found the angular left-handed Bill Lawry a tireless, insatiable fellow on whom to blunt their energies. Doug Walters with two hundreds in his first two Tests was acclaimed – prematurely, as it proved – a batsman in the classic mould, while for England Barber played the innings of the series at Sydney – a chanceless 185 in five hours out of 303. I cannot remember when an England batsman treated the bowling with such lofty disdain on the first day of a Test Match. England had some belated compensation for the frustrations of the last Test at Sydney in 1962/3, for this time the wicket did go, and in the follow-on the old combination of Titmus and Allen confounded them.

However, once more only two Tests out of five were finished. Australia hates draws, and one began to think that the old formula of timeless Tests (over there, anyway) might be preferable.

The following summer the West Indies again beat England handsomely and if it had not been recognized before no one now surely could gainsay Gary Sobers's place as an all-rounder unique in the game's history. He came on to bowl in whatever style the occasion seemed to suggest, fast left-arm with a lethal late-swing when there was still shine on the ball – or sometimes when there was not – slow wrist-spin as foil to the off-breaks of Gibbs, or orthodox slow-left; he fielded marvellously 'round the corner'; and his batting average for the series was 103. All this and captain too.

I wonder, by the way, what can have possessed Neville Cardus in his last, refreshing book *Full Score* to deliver the judgment, 'Your Sobers pants and toils after Rhodes in vain for all-round cricket skill . . .' The operative word is *all-round*, and what could possibly be more comprehensive than the range of Sobers's virtuosity? Genius is not measured by figures, and Gary has always been oblivious to them, but if any be needed he has scored three times as many Test runs as Rhodes with twice the average, and made twenty-seven Test hundreds as against two. As a Test bowler he has taken nearly twice as many wickets. In fact only six men have taken more Test wickets than Sobers, and in runs, topping eight thousand, he has outstripped Cowdrey and everyone else of whatever country or colour.

Wilfred Rhodes was a marvel, conscientious and dependable, a Yorkshire rock of solid achievement year after year, a bowler of classical style and a careful, gritty batsman, 'made' by his own determination to succeed, a safe, steady, unspectacular fielder. But as for Sobers panting and toiling . . . I really feel that my old friend and colleague, just this once, has not seen the past and the present in fair perspective. In other words he is talking through his venerable and illustrious hat.

In the mid-'sixties, little knowing the greater storms lying ahead, one found oneself having to record and comment distressingly often on instances of indiscipline and general strife. There was Fred Trueman getting a final and public warning from Yorkshire for disobeying the rule to which every player had now to conform requiring them to submit articles and books to the county concerned for approval. Ted Dexter was up on the same charge, and since it was his second offence he was actually suspended for a month, the only time the ultimate penalty has been imposed. Then Geoff Boycott after batting all the first day of six hours in a Test against India at Headingley for 106 was dropped by the selectors, who comprised D. J. Insole in the chair, A. V. Bedser, D. Kenyon and P. B. H. May. They had said they would not tolerate dull play, and were not moved to mercy by Boycott next day adding a further brisk 140 (undefeated) in three hours and a half.

These public rebukes to household names, though no doubt salutary and necessary, were distasteful evidence to the public at large that all was not well with the state of cricket. Then came a greater shock when Brian Close, who in 1967 had led

England with no small credit in the admittedly not very taxing series against India and Pakistan, blotted his copy-book in a county match immediately before the MCC team was due to be chosen for the West Indies tour in the winter. Close was hauled up before the Executive Committee of 'the Advisory' for delaying tactics in the closing stages of a vital Championship match between Yorkshire and Warwickshire. I was not there, but certain respected colleagues who had seen it all were still spitting with anger days later and the finding was unanimous that the Yorkshire tactics (which enabled them to avoid defeat by the margin of 9 runs) constituted unfair play. They held that Close was entirely responsible and therefore 'severely censured him'. According to *Wisden* Yorkshire, when Warwickshire were set 142 to win, bowled only 24 overs in the hour and forty minutes, and 'in the last fifteen minutes, during which they left the field to the umpires and the batsmen during a shower, sent down two overs . . . ' Close, followed and pestered for days no doubt by TV, radio and press, and accordingly perhaps upset, was ill-advised enough to declare that he would act in the same way again.

These were the glaring circumstances in which MCC had to choose their captain to make the trip to the West Indies where England's reputation for sportsmanship had been tarnished two tours previously. Small wonder that they preferred Cowdrey, but this let off all sorts of depressing stuff in articles and letters to the press about 'the old school tie' influence. I would have thought that at this distance of time few would maintain that MCC had not made an entirely right and proper decision. Yet at this delicate moment the chairman of selectors thought fit to announce that despite the censure of 'the Advisory' he and his three colleagues nevertheless had chosen Close rather than Cowdrey and had been outvoted. (Both Insole and May, by the way, were members of the full MCC Committee at the time.) It was this which caused Colin Cowdrey in a melancholy moment to say he felt as though he'd just come third in an egg-and-spoon race.

The theory of individual committee responsibility for decisions made as a body is generally followed in sport as in sterner affairs. It is on the same lines as the practice of corporate responsibility for Cabinet decisions, and the reasons behind it are similar. How an experienced man like Doug Insole, himself a pillar of the MCC establishment, and someone who had given good service to cricket over many years, could have added fuel to the controversy, and simultaneously made

216

Cowdrey's unenviable position as second choice even more difficult, can only be explained by the malaise that at this time was affecting the top echelons of cricket. Sound men said and did quite uncharacteristic things – such as this.

My own view was that Cowdrey, with seven MCC tours behind him, in four of which, including the last to the West Indies, he had been vice-captain, had been the obvious choice all along rather than Close, who had been abroad previously only as a lad of nineteen to Australia. Cowdrey had just led Kent to their best season for nearly forty years, and had finished as usual high in the averages. The qualities needed for leadership at home and abroad are not the same, as everyone in cricket knows. Yet Close would surely have got the job despite all had he gone to Lord's and said, 'Look, I'm sorry. It was a very keen match, and I overstepped the mark. It won't happen again.' MCC could scarcely have brushed aside a sincere apology. Maybe Brian was incurably obstinate: or perhaps he was unlucky in his advisers.

Wherever the truth lies I record for the first time my own tentative and earlier approach to the situation. When early in August and before the Edgbaston trouble it looked to me as though Close was going to get the job I had the presumption to offer my services quietly to MCC as manager of the tour if that should be considered helpful. My line of thought was that the captain would need someone at his right hand who knew the places and the people well, and I had been on five West Indies tours, including the two of my own which I had managed. I had known and liked Brian for nearly twenty years, without always approving of what he said and did. Anyway I was prepared to try if I was required. Candid friends at Lord's told me afterwards that I was thought to be 'too pro-West Indian'. In any case, unknown to me, Les Ames, who had been twice to the West Indies back in the 'thirties, was available, and, as might have been expected, he and Cowdrey did a perfect job in harness. Whether Close was ever sounded about my tentative offer I have no idea. If I had known Les was willing to be manager, I should not have indicated my own readiness.

There have been very few tours in my memory which the players have enjoyed as much, and which were successful into the bargain. Colin gave his answer to the Test selectors in deeds, while they for their part managed to retain the confidence of the counties, were elected for a further year, and in due course appointed him as captain the following summer against Australia. Brian Close came out to the West Indies with his delightful wife to write for *The News of the World*, fitted perfectly into the party, and caused never a moment of embarrassment. Knowing both the characters involved, this did not surprise me in the least. It is one of the blessings of cricket that among good-hearted men tensions, however taut, almost never threaten personal relationships. Most of the animosities darkly alleged, north *v.* south, 'old school tie' versus the rest, and so on, are quite fictional.

That MCC tour was notable in many ways. For instance the rehabilitation of Tom Graveney after he had been so strangely underestimated by successive selectors, begun by his triumphant return to the Test side in 1966, was completed by his appointment as Cowdrey's vice-captain. We had been given little chance of winning in the West Indies, but Tom's lovely innings in the First Test, I think the best I ever saw him play, not only enthused the Trinidadians and all who listened but impressed the West Indies generally with the quality of the English challenge. Cowdrey and Boycott batted admirably. Alan Knott midway through ousted Jim Parks and batted almost as well as he kept wicket, and has worn the gloves for England ever since; while John Snow, David Brown and Jeff Jones showed themselves more effective fast bowlers than the West Indies could muster.

England had a moral victory in the First Test, the West Indies being narrowly saved by the bell, and they must have won the Second but for the riot which took the heart out of the game. They had the better of the Third, and there was therefore a rare moral justice in their capitalizing on Gary Sobers's slightly over-generous declaration. It was only 'slightly', but only Sobers perhaps of modern cricketers would have had the courage to contemplate the risk of losing and make the challenge he did. Certainly it needed a mighty long rearguard by Cowdrey and Knott on the last day of the Fifth Test to hang on to the lead, but they just managed it.

The riot at Kingston was the worst thing of its kind, in my experience, made uglier than the disturbances in previous tours at Georgetown and Port-of-Spain by the police use of tear-gas. This cleared the troublous bottle-throwing section all right, but the wind was blowing the wrong way for the law-abiding majority who were soon spluttering away with their eyes streaming while the Jamaican Cabinet had to suspend their meeting half a mile away.

It was a wonderful bit of luck that this was the one and only time cricket writers have been provided with an air-conditioned press-box. We got whiffs of the stuff as people crowded in seeking sanctuary, but it was possible to type, and even though the Cable and Wireless operators (unprotected) had to cease work for a while most of us caught our early London editions. This was the first time a cricket story had ever led the *Daily Telegraph* (though it happened later with the South African tour cancellation). I never want to write another such, needless to say. There is a small, explosive element, without regard for law and order, in Jamaica, as in Trinidad and Guyana, that makes such a possibility on the cards, and the only thing the authorities can ensure is that there is sufficient force at hand to protect the players and the 95% who are as distressed and embarrassed by such behaviour as are the cricket Boards themselves. Barbados prides itself on the stability and self-respect of all its citizens. It likes to think that nothing of the sort could occur at Kennington Oval – but, well, I'm somewhat prejudiced.

From what one might call localized trouble the cricket story jerks unhappily on to the tragedy of 'the D'Oliveira Affair' with its world-wide implications and repercussions. It is a long and melancholy saga beginning in the summer of 1968, embracing the MCC's calling-off of their tour to South Africa once Mr Vorster had said that D'Oliveira's presence would be unacceptable, and ending with the last-minute cancellation of the South African tour to England by the Cricket Council at the request of the Government in May 1970. I cannot think of reciting the whole saga here. Nor do I need to do so since those for whom it still has a melancholy fascination can turn to two excellent sources.

One is *The D'Oliveira Affair* published in July 1969 by Collins which tells of the happenings up to the spring of that year from the point of view of the subject himself. The one thing about the affair not in dispute by any of the parties concerned is D'Oliveira's own conduct. When the President of MCC, Ronny Aird, said to the members of the Club at the Special General Meeting at Church House, Westminster, 'I am sure you would like me to publicly pay tribute to Basil D'Oliveira for the dignity he has maintained throughout this whole business' he got the only unanimous response of an infinitely depressing evening. This book deals with the whole story in a characteristically modest and fair-minded way, the author expressing on the fly-leaf his indebtedness to Robert Moore, of Hayter's Agency, a neighbour and close friend, by the way, of an earlier admirer and supporter of Basil, Ron Roberts, 'for his help in preparing the manuscript'.

The events from the publication of this book to their sorry end are recorded in full and meticulous detail in the 1971 *Wisden* by Irving Rosenwater in an article entitled 'The South African Tour Dispute: A Record of Conflict'.

But I must record some personal impressions, beginning with the last Test against Australia at the Oval where D'Oliveira's performance precipitated the crisis. He came in towards the end of an evenly and not excitingly-fought first day in this game which England had to win in order to save the rubber. Here he was, after an undistinguished season following an indifferent tour of the West Indies, brought into the England XI because several men were hurt, and thus providentially given the chance of winning a place in the MCC team for South Africa which was due to be chosen directly the Test was over.

If ever there were a case of a man seizing the psychological moment this was it. He batted confidently and briskly that evening, and carried on in the same vein next day until he reached his hundred in the remarkably fast time (in Test parlance) of three hours and a quarter. He had given one chance only (when 31) before reaching his hundred but, pressing on more riskily as the game demanded, offered three more before being ninth out for 158. It was a superb innings, and I only mention the details because there were those who were soon damning it with faint praise.

Next morning at the Oval I ran into one of the selectors, and as we talked about the state of the game and D'Oliveira's innings he asked whether I had read Crawford White's piece in the *Daily Express*. No, I was afraid I hadn't got round to it: my wife must have spent too long on William Hickey. He then said he thought that Crawford White had 'got it right', making the point that although D'Oliveira had played a valuable innings it should not determine his place in the MCC team for South Africa where conditions were very different. Remember Dolly had had a poor tour in the West Indies. What did I think?

I said I supposed that there were about twenty in the running for South Africa, including D'Oliveira. He had been lucky to get the chance of advancing his claims in this Test, but, as it was, he had seized it brilliantly.

When there is very little between several men, and on the eve of the decision one of the contestants with all 'the pressure' on him proves his temperament as well as his quality with an innings like this, I added, he pretty well picks himself.

So D'Oliveira was in my side for sure. Then – and only then – I finished: 'He's won his place, and if, after all the palaver about whether he would be accepted or not in South Africa, he isn't picked, you know what the world will say, don't you?'

My friend the Selector disagreed, and added something fairly strong about what 'the world' could do about it.

There, I registered to myself, is one vote against D'Oliveira. Later that afternoon another selector came up to the Oval broadcasting roof where there is an excellent view of the play and they are always very welcome.

'Well,' said he, 'what do you think about Dolly's chances now?' I repeated my summing-up of the situation just as I had put it to his colleague. Whereat he exclaimed, 'Jim, I couldn't agree more.'

That was obviously one-all, and for the duration of the match various other straws in the wind suggested to me that views were very mixed, with a quite strong anti-lobby. Before long this 158 in the deciding Test against Australia was apparently not much of an innings to write home about, riddled with five or six chances. And so on. Though born and brought up in South Africa he was even stigmatized as an 'English cricketer', not likely to be much good in his own country!

As it happened Basil had a further mark to make on the game, for on the last evening after the thunderstorm, when it looked as though Australia would hold out and so win the rubber, he broke the vital partnership, enabling Derek Underwood to polish off the tail with six minutes left.

A great victory it was, and of course, for Cowdrey, the captain, there followed the usual emotional paraphernalia of interviews for press, TV and radio, a reception given by the sponsors for the distribution of awards to players, and farewells to the Australians.

The time-table has some significance, since although previous experience had suggested it was not an ideal arrangement for selectors to sit down directly after a Test Match to pick a touring team they were summoned for 8 o'clock that evening at Lord's. The captain, coming off the field at 5.54, had two hours to do all his business, and get himself to Lord's for a meeting which went on until 1.50 a.m. If he was the most over-worked case all the four Test selectors, Insole, Bedser, Kenyon and May, were actively involved at the Oval. Those added to pick the side for South Africa were Cowdrey and Les Ames, already announced as captain and manager respectively,

A. E. R. Gilligan, President of MCC, and G. O. Allen, Treasurer. No one can say that, meeting fresh next morning, these men would have picked a different side, but at least the circumstances would have been more propitious.

There was a full meeting next afternoon of the MCC Committee, which approved the team, whereupon it was released to the press and the storm of protest broke. Most critics, myself included, thought there were several mistakes other than D'Oliveira's omission; for instance Colin Milburn, our most exciting prospect at the time, was left out, while John Murray was brought back as second wicket-keeper in front of several younger claimants. But, of course, the absence of D'Oliveira dwarfed all else in the public mind, and there followed such an explosion of feeling as no sporting decision surely had ever aroused. 'The world' was speaking, and no one, least of all the selectors, could ignore the tumult.

A few weeks later one of the full Committee which had approved the side, a man with a broader experience than most of the others present, said to me, 'When the side was presented to us with D'Oliveira excluded, I suppose, looking back, we should have adjourned for a bit, and talked over the implications.' He said that the omission had come as a complete surprise to him, and, he thought, to most of them. He had taken it for granted he would be in.

Maybe a 'cool look' at the situation that afternoon, and an appraisal by someone in 'the communications media', would at least have prepared the Committee for the public reaction, but it's hard to think they would have interfered with the selectors' choice, for their whole stand thenceforward was that they would not allow cricket and politics to mix.

I expect the events that followed will be easily recalled: the deluge of correspondence in the press; the protesting voices of MPs; the resignation of members of MCC; the formation of the 'Sheppard Group'; the explanations on television by Doug Insole; his subsequent announcement that because of Tom Cartwright's withdrawal D'Oliveira would go after all; Mr Vorster's riposte that MCC had bowed to pressure, and that 'we are not prepared to accept a team thrust upon us' by the anti-apartheid movement; the fruitless journey to London by J. E. Cheetham and A. Coy of the SACA; and finally, a month after they had approved the original selection, MCC's announcement that since their side was not acceptable the tour would not take place.

It was a dire catalogue of high passions, bewilderment on

one side, exasperation on the other, with the shadow lying ahead of the Special Meeting of MCC called by the group of members who had rallied round David Sheppard. Their three motions amounted to a vote of no confidence in the Committee, and they wanted no further contact on the field with South Africa pending evidence of 'actual progress' towards non-racial cricket. They also wanted a sub-committee of MCC to report to the next AGM any South African proposals towards non-racial cricket.

Knowing all the principals so well, feeling that the situation had been mishandled both by MCC and by the selectors, and being obliged therefore to say so in print, mortified at the great damage that was being done to the prestige of the Club and of the game itself, I hated every day of the autumn of 1968. Moreover, I knew in November from Lord Cobham of his meeting with Mr Vorster in the spring, and of his passing on to the President, Treasurer and Secretary the South African Prime Minister's assertion that it was highly unlikely D'Oliveira would be allowed in as a member of the team. In other words I knew that at least two of the selectors had had this information most of the summer, however hard they had no doubt tried to put it at the back of their minds. But I had been told in confidence. So, also in confidence and a good deal earlier – in fact immediately after D'Oliveira's non-selection – had David Sheppard been told by Lord Cobham.

It was this knowledge, so David said in a *Sunday Telegraph* article written in the following April when the Cobham story was blown by Ian Wooldridge in the *Daily Mail*, that helped steel him to carry through with the Special General Meeting. But, of course, we could not use the information. If he had been able to, the moral victory which he and his supporters won at the SGM at Church House, Westminster, would surely have been more conclusive than it was. It is not the least sad aspect of the whole deplorable business that as a result of his part in it, the name of David Sheppard (now, of course, Bishop of Woolwich) has become anathema to so many in the once sunny and peaceful world of cricket. When he was consecrated bishop a year later I saw George Cox, alway's David's faithful supporter, and Bet his wife, and there must have been a few more cricketers tucked away in Southwark Cathedral, but it seemed otherwise sadly bereft of representatives of the game which had been such a large part of his life, and to which he had given such distinguished service.

One day that autumn, before they had formulated the three

Resolutions which brought about the Church House meeting, I wanted to know the exact standpoint of the Sheppard Group, and so asked him, Peter Howell, the actor, who subsequently spoke extremely well at the SGM, and Robin Knight, a young man of liberal opinions who is an occasional contributor to *The Cricketer*, to lunch at the Bath Club.

After lunch an old friend, the late Harold de Soysa, Bishop of Colombo, whose hospitality has been known to many MCC cricketers passing through Ceylon, and who had been in London for the Lambeth Conference, dropped in to say goodbye before leaving for home. As we all sat in the Smoking Room over coffee I happened to notice an MCC member up from the City at the precise moment when with a look of surprise and alarm he spotted us. By the time the Stock Exchange closed news of the meeting of this terrorist organization was no doubt all round the House. The black Bishop's scarlet stock was clearly the red flag of revolution.

I tried to fulfil, but with scant success, some sort of catalyst function between the Establishment and its critics. Neither seemed to understand the language of the other. This was largely the case, so far as the speakers were concerned, at the SGM at Church House on 5 December. But if there were at least some among the thousand or so members of MCC who went with open minds the speaking would have won over most of the doubters to the opposition. Sheppard himself, who as usual went in first, Howell, Lord March, and Jeremy Hutchinson, QC, had had all the better of the exchanges before, right at the end of the long evening, when for many hunger and thirst had won the battle, Aidan Crawley and Raman Subba Row did something to restore the balance.

The level of much of the argument was terribly second-rate. One gentleman in a red and yellow tie indignantly queried Sheppard's right to continue as a member. Another announced he had marched behind Martin Luther King wearing the colours of MCC. The relevance of this comment was hard to follow, but he at least provided the only comic interlude in a singularly humourless evening. The occasion lost immeasurably through the absence of Sir Alec Douglas-Home, President two years before, who after seeing Mr Vorster while on a visit to South Africa had given the crucial advice to the Committee. This was that they should not insist on an answer to the letter they had written in January asking for a confirmation 'that no pre-conditions will be laid on the selection of the MCC team'.

Nor was Lord Cobham present, who had returned from the

Cape shortly after Sir Alec. During a last-minute courtesy visit to Mr Vorster the subject had been mentioned, and Charles Cobham had gathered a completely different picture of the situation. Ex-Governor-General of New Zealand, he was now the Queen's Lord Steward, and high officers at court are not expected to become publicly embroiled in contentious issues.

The person who was most often in my mind at Church House was Harry Altham: the proceedings would have distressed him immeasurably, though he might have been relied on to lift them to a considerably higher plane. As it was, the postal votes ensured the Committee of a substantial victory – for instance on the accusation of 'mishandling' they won by 4,357 to 1,570; but of members voting at the meeting (many of those present had sent their papers by post) Sheppard's resolution gained 314 supporters against 386 for the Committee.

For Ronny Aird who took the chair as president (Arthur Gilligan's term had ended on 1 October) even the most critical member must have had much sympathy. Here was a devoted servant of MCC all his working life given the highest reward that is in the power of the Club to bestow one minute, and next finding himself in a situation of unprecedented difficulty that would have taxed the powers of a Lord Chief Justice. The days when the Presidency of MCC was an honorific post making little but social demands are long over. Anyone who is nominated nowadays must expect to guide and inspire a lot of taxing and time-consuming Committee work. But to be saddled with a public meeting such as this! There was a special irony in Ronny's case in that he is the most pacific of men; nor is there anyone prouder of MCC's history or more sensitive to its good name. To see this reputation besmirched, in the light of all that MCC had done for a century and more to spread the game throughout the world, and to guard its traditions, was a bitter blow to many, and to none more than to him.

My thoughts around this time were already turning to the visit of the South Africans to England in 1970, and it already seemed then as though public opinion was unlikely to allow the tour to proceed peacefully if the side was chosen on an all-white basis. However in 1969 Wilfred Isaacs, a well-known personality in Anglo–South African cricket circles, was due to bring a side to England to play a varied programme including several first-class matches. Suppose he were to blaze the trail by including some of the best non-white players in his side. I wrote to Isaacs suggesting this and adding:

It seemed when your Government decided to allow a multi-racial athletics team to come together outside South Africa to compete as one unit in the Olympic Games that it opened the way for teams similarly constituted to compete 'away from home'. Of course, there are those who may think that the upshot of the Olympic business – to say nothing of the MCC cancellation – will have disinclined Mr Vorster from any such 'concession' to liberal feeling. Nor do I know what your own attitude might be towards an experiment of this kind. What I think I do know is the response that such a thing might evoke over here, and in other cricketing countries.

As I see it, this would be a practical illustration of South African desire to participate in the full kinship of cricket, and as such infinitely welcome. If some of your foremost players were to take part in company with a few carefully chosen non-Europeans in a tour freely organized without pressure from anywhere only the extremists (on both sides of the fence) would be other than delighted.

I have felt strongly, ever since the proclamation of withdrawal from the Commonwealth, that the SACA's one prospect of getting back into the ICC was to establish some sort of diplomatic link with the non-European Board, and to do what was possible to encourage them within the law.

I think it would be the greatest pity if political pressures were to prevent the 1970 series over here; but I also think that, especially now the D'Oliveira affair has made opinion so sensitive on the whole matter, practical gestures are very important in bettering the atmosphere.

Wilfred's friendly answer was understandable but disappointing. Writing on 4 December he said that such sides to England had to be chosen many months in advance to enable those concerned to save up towards the cost, and his was already complete. In the event his tour took place amid some harassment – at Oxford for instance undergraduates dug up the pitch.

Would a multi-racial tour in 1969 have improved the chances of the official tour the following summer? One cannot say, but there is little doubt it would have been a great advantage if the white SACA had already enjoyed diplomatic relations with the non-white Board of Control when the D'Oliveira row blew up. If they had gone to the South African Government together and said they wanted multi-racial trials with a view to picking the best side most of the anti-apartheid fire would have been drawn, whatever the outcome. But that is going forward a bit, and the dreary chronicle must now record the disclosure in April of Charles Cobham's part in the affair, which involved more newspaper comment generally critical of MCC.

Almost simultaneously was revealed the large financial inducement made to D'Oliveira during the summer of 1968 to take up a coaching job in South Africa, the condition of this being that he should forthwith declare himself unavailable for the MCC tour. There was evidence of clandestine talks and meetings including one in a lay-by off the M1 between Basil and Martinus Oosthuizen, the latter reputedly speaking on behalf of the Sports Foundation of South Africa, a charity financed by big tobacco interests. The size of the offer, £40,000 spread over ten years plus house and car, the cloak-and-dagger atmosphere of the negotiations and the pressure on him to decide on his future before the team was picked, increased, if that were possible, public sympathy for D'Oliveira, and helped explain his moderate form. No one succeeded in implicating MCC in this, which was some comfort, but of course it was more appalling publicity for cricket.

It was with this bitter background that the anti-apartheid forces now got to work to try and prevent the visit of the South Africans to England in 1970. I thought the best hope of improving the atmosphere, and at the same time bringing good out of evil, was for the South Africans to bring over a mixed party of sufficient players to make two sides, playing concurrently, the second being a sort of 'A' XI fulfilling fixtures just short of county class. There were assuredly coloured players good enough to form part of an enlarged party, and the SA Government's Olympic Games decision had made a precedent they would have found difficulty in disowning. I wrote to this effect both in England and for the South African Morning Newspapers. But another ICC meeting came and went without any change in the position and it was December before Jack Cheetham announced the SACA decision that in future selection would be 'on merit alone'.

Messrs Cheetham and Coy had just previously been to England and it was after they had tested the atmosphere that the decision was made known. They also announced a substantial money offer for the encouragement of non-white cricket, but they did so without prior consultation with the non-white Board of Control who said they were not short of money and turned it down. As usual these gestures were 'too little and too late' to influence the course of events, and opposition to the tour built up steadily and formidably.

I thought it was important to know what considerations would persuade the 'Stop the 70 Tour' people to suspend their propaganda operations, and so asked the two chief figures, Dennis Brutus and Peter Hain, to talk the subject over with Raman Subba Row and 'Bernie' Coleman, a member of the Surrey Committee, and of certain Lord's sub-committees. We met at my office at *The Cricketer*, it being agreed that what passed should be confidential. So I can only say that I gathered an impression of personal sincerity, and tried to imagine what my own attitude would have been if I had suffered similar experiences to theirs in South Africa.

But, however fervently these two might say that they were committed to 'direct but non-violent action', there were others who would stop at nothing. A dozen county grounds were damaged in a night, MCC bought 300 reels of barbed wire, and the Cricket Council dug in to the extent of announcing a shortened tour of twelve matches on eight grounds. The Prime Minister, Mr Wilson, on TV called the tour 'a big mistake', and the decision to carry on 'very ill-judged'. The majority of the county members and of the players still wanted the tour to go on, but the Cricket Council were urged to stop it by a cluster of MPs, the United Nations Association, the British Council of Churches and the TUC. Thirteen African countries threatened to withdraw from the Commonwealth Games due in Edinburgh in June. Then Harold Wilson went further and said that anyone should feel 'free to demonstrate' against the tour if they so pleased.

This to me was practically an open invitation to disorder from the leader of the Government, and it was the moment when I felt that the Cricket Council might have extricated themselves honourably from a situation that had become impossible, if only on the grounds that as hosts they could not allow the South Africans to submit themselves to the indignities and dangers that lay ahead. The tour was no longer a sporting exercise. It could give neither pleasure nor profit to players or spectators, or indeed to anyone save those bent on violence.

On 14 May, less than three weeks before it was due to start, there was an emergency debate in the House of Commons on the tour, which I attended and followed with gloomy fascination. It broadly followed party lines, Labour members following the Government in opposing the tour, the Tories declining to be dictated to by a minority. Certain Tories however spoke earnestly against the tour, including Sir Edward (now Lord)

Boyle, a passionate supporter of Sussex whom I had known since Pusey House days. He was a member of the Fair Cricket Campaign which David Sheppard started as a more moderate alternative to the activities of Hain. I came out against the tour in the *Daily Telegraph* on 15 May, the day after the Commons debate, and was promptly invited to repeat my views, which I did, on *The World at One*. My line was that the issue concerned a balance of evils. However distasteful it was to suffer dictation by what was still probably a minority, the alternative was sure to be more disastrous for cricket. It is the easiest of all games to disrupt. The cricket grounds of England would have become battlefields to which no one would take women or children. No one could guarantee the safety of the players – least of all the South Africans. As for pleasure in the play there would be little or none.

Those who thought the tour should be forced through at all costs, it seemed to me, were pursuing a political principle at the expense of the game. And expense was the word, in every sense. One's correspondence was divided between many who felt I had 'sold the pass' – 'You of all people' – and those who for a variety of reasons, both moral and practical, wanted the tour called off. The Chairman of the Race Relations Board, Mark Bonham-Carter, wrote a note of congratulation.

Though the Cricket Council on 19 May once again confirmed their intention of proceeding with the tour the climax was now near. Two days later M. J. C. Allom, who as President of MCC was now Chairman of the Cricket Council, and Billy Griffith, the Secretary, were invited to the Home Office by James Callaghan and in a three-hour meeting requested to cancel the tour 'on the grounds of broad public policy'. The Cricket Council considered that the letter in which Mr Callaghan set out the arguments against the tour ('relations with other Commonwealth countries, race relations in this country, and the divisive effect on the Commonwealth', the strain on police resources, and so on) to be tantamount to a Government directive, and promptly complied.

It so happened that over this last period I was at Cardiff watching Glamorgan and Hampshire and sharing the TV commentaries with just about the most die-hard member of the Cricket Council, Wilfred Wooller. Since he had to attend the final meeting in London I found myself on the decisive Friday with about three hours' talking on the air, in addition to writing my comment on the cancellation and report on the match.

Back in London that evening I agreed to go on David Dimbleby's 24 Hours programme with Helen Suzman, and on arrival at Lime Grove found that Peter Hain and a man who was proposing to sue him were also on the programme. This diversionary topic rather ate into the time available – there's never enough – but Mrs Suzman appealed to the vast audience not to underestimate the growing strength of liberal opinion in South Africa while I said why I was relieved by the decision, and how much I hoped eventually to see a multi-racial side here. I looked full into the eye of the camera, and said I thought that lovers of cricket might never forget Mr Wilson's recent remark on television that opponents of the tour should feel 'free to demonstrate' against it. By the time a BBC car had deposited me at Sandwich some time after midnight I reckoned I had had quite a day. One's predominant feeling was one of overwhelming relief and in the days following it was evident that, whatever their opinions, this was common to nearly all in the cricket world who would have been closely concerned, players and officials particularly. Thankfully the barbed wire and the barricades were taken down.

A month later Ann and I were at the *Daily Telegraph* Election Night party at the Savoy, and luckily found ourselves at supper with Christopher and Ann Chataway, he having won in a canter at Chichester. I had known Christopher at Oxford, where he was President of Vincent's and of the OUAC, as one of the most glamorous members of that vintage post-war sporting generation, and had since followed his career with much admiration: 5,000 metres world record holder, television reporter and commentator, MP at twenty-eight and junior minister in the Macmillan administration two years later, a high flier who as this night wore on saw an even more glowing future unfolding. As we watched the television, fascinated by the results, some of my friends seemed genuinely surprised by my enthusiasm. 'Oh,' they said, 'we thought you'd gone over to the enemy.' My editor, Maurice Green, then and only then told me categorically what more than one of the leaders had indicated, that he had not always agreed with my opinions on the South African affair. I do not say there are no other papers where in such a situation not a comma of the correspondent's work would be altered, nor any suggestion made – but I hardly think there are many.

It is a relief after so many pages to return to the cricket field, but not unfortunately to a scene free from discord. As the summer of 1969 dawned, the reigning England captain was Cowdrey, as secure in his position as ever May and Hutton had been. He had led England in the last twelve Tests, including the three in the politically tempestuous and nerve-wracking tour of Pakistan arranged when MCC's tour to South Africa fell through (the last of these games at Karachi ended in a riot completely unconnected with the cricket). Tom Graveney had been vice-captain throughout this period, and had led England against Australia at Headingley when Cowdrey was unfit.

Cowdrey has suffered more disabilities than most one way and another and at the end of May 1969 came one of the worst and certainly the most personally disastrous, the tearing of an Achilles tendon when batting at Maidstone in a John Player League match. The selectors therefore had hurriedly to find a new captain for the series against the West Indies and New Zealand. Graveney was next in line, but Illingworth, who had been reputedly the brains behind the Yorkshire side, had had a disagreement on terms with them and was now experiencing captaincy for the first time with Leicestershire.

The selectors to the general surprise plumped for Illingworth who in the three home seasons since has held his place and done the job very well. However the change-over was not effected without yet another row, for Graveney first heard of Illingworth's appointment over the wireless or from the press, and was so nettled that on the Sunday of the First Test he unwisely defied the well-known rule and, despite specific warning, went off to fulfil an engagement to appear in a match for his benefit. A fee of £1,000 hung on his appearance.

Alec Bedser reported him to the TCCB, and the TCCB issued a severe reprimand, and banned him for the next three Test Matches. As it turned out his 75 at Old Trafford against the West Indies was Graveney's last Test innings. He was never chosen again, and at the end of the 1970 season retired from English cricket to serve as a coach to Queensland. So passed on the best professional batsman in my estimation – though Ken Barrington runs him close – produced since the war: the best and, out of question, the most stylish and delightful to watch.

There used to be a terrible Army phrase called 'man-management', under which heading were set down certain elementary guide-lines for the handling of people. It all boiled down, of course, to commonsense and consideration for others. Top-class cricketers are no less sensitive than other men – rather the reverse – and most will respond to the personal approach.

If the shock had been broken to Tom in advance and his co-operation sought I like to think that he would have accepted the situation that someone very much his inferior in skill and reputation was being put over him, and that he would not have cocked a foolish snook at authority in the way he did. We might then have seen him in due course make the graceful exit from the Test scene that his achievements had deserved.

I couldn't help remembering how hurt Alec Bedser himself had been when in 1954/5 in Australia he, the destroyer with 69 Australian wickets in the previous two series, discovered he had been dropped from the Test side only when he saw the names pinned on the dressing-room notice-board. Not much 'man-management' there either!

With the tour to Australia due after the 1970 season it was inevitable that the decision regarding the captaincy there should become one of the chief topics of the summer. Had there been no substitute for the South African Tests probably Cowdrey would have got the appointment, perhaps with Illingworth, who had stood in for him successfully in 1969, as his deputy. But the Rest of the World series was announced, five games sponsored by Guinness, which would have the same status of 'Unofficial Tests' as those arranged against South Africa.

There was some hostility on the part of some of the counties to this project – yet more acrimony on the cricket front – and Cedric Rhoades, the Lancashire chairman, in advance of the First Test stigmatized it in a newspaper interview as a 'pantomime series'.

The gates in the early matches were disappointing for various reasons: the lack of time (only three weeks) between the announcement of the series and the First Test; the General Election; the lack of TV coverage; the counter-attractions of the World Cup and the Commonwealth Games. But in the end the quality of the cricket overcame all handicaps, the crowds increased and the counties had £43,000 to share in part compensation for the absence of the South African team. Five of their number played in the games, by the way, and with much distinction; and not the least value of the enterprise was that with Gary Sobers as captain and Eddie Barlow as his deputy it was as admirable an illustration of multi-racialism in practice as could be imagined. Both Freddie Brown and Les Ames, who with the captain chose the teams from five nationalities, said they had never known a better team-spirit.

So far as the leadership issue was concerned things went

232

Illingworth's way. After almost a season out of action, and no doubt over-anxious to do well, Cowdrey started the summer very poorly, and with scarcely a run to his name asked (as also, surprisingly, did Geoff Boycott) not to be considered for the First Test. By the latter part of the summer he had quite recovered his form and not only led Kent to the County Championship but finished top of their averages. However, Illingworth thus had his tenure renewed and again he took his chance with both hands. In the First Test when England fielded one of the weakest batting sides in her history Ray made 63 out of the total of 127 in the first innings, 94 out of 339 in the second. The improvement in his batting since he had first led England the year before is one of the most startling developments in a mature player I can remember.

By the time the announcement of the MCC captain for Australia was due to be made during the Third Test England were all square in the rubber at one-all, and though Cowdrey was now back in the Test side most of the limelight fell, properly indeed, on Illingworth who had imbued his men with the proper degree of determination against opponents technically far superior (Barlow, Richards, Kanhai, Pollock, Lloyd, Sobers, Procter . . . what a batting order!).

I was pretty sure, weighing up all the factors and the evidence, and knowing the two men as I did, that the right captain for Australia was Cowdrey. At this stage of the book I need not recite again the attributes needed in a touring captain. If the choice had been made by the old method, with a few senior MCC officers supplementing the four selectors for home Tests and their recommendation passed for approval to the full Committee, the answer might have been different. As it was, however, for the first time – and by a 1971 decision it is to be the last – the choice was made by the four alone, with D. G. Clark, who had already been appointed manager in Australia.

The four were Messrs Bedser, A. C. Smith, Kenyon and Sutcliffe (Billy, son of Herbert), of whom only the first two had the advantage of first-hand experience of playing in Australia. They appointed Illingworth, and offered the vice-captaincy to Cowdrey, who after great misgiving and rather too much delay accepted it. Some thought that on grounds of compatibility the combination wouldn't work well. I was more optimistic, but they proved right. The trinity of Clark, Illingworth and Cowdrey did not produce the happiest results, though to the best of my knowledge there was no personal friction. It was just that the mixture didn't 'gell'.

This was my seventh tour of Australia, and as Michael Melford was also covering the tour, as he had in 1965/6, I did not appear on the scene until immediately before the First Test. How glad I was to have missed the preliminaries! Beginning at Adelaide, MCC were a couple of hundred behind on first innings against South Australia, were beaten by Victoria by six wickets, followed on against New South Wales, and gained first innings lead over Queensland only after the weakest of the states had made 360. They were the only side MCC had bowled out. Boycott was full of runs and the other batsmen had all made enough, but the attack was apparently too moderate for words to describe. It was just about the poorest start ever made to an MCC tour of Australia.

The prospect looked bleak, except that no one rated Australia very highly either. They had been saved by the weather in England in 1968, and in South Africa in 1970 had been annihilated in all four Tests – a thing that was without precedent in their history. In the event England after an inauspicious first day at Brisbane had, on balance, slightly the better of things, chiefly because they had much the most effective fast bowler in John Snow, who was correspondingly better supported than Thomson and McKenzie, both of whom were themselves dropped before the end of the series.

On a pitch that no one trusted at Sydney Snow in the Fourth Test excelled himself in the second innings, and England deservedly took the lead. At Adelaide they should have clinched the rubber had not Illingworth, with a lead of 235 and thirteen hours of the match to go, neglected to enforce the follow-on. The Australians could scarcely believe their luck, which would in all probability have saved them the Ashes and the rubber but for their selectors making two obliging omissions from the last Test at Sydney. They dropped Bill Lawry, the captain, appointing Ian Chappell in his place. On another suspect pitch and to England's great relief they also omitted to restore Graham McKenzie.

It was understandable that, before the series ended, and with the future in mind, they should want to brighten the image of Australian cricket by finding a more adventurous figurehead than Lawry; but there is scarcely a more valuable batsman in the world when the going is tough and time is no object. There was still no Australian batsman England wanted more to see the back of. Lawry's elderly replacement as No. 1, Eastwood of Victoria, made 5 and 0, and England won a narrow victory by 62 runs.

The Ashes at last! And if that were the whole story it would have been a rare moment to savour. But the result in this 210th Test Match between England and Australia was secondary to the unprecedented scenes on the second afternoon when Illingworth first argued and gesticulated at Umpire Rowan on the latter warning Snow for intimidation, and then, after an incident on the picket fence involving Snow, a brief tangle between him and a spectator, and the throwing in this section of a few beer-cans on to the field, led his men off without reference to either umpires or the batsmen. Technically Illingworth might have surrendered the match there and then by 'refusing to play'. As it was, when the umpires came back to the pavilion they issued a warning that the game must be continued forthwith. The field was cleared of litter in a few moments, and to further boos the England XI returned to the fray.

The scene, shown and replayed many times on television will be too fresh in the minds of most readers of this book to require much further analysis. It could have been avoided by an ounce of tact or a single friendly gesture at any moment after a bouncer from Snow had felled Jenner, the Australian spin-bowler. The reaction of both Illingworth and Snow on the other hand was provocative and, to English eyes, embarrassing to a degree.

Yet it was symptomatic of a truculent spirit that had developed during the tour among just a few of the leading players which in my experience was quite new. I had marked it seriously for the first time at the New Year in Melbourne, when the Test there had to be abandoned because of rain – an unprecedented thing in Australia – without a ball bowled.

The Australian Board accordingly asked the English authorities present, who happened to include Sir Cyril Hawker and Gubby Allen, Chairman and Vice-Chairman respectively of the Cricket Council, in addition to David Clark, whether they would agree to Melbourne being given a Test after all instead of MCC's return game against Victoria. There were six Tests this time anyway because Perth had been brought into the rota. One had been lost, and the proposition was to restore it, the effect of which would be to have four Tests in six weeks. In the general interests of the game – and not least to compensate the largest cricket community in the world which gets on average only about a Test in two years – England said yes.

On the Saturday afternoon that the news was announced I was unlucky enough to run into one of the militants who had already had an hour or two to digest the situation. In the foyer of the Windsor Hotel he informed anyone interested that the decision was disgraceful, that 'we' hadn't been consulted, that the rubber had been handed to Australia on a plate, that the sooner these things were managed by professionals the better, and what about the extra money anyway. No one had mentioned anything about that.

It was a cricket-writer, I fancy, who remarked that to listen to a few of these fellows talking was, he imagined, rather like a meeting of shop-stewards; if he did not say it Cyril Hawker must have been thinking much the same thing. Having flown in in his year as President of MCC to enjoy the supreme sight of the New Year Test at Melbourne he saw no cricket, and found himself instead involved in hours of arbitration and argument.

The decision not to follow-on at Adelaide was partly induced, I believe, by a sense of grievance about the extra Test, while the throwing-down of his bat there by Boycott when he was (rightly!) given run out reflected the lack of discipline and self-control.

Soon after MCC returned home the Cricket Council issued a statement recording 'their grave concern about incidents involving dissent from umpires' decisions by word or deed. While appreciating the strains and stresses under which cricket at the highest level is played, the Council must warn all players that such conduct, which is contrary to the spirit and tradition of the game and brings it into disrepute, will not be tolerated.' The TCCB Disciplinary Committee would not 'hesitate to use their wide powers which include the termination of the registration of a player'.

Within a few weeks of this broadside Snow in the Lord's Test against India was demonstrating the sort of behaviour that the authorities were determined to stamp out, and Alec Bedser was responding by saying that Snow had not been considered for selection for the next Test.

I happened to be standing in the Long Room with Sir William Collins, Chairman of Collins, in direct prolongation of the pitch as Gavaskar, the non-striker, backing up for a quick single, and Snow ran towards us and the latter swerved, knocking his small opponent headlong. Billy Collins, an old cricketer, could scarcely believe his eyes, though having been in Australia at the end of the MCC tour he had heard enough to make him highly uneasy about the behaviour of the team. Every time this sordid incident was shown again on television it seemed to look worse – and it was replayed *ad nauseam*.

I must endeavour to end this chapter of accidents on a more agreeable note, and this is not difficult. The example set to young cricketers by those at the top cannot be underestimated today when the camera picks up every action and attitude. But the tradition of chivalry and sportsmanship in cricket runs too deep to be shaken seriously by a few incidents, however blatant. County cricket is still waged in a good spirit, even if it tends to be short of personality and humour. The clubs, the leagues, the villages, are flourishing well enough – stimulated, many of them, by the new competitions that have recently sprung up and proved their popularity. The face of cricket may be changing, but its heart surely remains sound.

12

The Personal Tours

As I look back on something like half a century's involvement in cricket from all angles it seems that (leaving Arab activities out of account) the happiness I have had from the game has been best personified in the three 'private' tours which I have arranged and managed, and, in the Duke of Norfolk's tour to the West Indies in 1970, for which I acted as Treasurer. There's a lot of administrative work involved before these expeditions get under way, for they are essentially pioneering efforts which have to build up from the initial idea. But once all is settled, and the side has been finally agreed on, the drudgery is over and only the fun and excitement lie ahead.

Obviously the choosing of the players is one of the most important items, and it was not always easy. One had to keep within a budget, which put a limit on the number of professionals, and it was important to find a side strong enough for the purpose. One tried to avoid difficult or temperamental fellows if only because there was no sanction that could be applied to any such, in case of trouble, apart from the extreme step of sending a bad boy home. Naturally the ideal was a good cricketer and an easy mixer rolled into one, and these were plentiful enough. I find that we had forty-six players altogether on these four tours, and there is not one I would not be delighted to invite again, if the chance arose. A heterogeneous bunch they were, made up of thirty-four Englishmen, four Australians, three West Indians, three Indians, and two Ceylonese. Several, Colin Cowdrey, the Nawab of Pataudi, Mike Griffith and Ian McLachlan came twice, and Colin Ingleby-Mackenzie three times. Every county has subscribed one or more, and I'm glad to say all were returned to them fit and well. Of the forty-six exactly half were Test cricketers when they toured: several others became so, most of them being, I think, helped towards their caps by the experience.

I was put in some difficulty by the circumstances surrounding the first tour, in 1956, since the West Indies Board had invited me to bring a side ostensibly to give experience to their up-and-coming players but chiefly, in fact, to provide some antidote to, or to blunt the memory of, the MCC tour of two years before. My correspondence with the Board was naturally confidential, but since the visit of Len Hutton's side had been accompanied by such a rumpus, and seeing that I had been critical in some respects of their attitude and behaviour, it did not take the press long to put two and two together. There was some caustic comment from the sort of quarters whence it might have been expected, the *Daily Mirror* leading the way with a banner headline calling it *The Tour with the Tact of a Cactus*.

It was a 'piffling expedition', they said, condemning this 'Caribbean Carnival', the particular point of criticism being that Cowdrey and Frank Tyson were coming with me, just in advance of the Australian visit, both having had foot trouble the previous summer. Peter Wilson, billed over the article as 'The Man They Can't Gag', summed up the situation thus:

Swanton is a cricket writer and television commentator of some note. I suggest he has struck a sour note by trying to organize a completely unnecessary tour.

And I should not like his responsibility to be mine, if in particular either Tyson or Cowdrey broke down as a result of this out-of-season flummery.

Another national paper quoted Alf Gover, the sage among bowling coaches, as saying that Tyson had made a mistake in accepting. Alf's remarks were said to have 'crystallized adverse comment', so it was something of a relief to hear promptly from him that his remarks had been completely turned round. The *Morning Advertiser*, journal of the brewers, was equally forthright about this 'cricketing junket', declaring that 'for current international cricketers facing an Australian season to take places on Swanton's holiday cruise is indefensible'.

I tremble now – more, I'm sure, than I did at the time – to think what further opprobrium would have fallen not only on me but, much more seriously, on Cowdrey and Tyson, if either (or both) had come back a cripple from this junket or flummery. Ah, well, time is the great healer, and I certainly bear no resentment on the score of opinions honestly expressed. There were other less strident voices. My own paper naturally gave moral support, Peterborough drawing attention to this comment made by Keith Miller, vice-captain of Australia on their West Indies tour of 1955, in the *Sydney Sun*:

Even the staunchest English cricket supporter would still

have burning ears if he had toured the Caribbean with the Australian team which followed in the wake of the MCC team . . . Swanton fully realizes that England needs some urgent diplomatic patching-up in the West Indies. He could have made no better choice of diplomats than Cowdrey and Tyson.

In the provinces the *Yorkshire Post*, the *Birmingham Post* and the *South Wales Argus* gave the tour polite notice, while *The Times* did us proud, starting us off with a 'good luck' leader and commissioning Hubert Doggart, my vice-captain, to cable back five long pieces, which actually covered more space than my own reports to the *Telegraph*. That the tour was well received in the West Indies I have a cuttings-book full of enthusiastic press notices to bear witness, apart from a letter of appreciation from Sir Edward Beetham, Governor of Trinidad, which with his permission I shall quote:

Government House,
Trinidad.

Dear Swanton,   27 April 1956

I have waited until now to write to you in order to make sure that the wonderful atmosphere created by your visit at the head of your XI was not just temporary excitement after a series of matches which everyone enjoyed immensely. I know that you will be as pleased as I am that the effect has remained solidly with the Trinidad public throughout the island and that you and all the members of your team will long be remembered with great friendliness and with a firm feeling that all is still well with British cricket. In other words, the tour could not have been more successful.

May I say a very heartfelt personal 'thank you' to you for having conceived the idea of the tour and then carried it through to such a wonderful conclusion? You and your chaps have done something, and something *very* valuable, which could have been done in no other way, and anyone who really *thinks* must be as grateful and happy as I am.

This letter is of course quite personal to you but perhaps, if you think fit, you would pass on orally to Cowdrey and the team, when you see them, a word as to my own very deep appreciation for all they did in the sun and heat of Trinidad. I can only hope that they got a tenth of the enjoyment all of us got.

With very best wishes from my wife and myself.

Yours very sincerely,
Edward Beetham.

Of course a tribute such as this, with other kind words from the cricket folk of Barbados and Trinidad were much more than a counterweight, so far as I was concerned, to the press criticisms in advance.

This was the side: M. C. Cowdrey (captain), G. H. G. Doggart (vice-captain), T. W. Graveney, F. H. Tyson, J. J. Warr, D. E. Blake, G. Goonesena, A. C. D. Ingleby-Mackenzie, R. C. M. Kimpton, R. G. Marlar, A. S. M. Oakman, M. J. Stewart and Swaranjit Singh. The party was made up to fifteen by the addition of John Haslewood who came, in a strictly honorary capacity, as treasurer. Not many of these will need introduction. For Roger Kimpton, who came at his own expense from Australia, it was a temporary return to the first-class game which he had last graced with such brilliance for Oxford and Worcestershire in the 'thirties. But for the war, in which he won the DFC, he could easily have played for his country. David Blake played for Hampshire as wicket-keeper batsman when he could get away from his dental surgery. Swaranjit Singh was a Cambridge all-rounder second only in quality to 'Gammy' Goonesena, a notable figure among those who toured with me in that he is the only man ever to have suggested his own inclusion! This he did in a letter of due modesty saying, 'As there is no harm in trying I offer myself for your kind consideration. Perhaps you may like to have colour and gaiety, which I can provide . . .' And so he did, starting literally with turbans of a different hue for every day of the week.

Tom Graveney, Colin Cowdrey and Micky Stewart batted admirably, and Frank Tyson and Goonesena bowled with great success, and everyone contributed their fair ration of runs and wickets except for poor Robin Marlar, second only to Jim Laker around this time as an off-spinner, who with Wendy his wife came on the tour as their honeymoon. This fact naturally caught on, and the cry was heard round Kensington Oval: 'Him honeymoon bowler, Clyde, give him licks.' And I'm afraid everyone did.

Frank Tyson was the great draw, and how he gave value for money. The first time he faced Clyde Walcott, then at his very best, he shattered his stumps first ball. The next time Walcott lasted three balls before, with his slightly circular back-lift, he was seconds late and Frank spreadeagled him again. Pandemonium! At the third encounter honour was restored when Clyde got a hundred. Wes Hall, by the way, was introduced to first-class cricket against us in Barbados. Hall, an eighteen-year-old telegraphist with Cable and Wireless, was not yet truly fast, but Conrad Hunte, who had played one match previously for his native island, made his mark directly with an innings of 151.

At Trinidad Tyson, bowling almost if not quite as fast as he had done in Australia the year before, against the full island strength took ten for 78 in the match, and had enough in hand in the last over of a baking six-hour day to uproot the last two men and bring us a thrilling victory. When we found ourselves pitted in a five-day match against a West Indian XI whose batting order started, if you please, Hunte, Rae, Kanhai, Weekes, Walcott, Sobers and 'Collie' Smith, there were 17,000 on the Saturday around Queen's Park Oval. My cuttings-book contains this choice item:

> Not even his client could have kept Mr L. L. Roberts, solicitor, from going to the Queen's Park Oval yesterday. When his case was called, Mr Roberts told Mr Alcindor: 'Sir, it is Weekes, Walcott and the "Typhoon" duel, and I am asking for an adjournment in this matter.'

The adjournment was granted. A delightfully West Indian touch!

Incidentally Peter May, the reigning England captain, asked me to try and persuade Colin Cowdrey to go in first on this tour, because the idea was that he should do so in the forthcoming rubber against Australia. Colin never had opened but he duly obliged and went on to do so throughout that summer's Test series. So possibly our tour was rather more a help than a hindrance to English cricket after all. Everyone was in rare form on return to England, as I noted in a commentary. In one week in May our top six batsmen made 1,200 runs between them and the chief bowlers collected 30 wickets. As subsequent tours have emphasized, there is nothing more likely to get cricketers into the groove than an April in the sun.

On our way home we stopped off for a one-day game in Bermuda which was only slightly less than perfect in that an aircraft delay fetched us up at Bermuda about 0300, and by an extraordinary arrangement we were due to start play at 10.30. I not only captained the side but as there was little competition for the job went in first with Alan Oakman and almost survived the hour before what was best described as 'brunch', being caught at short-leg in the last over for 13, foolishly 'playing for the interval'.

There was one further front-page echo of the tour after it was over when Frank Rostron of the *Daily Express* discovered that many months before I had privately enquired of the West

Indies Board whether they would welcome the inclusion in my side of the South Africans, John Waite and Roy Maclean, two very cheerful characters and highly attractive cricketers, both of whom were keen to come. After deliberation the Board, centred then in Trinidad, regretfully decided against it, on the ground that there *might* have been a bad press reaction and the risk was therefore not worth taking. This was accepted without demur by me and the men concerned, though when we arrived at Barbados the President, old Judge Colleymore, said they would have been well received there, and he regretted their not having come. Perhaps it was a naïve idea of mine, but remember this was 1956, not 1970.

The nearest thing to friction on any of my tours suddenly blew up on this one, at – of all places in the world – the Robinson Crusoe island of Tobago. It was really a very small affair, but interesting perhaps as an example of how on tours both major and minor managers can walk innocently into trouble.

At the last moment the Board of Control asked if we could possibly add to the fixtures by playing a game in Tobago. They'd never seen a touring side in Tobago, and it would be a wonderful boost to cricket there. Rest days are precious to the players, and the only possible day was the one immediately before our five-day 'Test'. So I said I couldn't promise my key men but would bring a mixed XI from both teams if that would do. The Board said fine, and so we set off with a marvellous side for little Tobago including half-a-dozen of mine plus Gary Sobers, Rohan Kanhai, 'Collie' Smith, Sonny Ramadhin and Gerry Gomez.

On the runway a full dozen of the cricket hierarchy were lined up on the tarmac, all in formal dark suits grilling in the sun. It happened I was last out of the plane, and as I stepped out it was at once plain something was wrong. The President was grave, unsmiling. 'Welcome to Tobago, Mr Swanton,' he said, then with anguish in his voice, 'but where is Mr Cowdrey, and Mr Tyson and Mr Graveney?'

I explained exactly what I had contracted with the Board to do, but clearly the arrangement had never been passed on, and the clear impression was that on its great cricketing day Tobago had been slighted. Happily there had flown over with us the old Test cricketer, now dead, Ben Sealey, one of the most charming men I've ever met. He was due to talk to the crowd on the match over the public address system, and he had so winning a way with him and introduced us all so flatteringly that all in the end was well. After a morning rum-punch or two the smiles returned.

This 1956 tour gave me even more of a taste for the West Indies than I had had before, and while I was out there with MCC in 1959–60 I therefore tested the ground to see whether another visit would be acceptable. The idea this time would be to concentrate more on the smaller islands though in order to balance the books, apart from anything else, we would need to play at least two of the main territories. When it came to estimating the cost, I found it necessary also to call on firms with Anglo–West Indian interests. Even so, since for several reasons I did not contemplate accepting any financial aid from the West Indian Board as such, I was still short of cash when the MCC tour was finishing.

It was then that the Prime Minister of Trinidad came up and said he'd heard about my difficulty. 'If it would help you my government – on one condition – will guarantee you to a limit of £2,000.' I asked the condition and he said 'that you'll play a match in Tobago'. So all was fixed, and I made up a programme involving ten separate journeys adding up to nearly 12,000 miles, and nine matches in six different centres. As I was also responsible for the itinerary and collected the money – which came from more than thirty sources of all kinds – as well as the players – I was kept pretty busy.

Dr Eric Williams has been a stern critic of many aspects of Imperial rule, and around this time he considered the interests of Trinidad incompatible with the British-imposed Federation of the West Indies. It was on the non-co-operation of Trinidad and Jamaica in fact that the whole wide concept foundered. But I always remember that it was his friendly intervention that enabled my predominantly English side to make our 1961 tour.

This time Colin Ingleby-Mackenzie, now captain of Hampshire, led us and did so superbly, aided by two much senior old hands from the Commonwealth in Ray Lindwall and Everton Weekes. Again John Haslewood, as treasurer, brought the party to fifteen, the side being as follows: A. C. D. Ingleby-Mackenzie (captain), E. D. Weekes (vice-captain), A. A. Baig, R. W. Barber, R. R. Lindwall, H. J. Rhodes, P. M. Walker, R. A. Gale, I. M. McLachlan, Nawab of Pataudi, A. C. Smith, B. D. Wells and O. S. Wheatley.

Starting in Barbados (the natural kicking-off point for all such tours in the Caribbean with its dry heat, excellent practice wickets and unique cricket atmosphere) we proceeded in turn to Grenada, Trinidad, British Guiana, Trinidad again, Tobago, and finally St Kitts. Grenada provided not only about the finest bathing anywhere in the world, on the Grand Anse beach, but a unique field with blue sea on one side and mountains thick with tropical vegetation on the other. Grenada, by the way, has been British since the French garrison surrendered to the squadron commanded by a presumed ancestor, Commodore Robert Swanton, in 1762. The island was ceded to Great Britain at the Treaty of Paris the following year.

Grenada, island of nutmeg and spices, we found luxuriant and lovely. Thence to the more sophisticated delights of Trinidad where Ray Lindwall showed himself an adept at the jump-up after my wife's heart, and where she and I had the honour of staying for the first of several times with the Governor, Sir Solomon Hochoy, and his wife.

The appointment of this remarkable man was, I suppose, the last but assuredly not the least function of the Crown in respect of the emergent nation of Trinidad. Considering that the population of the island is, broadly speaking, 40% of African descent, 40% Indian, there were obvious merits in picking one of the minority Chinese element if such a man could be found. The genius lay in the choice of this modest, humorous philosopher who began life humbly enough as a government clerk. Governor-General now, since the collapse of the Federation, he is as I write in his thirteenth year of office, a quiet fount of Oriental wisdom in the midst of a sometimes turbulent community.

At Berbice in the hinterland of BG we hunted alligators by the light of torches and played on a ground in the middle of the Rose Hall sugar estate good enough for a Test Match. At Georgetown over Easter we were beaten narrowly and honourably by the West Indian champions, British Guiana, our only defeat.

The Tobago 'high-spots' of Pigeon Point and Buccoo Reef, a mile or two out to sea, on which at low tide one wades about watching through snorkels tropical fish of a thousand colours, are famous tourist haunts of the Caribbean.

Our guide was the vast and genial Anthony, who for the film 'Robinson Crusoe' swam under water lassooing sharks and bringing them up by their tails. That, let me quickly add, wasn't on the programme this time and, come to think of it, one scarcely hears or thinks of sharks in the West Indies. I believe I'm right that no one has been 'taken', as the

Australians say, in the Caribbean for fifty years. Down Under, by contrast, it is not so rare to read of some poor creature swimming to his death. Generally it's a New Australian and only the more horrendous examples rate the newspaper front pages, such as that of the man who dived off the quay-side and never came up. The blue water just became suffused with pink.

St Kitts had not been visited by a touring team since Lord Hawke's in 1896, and were so stimulated by the prospect of our arrival that they had had their ground, Warner Park, levelled and a fine pavilion built. Here as in all the smaller centres the crowds tested the accommodation, and the whole island went *en fête*.

The keenness started as usual at the top with the Chief Minister, Mr Southwell, who was a player of some note. All premiers or equivalent heads of government are cricket enthusiasts in the West Indies. Perhaps they dare not be otherwise! At all events the time-honoured cliché about this game being a breaker-down of barriers between colours, classes and creeds is nowhere so relevant as here, as visiting cricketers have every opportunity to know. Cricket is the *lingua franca*, and the touring players are Very Important People indeed.

Of the ones on this trip Weekes and Lindwall provided the fame and the class, though Ray had a back which sometimes cramped his performance. But there was still that superb thoroughbred action, and occasionally the late swing, both in and out, undetectable until too late. Bob Barber, Harold Rhodes, Abbas Baig and 'Tiger' Pataudi were either on the threshold of Test careers or just approaching them, fine cricketers all, as also was Ian McLachlan (an Arab among other distinctions) who got as near a Test cap two years later as being twelfth man against England at Adelaide.

Of the rest Peter Walker, with three Test appearances the previous summer, was very much of an all-round prospect at that time, as was Alan Smith who had just come down from Oxford after two outstanding years as captain of the University. 'Ossie' Wheatley, after a record-breaking season as opening bowler from Cambridge two years earlier, was just about to start what turned out to be a very successful captaincy of Glamorgan. Bob Gale and 'Bomber' Wells were top-class county players unlikely perhaps to be chosen for an official trip but sure to be excellent value as tourists – as indeed they proved. The 'Bomber's' ripe philosophical observations on the Caribbean scene, and on life in general, delivered in the rich burr of Gloucestershire, provided continuous entertainment. He and the West Indian crowds regarded one another mutually as figures of comedy – they enjoyed each other!

This was the Nawab's first tour and some of the last cricket he played before losing the sight of his right eye almost completely in a motor accident a few months later. It is pleasant to think that the Indian communities of Trinidad and BG had a glimpse of his brilliance before he suffered the handicap which he has fought against so bravely and with such success. This reminds me that a year later 'the Noob' was not only playing again in India but won his first Test caps and got a hundred against England. Gubby Allen was out there, and in congratulating him said:

'Tell me, when did you first think you might still be able to make runs despite having only one eye?'

'When I saw the English bowling.'

It was an answer worthy of his more flamboyant and extrovert father. The 'old Noob' as a batsman, however, was a conventional stylist in comparison with his son about whom there were distinct traces of the reputed wristy oriental magic of 'Ranji', which in my experience was best exemplified by C. K. Nayudu and the unpredictable but devastating Mushtaq Ali.

Talking of brilliance, almost the most gifted cricketer on this side of mine was Barber. He has played altogether 28 times for England and done some fine things. His 185 against Australia at Sydney in 1965–66 for sheer splendour and audacity of stroke has scarcely been matched in my time. Yet to some extent he has been a victim of his temperament – as also of the need to make a livelihood outside the game. If he had chosen to play as a professional, and had found himself under a captain he thoroughly respected, I believe Bob might be rated today as the best all-round England cricketer produced since the war.

All in all, this second tour, more ambitious in scope than the first, seemed welcome and successful, particularly in the stimulation it gave to the smaller centres. We certainly helped St Kitts and Berbice to be recognized as places of call for visiting teams. Tobago has since followed. There was no hitch there this time, and at the end of our game Learie Constantine, present with Dr Williams, promised them an island coach. Whether it was significant that in the election shortly afterwards Tobago changed sides and voted for the government candidate I would not know!

My life is full of instances when a chance remark or meeting has set plans and projects in motion, and the Far-East Tour of 1964 was one of them. Talking about cricket one day at Sandwich in early October 1963 my friend and neighbour, Alec Hill, said, 'If you want to do a bit of good politically why don't you take a side to Malaysia?'

Thinking it over I saw the idea as something of a challenge, the difficulty being that the following spring was the only time in the next few years when I would be free. I had no known source of cash, and no particular cricket contact in Malaysia though I did have in India and Hong Kong, which we would be able to take in. I wrote first to a childhood friend, Sir Douglas Waring, chairman of London Tin, who happened rather tiresomely to be in Nigeria. However he alerted J. M. ('Tiny') Mason of Edward Boustead and Co., President of the Malayan Commercial Association, who promptly sounded the British firms with Malaysian interests who formed his Association.

I said I wanted £5,000 from them, thinking I might get £3,000 or thereabouts from India and Hong Kong, plus something though not much from the profits on games in Malaya. 'Tiny' Mason and Pat Coghlan, of the Rubber Growers' Association, between them proved so persuasive that the rubber and tin people in about a month found £800 more than I had asked for, while M. Chinnaswamy, secretary of the Indian Board of Control, and John Leckie, a friend from POW days, in Hong Kong were equally forthcoming. So all was put in train. With an airways time-table permanently on my desk and the incredibly efficient and delightful Daphne Surfleet (now Benaud) beside it, an itinerary and match programme were made out (in the event we travelled on seven air-lines). The accent of the tour was on the Commonwealth, of which the newly-formed Federation of Malaysia was a recent acquisition. So we recruited Richie Benaud and Ian McLachlan from Australia, the Nawab from India, Gary Sobers and Seymour Nurse from the West Indies, Ken Taylor of Yorkshire from New Zealand, where he was coaching, and 'Sonny' Ramadhin from The Clogger's Arms, outside Oldham, of which he was – and I believe still is – the genial landlord.

Then came several young university players, Mike Griffith, Richard Hutton and Dan Piachaud, plus two good Arab cricketers who were responsible for all their own expenses, Tim Coghlan and Nick Pretzlik. Yet another Arab, Simon Kimmins, son of Anthony Kimmins, the playwright, was due to be thereabouts on business and made himself available for the early games before Benaud and Sobers were due to arrive. Not least Colin Ingleby-Mackenzie – who had led Hampshire to the county championship three years earlier directly after the West Indies tour – accepted the captaincy, and John Haslewood offered his invaluable services as treasurer. Piachaud being Ceylonese, we represented five Commonwealth countries. It was a fine mixed bag altogether, varying in experience from Benaud and Sobers to Pretzlik who had played for Eton and the Public Schools at Lord's only in the preceding summer. Only four were offered professional fees, Taylor and the three West Indians.

Colours were ordered (as before single palm trees on a green ground), bats, pads and gloves were generously provided by Slazengers, publicity material and photographs sent forward, tour cards were printed, marching orders issued, and on 15 March, six months after Alec Hill's suggestion, we flew off on the first hop from London to Penang.

Three days later in the steamy tropic heat of that gorgeous island we first took the field – and, incidentally, unacclimatized, had a narrow escape from defeat. School parties came to watch from places as far away on the mainland as Perak and Ipoh, and for our four-day visit Penang was in festal mood.

The Malaysian CA President's XI was a positive United Nations affair, with a strong Chinese flavour, several Indians also, and an Australian or two from the RAAF station on the island, as well as two or three expatriate Englishmen. The Chinese inhabitants of Malaysia took to the game, both in the playing and administrative side, much more readily than the Malays, who gave the impression of finding it rather strenuous for their taste.

Support for the tour however came from the Malays at the top. They all gave parties for us, while the Governor of Penang, His Excellency Raja Tun Uda El-Haj, fortifying himself with an able partner, successfully challenged Haslewood (a former Italian champion) and me to a round of golf before breakfast. In that climate it was the most sensible time to play.

It can be imagined with what a wealth of feeling I touched down at Singapore which I had last seen under Jap rule, as I was marched from River Valley Road past the cricket ground to the railway station *en route* for Thailand. One travelled now rather more comfortably in the Deputy High Commissioner's car – a Union Jack on the bonnet in front rather than a Jap bayonet disagreeably close behind. He was a friend of Oxford days, P. B. C. Moore, a member of the unbeaten University rugger side of 1946, and now Deputy Private Secretary to the Queen. John Haslewood and I stayed with Philip Moore, and both at Singapore and Kuala Lumpur, where we were entertained by the High Commissioner, Lord Head, all was done to make us welcome. In fact like most touring teams, if they give the impression that they appreciate hospitality, we were thoroughly spoiled. At Singapore it was fascinating going over such of the battleground as was recognizable, and playing golf on the course on to which I had directed several hundred shells twenty-odd years before.

The star match was at the capital, Kuala Lumpur, over Easter on the marvellously-situated Selangor Club ground in the heart of the city, overlooked by the government buildings. Apart from the pitch, which tended to crumble, it was fit for a Test match, as too was the ground at Singapore, also in a central cluster alongside the Supreme Court and the Anglican Cathedral. It was clear just where cricket stood with the nineteenth-century empire-builders.

We had four days' cricket in KL, wherein the most memorable performance (all-round!) was put up by Gary Sobers. In our first innings, going in No. 3, he was bowled first ball by what to him was a perfectly-pitched off-break. The bowler was Dr Alex Delilkan, a very good wrist-spinner. A crowd filling the ground was vastly disappointed. When All-Malaysia went in Haslewood said in jest, 'You've let them down pretty badly, you'd better go and do a hat-trick.'

Gary got his hat-trick with the last three balls of his first over, and with the first two balls of his second clean bowled two more. What is more the next batsman (No. 7) was so late on his first ball, an in-dipping yorker, that it screwed off the bottom of the bat almost into the stumps. The batsmen were all, at the worst, good Minor County standard – but, of course, Sobers with the new ball is a proposition to test the best, as Geoff Boycott would testify.

I've never before or since seen five wickets in five balls, and I suppose few people have. Anyhow an opening bat glorying in the name of Ranjit Singh, surveying the wreck of the innings from the other end, bravely carried his bat for 56, to retrieve his side's honour. Then when the Commonwealth XI went in again Sobers, determined to give the crowd something to remember him by as a batsman, was promptly caught in the slips for 1.

The pay-off came next day when Gary got loose with 18 holes of golf before the cricket, then in a temperature of 90° in the shade made a hundred in an hour and a quarter, and finally for luck threw in 14 overs. I've never known anyone with quite so much compulsive energy as this man.

It was pleasant indeed to hear from Philip Moore that 'this visit has done more good for the Commonwealth than any occasion during my four years in Singapore,' while Lord Head wrote congratulating us on the 'unqualified success' of our visit. He said: 'I have heard nothing but praise and appreciation on all sides, both concerning the spirit in which the cricket has been played and about the friendliness and understanding of all individual members of your side.'

I sent copies of some of the letters to those in London whose generosity had made the tour possible, and there is no point in pretending that one was not thrilled to read sentiments such as these and others like them from people in authority including the President of the Malayan Cricket Association, Dr Ong Swee Law, of whom we all became fond, and who with his hon. sec., Peter Selvanayagam and hon. treasurer, Cecil Cooke, did so much work on our behalf.

John Leckie and his friends were equally solicitous in Hong Kong, where we played four days' cricket, two on the £17m ground in the middle of the city where Pretzlik hit a six smack against the communist Bank of China, and two on the mainland at Kowloon. We also got in a golf match against Royal Hong Kong GC at Fanling from which you can see over the border into communist China. There is a vast fascination about Hong Kong which, partly at least, derives from the extraordinary situation of a British colony populated by 3½ million Chinese pursuing a flourishing existence right in the lion's mouth. It is almost the last relic of colonial power, and it is as though all concerned combine to show British rule at its very best.

The Royal Bangkok Sports Club had asked us to play a game on our way through from Hong Kong to Calcutta, and though the time was all too short they were two days that no one would have missed. This is one of the great sporting clubs of the east, catering for almost every variety of games-player. There were said to be more than 2,000 members of forty nationalities, but running clubs is one of the things that the British are said to be best at, as this tour and not least this club gave evidence. No one wanted to leave, but it was as well they did, for the evening entertainment was prodigal, to say the least. Future tour managers calling in may like to know in respect of so-called massage parlours that the phrase is an under-statement.

I thought I could not come so near without seeing some of the old places, and was generously provided by the Shell Co. with an air-conditioned car and driver. Ken Taylor came with his camera, and kindly took for me a film of some of the POW trouble-spots, now mercifully reclaimed by the jungle, and the huge temple with the golden dome at Nakom Patom where the so-called hospital was, and the graves in endless rows, beautifully tended, which were the chief object of my pilgrimage.

The War Graves Commission has done a wonderfully painstaking work in seeking out the graveyards in the jungle camps and reburying, with the names carved on row upon row of crosses, thousands in all, in two locations, one at Kanchanaburi, the other up-river near Chungkai. We went upstream to Chungkai in a rather superior pom-pom, not struggling much against the current since March is the dry season and the river was placid enough. Then we came back and ate a picnic lunch in the shadow of the Bridge over the River Kwai which now carries the railway up, I believe, to Tarso or thereabouts. Nature has possessed the rest, sleepers and rails long since purloined by the inhabitants. There is a marvellous peace in those cemeteries which the Thai curator takes much pride in looking after. Back in Bangkok I located the trader, Boon Pong, who at risk of his own life saved so many of ours. It was a joy to see that he was prosperously installed in King Rama I Road, proud proprietor of the Boon Pong Bus Company.

The climax of the tour, naturally, was the concluding four-day match against the Indian XI at Calcutta. We approached this match a bit warily not so much because the side fielded against us was going to be (apart from Pataudi, playing for us) virtually that which had just taken part in five Test draws against England but because old Anglo-Indians had warned us that to play cricket in Calcutta in April was a folly which we might easily not survive. There was a lot of well-intentioned warning about mad dogs and Englishmen, etcetera.

It was hot, infernally hot, on none of the four days less than 100° and on one 107°. But despite this the cricket was remarkably good, and the interesting thing was that my side, which comprised five Englishmen, three West Indians, an

Australian, an Indian and a Ceylonese, stood up to the conditions every bit as well as the home side. Play began each day at ten o'clock and lasted five hours, excluding an hour for lunch at the hottest time of the day.

MCC had recently gone home with a record of nine draws in ten matches – which perhaps was why the Maharajah of Cooch Behar – the amiable 'Cooch' – had laid me a thousand rupees to a hundred against our winning. But we did win, on the fourth afternoon, by seven wickets with ten minutes to spare, and it was pretty nearly a straight victory since Chandu Borde's second innings declaration was at 215 for eight, with no real batting left. They had led us on first innings by 348 against 321, and the target of 243 in three hours represented, we reckoned, five runs an over considering there were drink intervals every 45 minutes.

Gary Sobers with nine wickets in the match and 123 in the first innings was our trump card, but it's questionable whether even the physical effort required in this performance was as great as that of Seymour Nurse who made 106 and 135 not out and was on the field for the whole match less two hours. How Seymour must have longed for the shade of the Eden Gardens pavilion after he had reached his second hundred! But with great determination he held his end while Richie Benaud unleashed a finely-controlled assault on the unfortunate Bapu Nadkarni whom MCC had declared could not be got at. Against them in the Tests he had bowled 213 overs for 278 runs with his accurate slowish left-arm stuff: 1·3 an over! His analysis now was 10–0–60–0, the crowning blow being a broken wrist as he tried bravely to take a return catch of shattering velocity.

Let us not relapse into technicalities, but briefly Richie countered the suspicion of in-swing by hitting 'from inside out', as the golfers say, aiming at and over mid-off, instead of trying to 'work' the ball to leg through a strong cordon in the current English fashion.

Piachaud bowled admirably, and Griffith kept so well that both Benaud and Sobers thought him sure to be keeping for England – this of course was before Alan Knott had made his bow – within a year or two. But Jim Parks that summer took the gloves for England as well as for Sussex, and as I write he is still wearing them, and doing so ably enough. So for Mike the chance has never come.

The Indians took the result with their usual good grace, especially Berry Sarbadhikary, the doyen of the Indian writers, as also did 'Vizzy' – the old Maharajkumar of Vizianagram, who had led the first Indian Test side to England – over the air. He did the running commentary pretty well non-stop, while I, a cool drink at my elbow, answered up from time to time to 'What do you think, Jim?'

I thought it was all splendid, and it was a small matter that 'Cooch' had had to leave Calcutta before the last day. When I saw him in England he said, 'Those rupees are waiting for you in India – I can't get them out.' He is dead, alas! So they're waiting no longer.

The crowds were large, but in view of recent history I should have some qualms perhaps recalling that the profits from the match were devoted by the Indian Board to the National Defence Fund.

As to our cash position we finished the tour £1,000 up, after foregoing our percentage of the profit in Malaya. When therefore the Prime Minister of the Federation, Tunku Abdul Rahman, came to London in the summer of 1964 for the Prime Ministers' Conference, he accepted from me at a dinner of the Malayan Association, a cheque for £1,000 for the benefit of Malayan cricket, and I from him a lovely Kelantan silver tray with the coats of arms of all the member-states of the Federation embossed on the rim. It stands on my bookshelf to remind me of six crowded, happy weeks.

Apart from an Arab tour to Barbados to play the island clubs in 1967 – a not inconsiderable effort by a small club wherein all concerned paid their own expenses – my only personal touring venture since then was the organizing part in the visit of the Duke of Norfolk's team to the West Indies in 1970. Like many another good deed in a naughty world this one happened in a sense accidentally, or at least as a result of an apparently chance remark.

I was proposing the West Indies team's health at the British Sportsman's Club luncheon of welcome and therefore sitting at the Chairman's table as also, of course, were Gary Sobers, the captain, and the manager, Clyde Walcott. The Duke, talking nostalgically of the side he took some long while ago to Jamaica, said 'Perhaps it's time I took another.' I said, 'If you aren't careful someone might take you up on that.'

Thereupon the Earl Marshal remarked that he'd be pretty busy for some weeks preparing for the Investiture of the Prince of Wales, but let us talk about it after that. So it came about, Peter Short, secretary of the West Indies Board, confirming the willingness of that body to collaborate since it was established that the team would pay its own way.

Now that the annual Shell Shield gives the major territories regular competitive first-class cricket there is less room in the calendar, and rather less need, for the visit of other touring sides to Barbados, Trinidad, Guyana and Jamaica. The smaller islands of the Windwards and Leewards however, who only compete in the Shield as one combined team, are another matter. They stand much in need of the sort of fillip that only a side from overseas can bring. So we arranged to play at four of the smaller islands, St Lucia, Dominica, St Vincent and Tobago, in addition to Trinidad and Barbados.

Part of our manager's object was to give hard-wicket hot-country experience to as many as possible who might be in the running to go on the MCC tour of Australia the following winter, and of these Derek Underwood and Alan Ward went (though the unfortunate Ward was soon laid low and had to come home), while of the rest Mike Denness, Tony Greig and Robin Hobbs can only have missed selection by a little. Many unofficial selectors would have had at least one in their side, or indeed all three. There were six England cricketers among the fourteen when we travelled, while Greig and Old won caps the following summer.

The only man unknown to the cricket public was the twenty-one-year-old Lord Cottenham, who came on an amateur basis and bowled fast enough in the one-day games and in practice to surprise some of the older hands who nowadays have no means of knowing that there are plenty of very good cricketers outside the first-class game. On this evidence there was not very much difference in speed between Ward and Charlie Cottenham.

Not the least happy aspect of the tour, coming as it did in late February and March, was to give Colin Cowdrey the chance of getting back into the swim after having lost most of the 1969 season with a torn Achilles tendon. He was keen to come, so the Duke had a ready-made captain.

It needs no saying that the tour under such management went like a bomb, giving the treasurer a singularly easy ride and the chance of a good look at St Lucia and St Vincent, two islands in the friendly, luxuriant Caribbean tradition neither of which I had seen before. The same was true of Dominica, only more so in terms of scenic magnificence, but I had only been able to organize a twenty-four-hour stay there, for which I was quite rightly blamed by all and sundry.

The Dominican game was unforgettable – even to an old sweat like me who can remember ancient cricket history fairly readily but all too often fails to recall what happened yesterday or the day before. Surviving not without moments of peril a winding coast-to-coast drive over the high spine of Dominica from the airport to Roseau, the capital, we suddenly found ourselves in a ground of unbelievable loveliness surrounded by palms and exotic flowering trees in the middle of the Botanical Gardens. They had never seen an overseas side before, and presumably therefore very few Englishmen, though Glamorgan were due to give them the equally strange sight of a lot of Welshmen a month or so later. So every possible vantage perch was occupied by a crowd of five thousand – which we worked out as one in twelve of a population scattered over an island measuring 300 square miles.

Dominica boasted five of the Windward Islands' team, and they gave us a rousing game, every aspect of which was scrutinized with the fervour one associates with a West Indian Test match – which in a sense it was. When at the climax Grayson Shillingford, the Test bowler, hit five sixes, most of which were still rising when they disappeared into the foliage outside the field, the joy and the excitement were alike unconfined. We won finally by 8 runs, 191 to 183.

Our manager was in high humour. Riotously received, he had gone out to field for a while, discreetly covered at first slip from the speed of Alan Ward by Mike Griffith on one side and Philip Sharpe on the other. At the end came his presentation of the Man of the Match award which we always made to the opposition in the Gillette-style games. Surrounded by the entire crowd, at the foot of the pavilion steps, microphone in hand, the Duke in his dry, bantering way struck, as he always did, just the right sentimental notes, and sent everyone home feeling that this was one of the great days of their lives. For our part we returned to the considerable comforts of the much-to-be-recommended Fort Young Hotel.

Returning at crack of dawn next morning by the precipitous road to the airport, and listening to Bernard Norfolk helping to dispel, by popular request, the perils of the journey by reminiscing about the Coronation and Churchill's funeral and other high occasions of State, one felt that this visit alone had made the whole expedition worth while.

The same could be said of our stay in Tobago, where Pat Coghlan's hospitality to us all over our three-day stay was prodigious. His Mount Irvine development there, comprising hotel, golf course, club-house serving a dozen cottages, and residential estate around the perimeter, is the best thing of its kind I have come across anywhere. The course is championship quality, with fairways (though only two years old when we were there) already better than I have ever encountered – which, as it happens, is saying a good deal. On this flawless Tifton Ormonde turf the ball simply sits up and looks at you.

The Duke's side was M. C. Cowdrey (captain), J. Birkenshaw, the Earl of Cottenham, M. H. Denness, M. J. Edwards, A. W. Greig, M. G. Griffith, R. N. S. Hobbs, B. Leadbeater, C. M. Old, P. J. Sharpe, D. L. Underwood, A. Ward, with C. S. Elliott accompanying as umpire.

This party, like the three earlier ones mentioned in this chapter, was picked with an eye to avoiding discordant elements, and four utterly harmonious tours were the result. But however carefully a side is selected a very great deal rests on the choice of captain, and here all concerned were extraordinarily lucky in the two Colins, Cowdrey and Ingleby-Mackenzie. It was characteristic of the former that he was diffident about leading my 1956 side. At twenty-three he was younger than most of them, though he had his first triumphal Australian tour behind him, and, of course, had led Oxford, and was just about to captain Kent.

I will not embarrass Colin by reciting a catalogue of his virtues but must mention one. I have never known anyone more considerate for the feelings of others, of all ages and types – which, of course, is why he has always had the maximum response from all the many sides he has led. Incidentally, it helps also, I think, to explain what is sometimes levelled against him as a weakness, the difficulty of making up his mind. He simply dislikes disappointing people.

It is an indication of how diverse the personalities of good captains can be that Ingleby-Mackenzie and Cowdrey have both been so successful, for in style and outward expression they are so different. Ingleby-Mackenzie's debonair sparkle is genuine enough, for in his philosophy life and cricket are equally to be savoured and enjoyed. But there is a good brain and a shrewd assessment of people behind the façade.

We were having tea one day at the beginning of August 1961 at Canterbury when a serious young man from the BBC asked for a word with him. The Hampshire captain excused himself and was soon back, smiling as usual, to resume our conversation. That evening on the television news one heard the exchange by which many remember him.

'Hampshire are having a great season. Have you any particular training schedule?'

'Certainly,' says Colin. 'In three words, wine, women and song.' The young man, rocked by this revolutionary recipe, can only murmur something about a curfew. Are there any restrictions?

'Oh, yes, we all have to be in bed by breakfast.'

As I have indicated this sally was completely spontaneous. And, of course, Colin was making a perfectly serious point. He had led Hampshire on a loose rein, according to his nature, and I don't suppose that they kicked over the traces any more often than those of any other side. They respected their freedom without abusing it. As they neared the title I believe there was a move towards curfews and taboos, but the captain would have none of them. 'We've relaxed so far,' he decided, 'and we'll go on playing that way.' They did and they won the Championship, and no success could have been more popular. Even in the early 'sixties Ingleby-Mackenzie stood out from the average run of county captains.

'Atmosphere' is something that no one can define but all except the least sensitive can detect. With Ingleby-Mackenzie in charge it was always easy, and often hilariously funny: which is the best tribute I can pay him.

13

On the Air

The broadcasting of games is about as old as my adult recollections of them. I joined the *Evening Standard*, aged twenty, in September 1927, and earlier that year rugger, soccer and cricket had been put over the air for the first time. Lawn tennis soon followed but golf seems actually to have waited until well into the 'thirties for its first coverage. There is a certain vagueness about the early history of sports broadcasting because so many of the BBC's records were destroyed by bombs. H. B. T. Wakelam, the famous Teddy, was however indubitably the first man to broadcast a game, and it was England v. Wales at Twickenham, on 15 January 1927. The very next Saturday he found himself describing the other code at Highbury, the match being Arsenal v. Sheffield United. John Arlott has some interesting things to tell about the pioneer efforts of Wakelam and others in *Armchair Cricket*, the BBC publication edited by Brian Johnston. I can add a little to this, and in particular a detail which Teddy himself thought extremely important.

The BBC staff man in charge at Twickenham on that red-letter day was Lance Sieveking, and it was this versatile and highly-talented figure in early radio who thought of the brilliant gimmick of sitting a blind man from St Dunstan's in front of the broadcast box and telling Teddy simply to describe to this person what was happening out on the field. Sieveking himself also devised the system of dividing the ground into squares to make it easier for the listener to follow the game, and he was there in the box as the anonymous voice interpolating from time to time 'square two' or wherever the ball might be. Wakelam, as I say, set great store by the technique of telling the blind man all about it, and this is easy for me at least to understand since the first thing I was ever told about broadcasting (I expect by S. J. de Lotbinière, the mentor of all of us in the 'thirties) was to remember that I was talking to each separate single person. Think of someone who might be interested, if you like, and describe what was happening to him. Don't ever imagine you're talking to the wide, wide world.

My own first broadcast in the old Empire Service was on a Saturday evening, and I saw no reason to forgo the Blackheath Football Club's Annual Dinner at the Café Royal. I therefore slipped away, took a cab up Regent Street to Broadcasting House, and – relaxed by the dinner and the company – said my piece and returned to the party. Having got over the first talk, I never remember being nervous of the microphone since. Almost everyone gets a little taut at times: the important thing is that no sense of strain should get across to the listeners or viewers.

Lord Bernstein (a Barbados neighbour) was less lucky in his introduction to the microphone, as I recently discovered when we were exchanging memories of early broadcasters and discussing the technique of talking on the air. His first performance was in the old Savoy Hill days, back in the 'twenties. He duly presented himself, and in a sober suit, script in pocket, was ushered into the presence of a very superior person, immaculate in a dinner jacket, who did not trouble to disguise the fact that he considered him distinctly under-dressed.

Bernstein's confidence, though fortified also by a good dinner, at the Savoy Grill, ebbed further when he found himself in a large room with a lectern and microphone in the middle, and, facing him on the wall, a bold notice which said: 'Remember, when the red light comes up the world will be listening' – or words to that effect. Luckily, said the boss of Granada television, he remembered that his mother would be listening through the headphones, and so he just talked to her.

By the way, the Rugby Union, not always regarded in those days as a particularly go-ahead body, at once recognized the importance of the new medium, and installed the broadcast box in the best possible position above the dressing-room 'tunnel' in the middle of the West Stand. Howard Marshall by contrast, when he first broadcast about cricket at Lord's, was not even allowed to do so from the ground. According to Arlott 'he had to dart off at lunch, tea, and the close of play and broadcast his account from a house in Grove End Road, where the microphone was installed in a semi-basement, completely unscreened from local noise so that, on one occasion, he found himself competing with the sound of a child's piano lesson in a room above'.

Wakelam covered cricket as well as the two codes of football in that initial year of 1927, though the very first man to talk about cricket over the air, appropriately enough, was 'Plum' Warner, who gave summaries of the first match of the first tour by a New Zealand team to England, against Essex at Leyton. Note that these were summaries, eye-witness accounts related afterwards, since cricket was considered too slow to lend itself to running commentary. When Marshall told the story of Hedley Verity's great triumph at Lord's against Australia in 1934 – he was allowed into the ground by now, though the BBC had to make do with a room on the top floor of the Tavern over square-leg – it was only in retrospect. Lobby initiated cricket running commentaries, as he did much else when he became Director of Outside Broadcasts in 1935.

Just as games were lucky in the early signed writers so they were in the first broadcasters. The backgrounds of Teddy Wakelam and Howard Marshall, as it happened, were much akin. Both were Harlequins and both chiefly footballers and very good ones, though both were also reputable club cricketers. They were more or less of an age, Wakelam from Marlborough and Cambridge, Marshall Haileybury and Oxford. Players themselves, they presented the games they talked about with enthusiasm, with sympathetic understanding and withal an occasional dry humour. Consciously or not broadcasters borrow from one another, and those that followed owed much to these two, who were after all developing a new art-form – out of thin air. Both, incidentally, for many years broadcast and wrote simultaneously and regularly, as Arlott and I, and a few but not many more, have done since. Howard had a marvellous voice, rich, deep and mellow, which added dignity to whatever he was describing. It was eminently suitable for Coronations – and, of course, cricket. The pace of his delivery by modern standards was slow – measured is the word – which does not mean he could not engender excitement. One could not imagine him 'fluffing', still less getting flustered. There was a balance both in his estimations and in the language in which he conveyed them – and, talking of language, he would not have dabbled in the technical jargon, much too much of which surely has drifted into the broadcast box from the dressing-rooms.

It was in 1939 that I joined Howard Marshall and Michael Standing in broadcasting the Tests against the West Indies. These were the first Tests in England covered ball by ball throughout the day, this being due, so the story had it, to a rash promise made by a Governor of the BBC on a winter cruise of the West Indies. When he came back to Broadcasting

House there was some consternation at what he had let the Corporation in for. Standing similarly was a club cricketer, a bowler of some distinction, and unlike Lobby both an inside and an outside man. He had a light-hearted programme called 'Standing on the Corner' wherein he roamed with a microphone chatting to willing passers-by on any subject that struck his fancy – or theirs. Michael succeeded de Lotbinière as Head of Outside Broadcasts, after which both travelled steadily up the BBC hierarchy, a Director of this, Controller of that, until their respective retirements a few years ago. I allow myself the thought that if, in the 'sixties, the luck – or the politics – of the business had landed either at the summit the BBC would have stuck a good deal more closely to its earlier ideals, and Lord Reith would assuredly have died a happier man.

Lobby's first-hand OB experience was said to have been limited to a broadcast of the Boat Race when the running commentary of John Snagge (the original and inimitable 'In-Out-In-Outer') from the BBC launch was supplemented by impressions by Lobby from an aeroplane.

This was no doubt a splendid idea in theory, but the aircraft was very flimsy, and there was a lot of turbulence over the Thames. The comments from above grew briefer as the broadcaster's health deteriorated, and the last hurried 'Back to the launch!' was said to have been gasped out in the very nick of time.

There is not an outside broadcaster of my generation who will not acknowledge a real debt to de Lotbinière. He listened a lot and never failed to make some constructive, helpful comment on one's performance. Once he conducted what today would be called a teach-in, illustrating his lecture with commentary recordings. Thanks to Robert Hudson, the present Head of Outside Broadcasts, himself, by the way, a broadcaster of unusually wide range before he took the reins of administration, here is a list of those who attended at Broadcasting House on 26 November 1951 :

Harold Abrahams, Rex Alston, Eamonn Andrews, W. Barrington Dalby, Michael Barsley, Patrick Burns, Jack Crump, Richard Dimbleby, Peter Dimmock, Charles Gardner, Arthur Gilligan, Raymond Glendenning, Billy Griffith, Michael Henderson, Robert Hudson, C. A. Kershaw, John Lane, David Lloyd James, Howard Marshall, Richard North, Daphne Padel, C. Parker, Robin Richards, Max- Robertson, Audrey Russell, Berkeley Smith, John Snagge, David Southwood,

E. W. Swanton, Wynford Vaughan Thomas, Graham Walker, Peter West.

There are not many of these names which fail to strike a chord more than twenty years later.

The art of the running commentary has changed somewhat since some of these were in their prime, especially in cricket where the modern programming generally gives little scope (Test Matches excepted) to the essayist, more to the crisp reporter. County cricket, whether the three or one-day form, is now fitted into a swiftly-moving sporting kaleidoscope, and the half-hour devoted to a single match, or to two, is no more. In the first twenty years after the war I broadcast a great many of these longer pieces including some hardy annuals such as one of the two Roses' Matches, Middlesex v. Surrey, and the Lord's Week comprising the University Match and Gentlemen and Players. The last of these frequently produced some of the best cricket of the summer – which is not to say the scoring might not sometimes be slow.

Once as I finished a half-hour stint, Roy Webber scoring beside me almost exploded with excitement. 'Did you realize that in the whole time they only scored one run?' he asked. No doubt I ought to have noted it, and perhaps it was on one of the slips of paper which the scorer passes across. But I had been too absorbed in the struggle to register the fact. Never, I expect, had it happened at Lord's on a Thursday in July. I used to feel guilty sometimes failing to avail myself of the tit-bits of esoteric information painstakingly acquired, but I was reminded recently, coming across a cutting from *The Spectator* of 1960, that I was not immune, on television anyway, from the fault of purveying too much fact. The author is Peter Forster:

> John Arlott over on steam is still the best of the commentators, with that rustic Bruno voice which occasionally takes wings, but the admirable E. W. ('Jim') Swanton does viewers pretty well, with his suitably housemasterly manner and line of discreet euphemism. ('Dexter's been hit in the bread-basket, perhaps slightly below.') My main reservation is that he and the others in the commentators' box tend to befog us with statistics, too few of which are vital. I would rather watch for a moment in silence than know that this was the first maiden over bowled by a left-handed spinner with brown hair immediately after lunch at Trent Bridge on July 9 – since 1911.

This criticism has my sympathy, but it is – or used to be – hard to ignore the zeal of the scorers who now are dignified by the title of statisticians. Poor Roy Webber – who fell down dead in the street at the age of forty-eight outside the office of *Playfair Monthly* – was as near infallible as makes no matter, as also was the first of the tribe, Arthur Wrigley, who also died suddenly and in early middle age.

Strangely, many of the broadcast memories that are clearest concern not Tests but County games and the classics at Lord's: I can see Emrys Davies, the pride of Llanelli, making a hundred and plenty in the summer before the war at Swansea, my 'No. 2' on the pavilion roof being a recent BBC recruit soon to become famous, Wynford Vaughan Thomas. There's no more fervent or responsive crowd than that at Swansea – they could well play a Test Match there. At Canterbury I was lucky enough to be on the air when Les Ames, against Middlesex in the Week, was completing his hundredth hundred, a great sentimental occasion. There was a wonderfully exciting finish at Southampton in 1949 when the New Zealanders scored at a tremendous rate to beat Hampshire with a minute or two to spare. The Overseas Service took a long commentary – perhaps half-an-hour – right up to the finish, and when I was in New Zealand nearly two years later I was usually introduced as the chap who had been on the air the day of the exciting win over Hampshire.

Opinions vary among commentators as to whether they prefer a closed-in box aloof from crowd noise and contact or to identify themselves more closely with the scene. I liked to be surrounded, in order to pick up the atmosphere. Also the presence of knowledgeable spectators was something of a challenge and a stimulant – especially in Yorkshire. Sheffield was best for this, and soon after the war there was a tremendous last day of a Roses' match there at Whitsuntide when in my pre-lunch session I told all who could do so to come along to Bramall Lane for an afternoon to remember. Over the interval the gate which had been good for a third day pretty well doubled, to the astonishment and delight of Yorkshire's ever-charming and helpful secretary, John Nash. The crowd got their excitement all right, but not exactly what they wanted since Lancashire, thanks to that admirable and underrated bowler, Roy Tattersall, won a narrow victory.

I always liked the company of friends in the box – someone specific to talk to. Entertainers of whatever sort seem to be attracted by cricket, and sometimes in Yorkshire Wilfred

Pickles used to join us. One day at Headingley I had with me not only Wilfred but John and Katharine Worsley who were taking me back for the week-end to Hovingham. No one could be utterly dull in the presence of Katharine, now Duchess of Kent, who moreover had had a thorough cricket education with two playing brothers and a father who had captained Yorkshire. Hovingham is the perfect private ground, on which the Arabs were privileged annually to play against Sir William Worsley's side with our host umpire at one end, dear Maurice Leyland at the other, and two or three Yorkshire or ex-Yorkshire players usually against us.

Talking of contact with spectators, when I first went to South Africa before the war cricket broadcasting was a complete novelty, and the open boxes at Cape Town and Durban were a great attraction. As many as could crowd round used to stay on to hear my close-of-play summaries back to England. So far as I was concerned the more the merrier.

One of the pleasantest parts of the job was broadcasting good news from Australia to a cold and gloomy England, to an audience getting up or having breakfast. In 1950 Freddie Brown's side had been very much up against it in the early State matches, and no one gave them a chance in the Tests. But on the first day of the First Test at Brisbane they put up a tremendous performance, bowling out Australia on a plumb wicket (Bedser and Bailey chiefly) for 228.

Gosh, this will please them at home, I thought, and for ten minutes in my close-of-play summary I let myself go. As I came out of the box, limp and thirsty with the effort, the bored engineer said laconically, 'Suppose ya know we never got through?' The Australian Broadcasting Commission was a more haphazard organization then than it is today.

I recall another misfortune of a minor kind when I was doing an 'in vision' television summary at Trent Bridge. The new electric scoreboard had been recently installed in which the figures were picked out by light bulbs. I said my piece, concluding with the words 'Now let me just repeat the score, England are . . .' But when I glanced over to the board to give the total nothing showed. They had switched off the lights. Brian Johnston says my expression at that moment was worth a lot. I was completely thrown, having foolishly relied on the board and not jotted the score down. So I had to make a shot at it, and luckily (I believe) got it right.

Such misfortunes are apt to be remembered, but what

tickled the viewers above anything was when, as sometimes used to happen where there was no convenient shelter within range of the camera, one had to do a summary standing in the rain. 'I saw you out there at Edgbaston' – or wherever it might be, they'd say with the utmost glee. 'You *must* have got wet.' It seemed almost a shame to spoil the fun by standing under an umbrella.

I have always enjoyed giving a summarized picture of the day at the close, whether on vision or sound, but it is a fairly concentrated exercise done off the cuff with a minimum of notes, and in this particular thing I can be easily put off by adjacent movements or conversation. The TV producer and his team of technicians (some 30 all told) do an excellent job presenting Test cricket, but often one used to feel that the last person they ever thought about was the commentator. I was doing a TV close-of-play summary one evening at Headingley when, immediately behind the camera I was looking into and only a few yards away, a fool of a stage-manager started waving his arms about like a lunatic. I stood this for a few seconds, then paused, pointed, and told him sternly to keep still. This must have looked strange to a million viewers, but I couldn't otherwise have continued to make sense. Anyway, one lady wrote in to say that my gesture had put her crying baby to sleep. The reason for the SM getting excited, it turned out, was nothing more serious than a man behind me, and therefore 'in shot', stacking chairs. A natural scene, surely!

It was at Headingley, too, where a far too personal aside winged its way over the air and gave poor Peter Dimmock, head of TV Outside Broadcasts, a bad turn. I was due to hand over midway through one morning to Henry Longhurst at the Open Golf Championship. Some seconds after I had done so and with our monitor showing the picture from Lytham St Anne's (or it might have been Birkdale) I added to Denis Compton '. . . And I bet he's got his gin bottle up there on the tower.'

Horror! We had gone over in vision, but someone had neglected to switch the sound, our microphone was still up, and my aside had gone out loud and clear. The golf commentators used sometimes to be marooned on their towers for ages, and it must have been dry as well as windy work. Who wouldn't be wanting a drink around lunch-time anyway? Certainly not Longhurst who was only amused by the whole thing. Peter was afraid he'd been libelled! But I'd broken a cardinal rule, talking before it was certain that the mike was dead.

Rex Alston once had an experience of this kind which caused much amusement. He had been broadcasting a match at Wimbledon involving an American called Miss Moran, more generally known as 'Gorgeous Gussie', whose frilly panties made no small sensation. After the broadcast ended Rex and his companions swapped views as to the lady's charms, and their comments were noted with interest by some of the top hierarchy at Broadcasting House. They had been listening to the tennis, and the mikes had remained live. Rex Alston too – the very pillar of decorum!

Rex Alston, John Arlott and I did the Tests on sound in the early years after the war before I began alternating between sound and television wherein our team was generally Brian Johnston, Peter West and myself. Subsequently many other names have been brought in. They include Robert Hudson, Alan Gibson, Freddie Brown, Trevor Bailey, Richie Benaud, Jack Fingleton, Denis Compton and Ted Dexter. All, of course, have their individual styles, and special qualities, but the ground-rules for each media, worked out in the early days, remain more or less constant.

I can't say I enjoyed one job more than the other, though nothing perhaps was quite so satisfying as giving the commentary on the tenser phases of a great Test Match on television, preferably in harness with someone from 'the other side', either Benaud or Fingleton. Television commentary in a sense is the more difficult since one is always aware that it is impossible to satisfy everyone. The knowledgeable cricketer looking in will need only the minimum of information and a technical point or two from time to time, while at the other end of the scale someone who knows little or nothing of the game will prefer plenty of talk, almost a sound commentary. These people in fact are better suited probably if they turn off the TV commentary and tune in to sound – as many do, for varied reasons. One cannot please everyone, but the golden rule is to say too little rather than too much. Hence the phrase 'the pregnant pause'. Leave the picture to tell the story unless you are sure you can embellish it.

Nowadays I stick to summaries at each day's close of play on sound, which I do with the score-card and the minimum of notes in front of me and the stop-watch in my hand. I always prefer talking *ex tempore* but in this case it is essential because the length of the summary is regulated by the start and duration of the last over. If a fast bowler starts the over at 6.29½ and you have to return listeners to the studio by 6.36½ there will be only about two minutes of summary. If the game ends prompt at 6.30 it will be three times as long. The rule that the next programme must begin dead on the minute is inflexible and there was one West Indian series when I was doing the TV summaries, and Wes Hall, with his enormous run, always seemed to be starting an over around 6.30, which meant one was keyed up ready but never got on the air at all. This was distinctly frustrating, and was probably one of the reasons why TV gave up the formal one-man close-of-play summary.

As I say, all these experienced men have their individual virtues and their particular admirers, but to one cricket owes a special debt not so much because he happens to have done more talking about the game over the last quarter of a century than anyone else but because in the post-war years his manner and style attracted a new and wider audience. I mean, of course, John Arlott who managed to weave together as much information about the progress of the game as the average listener wanted along with the fruits of his observation on players, spectators and the scene generally, all laced with humour and put across in an intimate, confidential way and a rich Hampshire accent. The voice evoked the village green and rustic England and leisurely days in the sun.

Arlott was not quite everyone's cup of tea – who is? – but his following broadened significantly the number of listeners interested in cricket. He made many converts, especially among women.

If Arlott is an enthusiast of a philosophical kind Brian Johnston, the first holder of the office of BBC Cricket Correspondent, is no less a one but in an entirely different mould. In a perhaps over-critical age Brian seems to set himself deliberately against the current trend. He sees the best in everyone and everything, and puts it all across with a gusto that many years in the game have not diminished a bit. He is the player's friend – indeed the friend of the whole world of cricket, and if that can be said with complete truth of anyone else the name escapes me.

Rex Alston, a more than useful player of several games as well as being an athletic blue, was for many years the all-rounder of OB sport, equally at home at Lord's, Wimbledon, Twickenham or the White City. He and the evergreen Harold

Abrahams did much to popularize athletics in the post-war years, and I recall especially one of the classics of sports broadcasting, his description of Roger Bannister's great race with John Landy, the Australian, wherein Landy led round the last bend. Rex's agonized cry of 'he can't do it' was followed by the description of Bannister's marvellous finishing burst and his coming up in the last strides to win.

Of sports that have been 'made' by the BBC I suppose that Show Jumping heads the list, with Dorian Williams, a great horseman himself, supplying the ideal commentary. The public for golf has been likewise vastly increased by television coverage; not merely of the Championships, but the recorded series round the celebrated British courses wherein Henry Longhurst conducts matches between the great players of the United States and the Rest of the World.

Not a little of the charm of these broadcasts is that the players as introduced and presented by Longhurst appear to be such pleasant, civilized people. As I have indicated often enough in this book the public, generally speaking, want to be able to admire not only the skill of the master-players but also, if possible, their personalities. The modern generation of golfers are beset by 'pressures' at least equal to those of any other game, but their sportsmanship and good manners almost without exception are exemplary – that is exactly the word.

In the world of soccer the better they play the worse, it seems to me, they are apt to behave. In cricket there are standards to restore in this respect. In golf the very converse is true. Three pictures in illustration thereof stick in my mind. One is of the delightful Arnold Palmer saying a few appropriate words after having won the Open Championship and been presented with the prize by the chairman of the Championship Committee, T. C. Harvey, at Troon. Another is of the vast ovation that Roberto de Vicenzo, a prime favourite, acknowledged with Latin grace as he came up the eighteenth fairway at Hoylake, victor of the Open in 1967.

The third shows Jack Nicklaus and Tony Jacklin playing the last hole of the deciding match of the Ryder Cup at Royal Birkdale three years ago. The whole contest was even as these two approached the 18th tee. Both played perfect drives, and seconds to the green that gave them longish putts for birdie threes. Both very narrowly missed, Jacklin leaving himself perhaps two or two and a half feet past the hole. Whereupon Nicklaus with a smile picked up his opponent's ball, conceding the half – which left Great Britain and America level at 16 matches all – and the pair walked off and into camera close-up, an arm on each other's shoulder.

I may be rated old-fashioned and over sentimental but this for me was the perfect sporting picture, and it was taking place in the highly commercial, ultra-competitive world of 1969. To reduce the thing to crude terms, as an advertisement for golf its value was beyond measuring.

Bernard Darwin, as might be expected, is informative about the early attempts to broadcast golf. In *Life is Sweet, Brother*, published in 1940, he tells how at Birkdale in an English Amateur Championship 'talking out of the side of my mouth into an odious little pocket microphone, I tried to follow and describe the playing of a hole from behind. Birkdale is a place of giant sandhills and with my lame leg I felt very like John Silver ploughing his way through the sand in the great scene at the blockhouse.' Only Bernardo would have described a golf broadcast in terms of Treasure Island! He concludes, as the BBC have since confirmed, that while golf does not lend itself to running commentary television is another matter 'for then seeing is the main point, and the broadcaster but an accompanist'.

He goes on to say he took part in the first televising of golf, the occasion being a match at Coombe Hill between Bobby Locke and R. A. Whitcombe. The year, I suppose, must have been 1938 or 1939. He says it would have been very enjoyable if the talking could have been done in privacy and not 'surrounded by spectators, who took a hideous interest in the performance'. He seems to have been walking about still, for he wishes the hills of Coombe had not been so steep – not surprisingly considering he was already lame and on the shady side of sixty. However, 'when it was finished it all seemed "wery capital" and I felt much as I had done years before when I had had a brief in a County Court and it was all safely over.'

This reminds me that it is said that Arthur Croome used to pull Darwin's leg, declaring that he only ever had one brief and that he had opened his case by saying 'My client's name is Mrs Winterwoman who is a washerbottom.' This seems to have been a stock joke, as indeed the story is an old chestnut, the pay-off line being the judge's remark: 'A gloomy name, and no doubt a depressing occupation.'

One has, of course, admired the technique of the broadcasters of various other games and sports. I happen to be not at all interested in racing, but the skill of Peter O'Sullevan and his colleagues greatly intrigues me. I always enjoyed John Snagge at the Boat Race or from Henley. His was the ideal combination of complete professionalism and a first-hand knowledge of the sport. John was also the senior news announcer, with the perfect Reith-era broadcasting voice, and it fell to him to prepare the world for the death of King George V in the memorable and completely apposite phrase: 'The King's life is drawing peacefully to its close.'

Cliff Morgan's utter involvement in the rugger scene and his infectious enthusiasm made him the ideal man to tell the thrilling story of the Lions' triumph in New Zealand. I always look forward, too, to Pat Ward-Thomas's crisp, clear summaries of the golf situation during the progress of the big tournaments and championships.

If one is a performer oneself one has a special admiration for Frank Bough, the anchor man of Grandstand, who preserves an easy conversational tone and a general air of unflappability whatever changes of cue, programme revision and other technical instruction are being simultaneously fed through his ear-phone by the producer. Frank seems never at a loss, though he told a good story against himself when compèring the last Sportsman of the Year party. He was at Fenner's for one of the Sunday Cricket Matches and, during the interval between innings, had asked a distinguished Cambridge figure to make a presentation to Ted Dexter. There the three of them were in front of the camera and suddenly – the nightmare of all public speakers – his mind became blank. Who was the fellow? The best he could manage in the way of an introduction when the moment came was 'My friend on the right'.

At this the producer's dry comment was, 'Well, at least you got his politics OK.' It was only Lord Butler, the Master of Trinity with a record of political achievement and public service a mile long!

This reminds me that when Walter Robins in 1937 was, as captain, presenting the England team to King George VI in front of the Lord's pavilion the name that escaped him was none other than Walter Hammond. In the Committee room afterwards, Robins apologized, whereat the King said, 'Oh, you mustn't worry about that. When we're about scarcely anyone remembers anything.'

I must not forget Lord Birkett, one of the great masters of the spoken word who was heard just occasionally over the air on the subject of cricket. I was organizing one of the Cricket

Writers' Club dinners at the Skinners' Hall and the BBC wanted to broadcast part of the proceedings. They were coming over, I think, only for quarter of an hour which would have to contain two complete speeches, so, duly apologetic, I asked the great man in advance whether he could possibly confine himself to eight and a half minutes. Though in fact he generally talked for twice this length and it was not a moment too long for his hearers, he said that eight and a half minutes would suit him admirably. Sure enough he spoke, perfectly as ever, without a note, every pause and cadence exactly as usual, finishing with a fine, long, rolling sentence, each comma and semi-colon distinct, and sat down, as I noted on my stop-watch, after exactly 8 minutes 30. There was the glimmer of a smile behind those steely spectacles as he glanced across the table at me, and I saw that his left hand also concealed a stop-watch.

Let me finally mention a few of the broadcasters outside the world of sport whose work I have specially enjoyed: Sir John Betjeman with his preposterous hats and faintly comical open-eyed expression and complete naturalness and command of his subject; Lord Clark also whose *Civilization* was surely the greatest individual *tour de force* in the history of TV; and, of course, the late and greatly respected Richard Dimbleby with whom every producer must have felt completely and utterly safe.

I loved *Animal, Vegetable and Mineral* with its quizzical relaxed chairman, Glyn Daniel, and Sir Mortimer Wheeler looking in turn, with his bushy moustaches, rather like the wicked Sir Jasper, inviting his viewers to enjoy the joke, and implying that they were as clever as he was to have spotted it.

Bamber Gascoigne (a cricket lover, incidentally, as also is Glyn Daniel) conducts *University Challenge* with brilliant speed and wit, and in a way only possible to a first-class scholar: the best performance of its kind, to my mind, on television.

I listen regularly on Monday mornings while shaving to Alistair Cooke's *Letter from America*, a perfectly balanced professional piece of work, a polished essay but conversationally delivered. Golf is his great sporting enthusiasm, and his tribute to Bobby Jones on his death last Christmas was a masterpiece.

Going back a long way I wonder how many recall a prewar series called *Foundations of Music*. My wife, a musician herself, has little regard for my taste in these matters. But these talks by Sir Walford Davies always fascinated me because of his manner of putting them over, easy, supremely natural, almost confidential. So we come back to where we started, with Teddy Wakelam talking to the blind man at Twickenham : one man conversing with another. To me that remains the secret of broadcasting.

14

Last Over

He is a fortunate man who can look back on a working life of not far short of fifty years (if the war be included) and recall such a large and interesting company of people met, so many journeys to pleasant, sunny places, such a variety of experience, so many happy days in the company of friends.

There have been seven tours each of Australia and the West Indies, four of South Africa, one of the Far East and nearly forty English summers, answering the call of cricket. On the roughest of calculations I suppose this all amounts to somewhere around a million miles travelled, and many times as many words written and spoken in newspapers and books and over the air. As I tried to show in the first chapter luck on the whole has been very much on my side and I hope I am duly grateful.

People and places. Though most of my acquaintance has naturally been with cricketers the game has opened for me all sorts of illustrious doors, beginning with Buckingham Palace. The investiture I attended attracted no ordinary attention, by the way, since Beatlemania was at its height, and the crowd extended away down the Mall. Messrs Lennon, Harrison, McCartney and Starr conducted themselves with reasonable decorum and were allowed to receive their insignia from the Queen four abreast.

When Kent won the Championship in 1970 the Prime Minister gave a dinner for the team and their wives, and a few others close to Kent cricket, and some sport-minded members of the Government, to the number of fifty-odd which is as many as can be comfortably got into the dining-room of No. 10. Mr Heath obviously enjoys giving parties and has a rare facility for relaxing on these occasions. What might have been a slightly stiff evening, at any rate for the players, became the friendliest possible one. He, a Man of Kent himself, of course, made an amusing congratulatory speech, to which Colin Cowdrey replied in the most sparkling form. Nearly all the present-day cricketers speak well, with a nice blend of humour and modesty, but Colin is rather in a class of his own. Among his contemporaries, by the way, I might mention Tom Graveney and Basil D'Oliveira, who at a Lawrence Trophy dinner a few years ago followed one another with speeches that brought a distinguished company to its feet.

My wife and I followed the Downing Street visit with one to Chequers, where the Prime Minister gave a small dinner in honour of Sir Robert and Dame Pattie Menzies before their return to Australia in the autumn of 1971.

The party was on the Sunday following the historic decision to go into Europe, and it enabled one, among other things, to get a brief insight into the ardours of life at the top. After many days and nights of debate the Prime Minister, following the vote on the Thursday evening, had taken the sleeper to Manchester for a hard political day there. He had then gone to Bradford on the Saturday for a full programme including the conferring on him by Harold Wilson, as Chancellor of Bradford University, of the honorary degree of Doctor of Technology. Sustained no doubt by this superbly ironic touch Mr Heath had proceeded by an aircraft of the Queen's Flight from Bradford down to Heathrow, in time to preside at a dinner for Mrs Gandhi, Prime Minister of India, who was staying with him at Chequers. A Sunday lunch party also for her, and here he was still at it.

When I asked Mr Heath whether he had *ever* had so tough a week he said he had not. Not least of the requirements of his office must be the constitution and energy of an ox. He confessed, in fact, to being pretty tired, and with the State opening of Parliament coming up on Tuesday there was no prospect of relief. However, he was still kind enough to show us many of the treasures which had accompanied the late Lord Lee of Fareham's gift of the house to the nation for the use of its Prime Ministers, these including Rubens's picture depicting Aesop's fable of the Lion and the Mouse.

The story told of how when the lion had spared the mouse the latter had said that one day he might repay the lion's mercy. Whereat the lion scoffed. Now, however, he was snared in a rope net, whereupon the mouse saved him by nibbling the rope away. The picture shows the lion enmeshed and the mouse on the task of liberation. Churchill however in his occupancy of Chequers protested that Rubens's mouse was too small to be able to do the job. He therefore clambered up and painted in a mouse in better proportion with the rope. So the vast canvas shows the lion by Rubens, mouse by Churchill :

a nice addition, surely, to the legend of the greatest of Englishmen.

There is no more sincere Anglophile than Bob Menzies and since his appointment as Lord Warden of the Cinque Ports he has never failed to come over each year, take up his residence at Walmer Castle, and attend all the functions demanded of him, and do a good deal more of a social kind than he strictly need have done. It so happened that on the Friday before Chequers he had spoken to a company of seven hundred at the Forty Club dinner, and subsequently accepted the Presidency of the Club.

Having entertained him at Sandwich just previously I was nervous about the strain that the Forty Club dinner would impose. He seemed in fact to take it in his stride, the sight of so large an audience perhaps inspiring the politician in him to pull out his best. It was a mighty good best too. But the effort had left an inevitable reaction, and at Chequers he confessed to being rather weary. When he said, 'You know I've either stayed or dined in this house with every Prime Minister since Ramsay MacDonald,' one sensed that he thought this might possibly be the last time. A month or so later, back in Melbourne, shortly before his 77th birthday, he had the stroke from which, as I write, he is struggling to recover.

While illustrious names are being bandied about, here in a different context are a few more. Some ten years ago, returning from Australia via the West Indies, my wife and I spent a week with Ian Fleming at Golden Eye, his house at Oracabessa on the Jamaican north shore. He used to write a James Bond book a year, doing all the work out there, and when we arrived late in February he was in excellent spirits having finished the latest that very morning. It would, I think, have been his last but one. There was a general picture current of Ian as a high liver, a sybarite for whom nothing but the best and most luxurious was good enough. As we knew his life in Jamaica and at Sandwich – he had a flat in Sandwich Bay, loved his golf at St George's and was captain-designate of the Club when he died – this was a mile from the truth. Golden Eye was utilitarian, the very reverse of plush – his neighbour Noel Coward called it in mock contempt 'the Eye, Nose and Throat'. You slid into your hard bench seat round a U-shaped dining-room table set in a stall like those to be found in old inns. The favourite dishes were land-crabs and hot pepper sauce, scrambled eggs and bacon with Jamaican vegetables, extremely well cooked by the admirable Violet.

paw-paw and melon all washed down with the Wine Society's claret.

Golden Eye is superbly sited at the top of a steep cliff with steps leading down to a small bay to which the only other access is by boat. One snorkelled about among the rocks observing the myriad small fish, which is the most fascinating and relaxing thing to do. In one of the Bond books there is a great under-water fight the theme of which must have been taken from this bay at the bottom of the garden.

One night we dined with Coward, whose sitting-room had two grand pianos face to face. When after dinner Ian Fleming said, 'Oh, Noel, Ann plays rather well,' the master's jaw tightened slightly as he invited my wife to the piano. I had a nervous moment or two, but soon our host was at the other piano and they were duetting away for an hour or more, recalling the songs and tunes of the 'thirties and playing them together, Ann whistling while Coward sang. Talk about reflected glory – it was my proudest moment.

Fleming always seemed to be more amused than anything else by the tremendous vogue of the Bond books which made him a rich man. He seldom spoke of his writing, and anyone who wore his success less ostentatiously would be hard to find. When he died the Durlachers, Esmond and Lou, used to rent Golden Eye, and it became distinctly less spartan. We went over with them to Blanche Blackwell's, nearby, and there found Charlie Chaplin to whom the Surrey heroes at the turn of the century, Bobby Abel, Tom Hayward, Richardson and Lockwood, were household names. He was born almost within sight and sound of the Oval. One thing Chaplin remembered about cricket had rankled over sixty-odd years. He had been playing as a young man at one of the Nottingham music-halls, and one Whitsuntide went to see Surrey at Trent Bridge. But though he had paid his hard-earned gate-money, rain prevented any cricket, and there was no refund. 'In the States,' he said, 'they give you a rain-check. Surely that's only fair?'

I have always thought the grim universal notice 'No play guaranteed, no money returned' was not only poor customer psychology, but both unnecessary and not exactly 'fair'. My opinion was fortified from an unexpected quarter.

This is a rather varied Last Over in which I must try to repair one or two omissions. I am conscious of not having written much about those essential people the umpires, but let me at least salute the most famous of them, Frank Chester. What a performer he was! As outstanding between the wars in his line of business as Don Bradman was in his. At the very end, when his health was failing, it could be said that he grew a bit dictatorial. The Australians of 1953 thought this, and complained strongly about one decision at Headingley which was almost the worst I ever saw. The central figure of this was Reg Simpson, who was given in by Frank when apparently run out by two or three yards. He, for his part, resented the Australians being, as he thought, over-aggressive. It so happened that, very early the morning after this Headingley Test, Chester and I met on the Leeds station platform. He looked terribly ill, and he told me he'd just wired Lord's and said he would be unable to stand in whatever match he was due for that day. As it turned out this was the last of the 48 Tests he umpired. He carried on for two years more, and died two years after that. At his best he came as near infallibility as any arbiter of any game could. Bradman rates him the best he ever played under, and the fact was that, coming into it young having lost an arm in the First War, he set a new standard.

Frank Chester and Maurice Tate were both addicted to the malapropism, the best collection of which lies in the memory of Alex Bannister. Pressed about some date or fact in dispute, Frank ended the discussion by saying, 'Never mind, it's immemorial.' And reciting the story of a knee injury he said, 'I knew at once it was me cartridge.' 'Was it a sharp, shooting pain?' asked Alex. 'Oh no, just a dull ache.'

One of the great joys cricket has brought me has been the visits to the West Indies, and a part-time home in the blessed island of Barbados. All the territories of the West Indies have their many points of difference, deriving from climate and history. Barbados, lying eighty miles to the east of the rest of the Caribbean chain, and so protected by the eternal and beneficent Trade Wind which blew would-be attackers harmlessly past, was, almost alone of the islands, never fought over. When an Englishman discovered it, in 1625, landing not a mile from where our house stands on the St James Coast, the island was uninhabited. There were no native Caribs, nor did Dutch, French, Portuguese or Spaniards settle and squabble over its fertile acres. There has been no Indian influx, as in Trinidad and Guyana. The inhabitants have been first English and then, from around the 1640s, following the planting of sugar, the slaves from Africa whose emancipation came with the Act of 1834.

When Barbados was accorded universal adult suffrage

in 1950, and control passed by stages out of white hands into black, with its natural culmination in the granting of Independence in 1966, there had been a history of uninterrupted English rule stretching back over three centuries. There are dark and shaming, as well as enlightened passages in the past of Barbados, as in that of all colonial territories, but this background has generated an individual self-respect and pride of island which, to my mind, set it apart from its neighbours.

The Independence celebrations, at which the Duke of Kent, accompanied by the Duchess, represented the Queen, were carried off with the utmost dignity and the mood, if I judged it right, was sentimental, prayerful, optimistic, rather than aggressively nationalistic. One of the three Ws confessed to a deep lump in the throat as the Union Jack, floodlit in the dark arena of the Savannah, was lowered for the last time and the bright sea blue and gold flag of Barbados, with its Neptune Trident, was hoisted in its place, as the massed throng sang the new national anthem.

There are more beautiful islands than Barbados (though it has beauty enough) and islands with more dramatic landscapes and more exotic vegetation (though to European eyes the well-tended Barbadian garden is luxuriant enough). But there is no better climate in the West Indies and, as I see it, there is no island in which such a sober and sensible electorate flourishes under such a sound, liberal political system. If we had not satisfied ourselves on this score we would have been foolish to make a capital investment.

What, you may say, of the threat of 'Black Power', a phrase which evokes such sinister fears in the United States and which has cast its shadow on some parts of the Caribbean. Some two years ago the *New York Times* carried a map in which the areas tainted by Black Power included Barbados. The newspaper, it is only fair to say, has since made due amends in at least two feature articles of a very favourable character, but even a little mud is sure to stick in nervous minds. The fact is that Stokely Carmichael arrived in Barbados apparently prepared to stay a while. He was allowed in after close interrogation at the airport, only on condition that he made no speech and attended no meeting, and when he had purchased an outward air ticket. He was thereupon tailed by the police, and departed next day. A disciple did carry on with a meeting at which Carmichael had been billed to appear. It attracted a meagre crowd which proved distinctly hostile.

'What's this about Black Power?' said the Bajans; 'we are black and we've got power.'

There was also a television programme in which two or three young men confronted the Prime Minister, Errol Barrow, who apparently in an avuncular sort of way wiped the floor with them. This is the beginning and end of the movement in Barbados at the moment of writing, and, since it is anathema equally to the Opposition as to the Government, for the forseeable future.

Among Commonwealth politicians Mr Barrow has a status away above the size of the small country he represents. He is a Bajan born and bred and through and through, but Englishmen remember also that as an undergraduate of London University at the School of Economics he joined the RAF during the war and has a distinguished record of active service, being finally Senior Navigator to Marshal of the RAF, Lord Douglas of Kirtleside. It probably doesn't need saying that his virtues, like those of his distinguished predecessor, the late Sir Grantley Adams, include a love of cricket – he was an opening bat, given apparently the nickname of Dipper after that old stalwart of Gloucestershire – which suggests his style may have been on the sticky side!

If I have pictured Barbados as a latter-day Garden of Eden I must add that, of course, it has its problems like everywhere else. A population of 300,000 in an island the size of the Isle of Wight with an all too healthy birth-rate and the highest educational standards in the Caribbean makes for a situation in which young men struggle for appropriate opportunity. As the University of the West Indies expands, and with emigration to Great Britain and the USA reduced to such a small quota, suitable employment for skilled men can only be provided by a steady flow of capital for development projects. I have given a fair picture of the political stability of Barbados, but inevitably foreign investors must see the island as one link in the Caribbean chain, and so to a considerable extent its prosperity is dependent on the reputation of its neighbours.

The natural cream coral stone, though now rather scarce and very expensive, is the perfect building material, giving a look of maturity as quickly as plants and the tropical flowering shrubs grow – bougainvillaea, oleander, hibiscus, alamander and the rest. Our house is built athwart the cooling trade winds, louvres controlling the strength of the breeze. The garden gives on to the ninth fairway on one side, Sandy Lane

Bay is two or three hundred yards distant on the other. In the middle of the bay stands Sandy Lane Hotel, coral built, and surely one of the most picturesque of its kind in the world. It is not the least of the jewels in the Trust House-Forte crown.

There are not many comparable environments and I find the regular recipe of a morning's writing, a swim, luncheon, a game of golf and a relaxed – or a social – evening the perfect preparation for the rigours of another English cricket season.

Knowledge of the West Indian people, and the feeling that I had some understanding of their background and their philosophy of life have made me coldly antagonistic to those who seem to see through blinkers the difficult and delicate issue of immigration to Great Britain. That there had to be control was obvious enough, and equally so surely that the atmosphere created by the controls should not be exacerbated by inflammatory sentiments uttered or written by people in authority. After the first of Enoch Powell's notorious speeches I was moved to write one of only two letters I have ever ventured to address to editors on a non-sporting subject. It was published in *The Spectator* in May 1968, drawing attention to some immediate effects of his recent tirade about 'rivers of blood'. I mentioned:

> Within the last few days an Indian student at Highbury has been set upon, kicked and slashed, by four sixteen-year-olds chanting 'blackman, blackman, Enoch, Enoch'. A respectable West Indian citizen at Wolverhampton celebrating a family christening has been attacked without provocation and injured by people also invoking the name of Enoch, the prophet. 'Enoch dockers' at Westminster have been putting their boots into students on the ground.

I called it 'a bloodthirsty, hateful speech lacking a single compassionate phrase towards fellow-members of our Commonwealth'. It was also utterly destructive, unless the voluntary repatriation scheme which Powell advocated could be considered a positive step to solve the problem. The point that is too often overlooked surely is that when the big influx of West Indians and those from the Indian sub-continent occurred in the 'fifties it answered an urgent need in our society. There was a desperate lack of men and women to fill every kind of hospital post, an equal shortage in the transport services. Was the Mother Country now to abuse and discriminate against those whom she had encouraged to come? Apparently, if the extremists had their way. Thank goodness, they haven't.

But it is time to move on to lighter matters; on two occasions during my career as a journalist I was faced with the threat of libel action. One incident was the outcome of a Peterborough paragraph written from Australia more than twenty years ago in which I had mentioned that a well-known actor and his wife had flown the four hundred miles odd from Adelaide to Melbourne to see a day's cricket though he was appearing in an Adelaide theatre the same evening. It seemed a notable example of the wide enthusiasm for cricket among the acting profession. About 900 miles to see a day's play! The upshot of this, as I thought, innocent note, was a cable from my editor, Colin Coote (since knighted), saying that Mrs X's lawyers had stated she was not in Australia and the statement was therefore libellous. Would I urgently cable the grounds for my message.

The fact was that the lady in Australia who was everywhere passing as such was not in fact Mr X's wife, though she later became so. It was obvious that I had acted in good faith, and the matter was not taken further, though whether the paper had to publish an apology I cannot now remember. It only went to show that one can't be too careful! The incident sticks particularly in my mind because Colin Coote had only just succeeded the venerable Arthur Watson in the editorship and we had never met. I was rather concerned that he might conclude he had in me a dangerous sort of chap on his staff.

Of all the unlikely places to which my association with cricket has brought me I suppose the pulpit at Westminster Abbey must easily top the list. The occasion was the Memorial Service to Sir Frank Worrell, the first time so far as I know that a sportsman had been so honoured. I was a great admirer of Frank, but so were a great many other more distinguished people, and the invitation from the Dean and Chapter to give the Eulogy came as a great surprise. For this talk at least – the service was broadcast back to the West Indies – I wrote my script. As it happens I have never been nervous over the air, but this was a very different assignment, and I confess to considerable qualms. Would I remember, having put my neck into the halter containing the microphone before I started, to remove it at the end? To have neglected to do so would certainly impair the dignity of my exit.

In the event all went well enough, and everyone seemed reasonably pleased, with the exception of a small part of the congregation quite nearby in the South Transept. Though far away in the Nave everyone heard perfectly there is – or was –

an acoustical freak which prevents those in this 'pocket' from hearing anything from the pulpit.

Even more strangely I have spoken also in St Paul's Cathedral. A few years ago when Canon Hood aforementioned was Chancellor he asked me to give one of a series of four lay sermons at the Evensongs in June. In declining I quoted Dr Johnson who compared the performance of women preachers to dogs standing on their hind legs, saying the wonder was not that they did not do it well but that they attempted it at all. I thought this applied to lay preachers generally. This was accepted by my friend, but a while before the date one of his selected four had to drop out, and so the spare man was sent for and with much misgiving obliged. I actually had to sign the Visitor's or Preacher's book below Donald Ebor (that is, for the uninitiated, the Archbishop of York), as well as autographs for the choirboys – altogether a humbling experience.

Recollection of Freddy Hood and Pusey House reminds me of a story told of his famous predecessor as Principal, Dr Darwell-Stone, whose bearded figure looked gravely down on us from his portrait in the dining-room. One day when he was presiding at a meal someone mentioned The Dolly Sisters. The learned Father looked up with a perplexed expression: 'Are you sure of the name?' he said. 'I know of no such religious community in the Anglican Church.' Freddy was not nearly as aloof from the world as that, and nor assuredly is the present Principal, Canon Cheslyn Jones, who gives his recreations in Who's Who as travel, swimming, music and bridge.

From Pusey it is a short cry to Exeter College, and I must say a word about an outstanding Oxford character during my residence there. He is Roger Bannister, only incidentally mentioned so far, who has recently taken on that post of high responsibility, the chairmanship of the Sports Council. At the University Roger seemed to pull off every medical as well as athletics prize, and on coming down won an open scholarship to St Mary's Hospital. He was anything but well off, and occupied a basement flat at the farther end of the Cromwell Road where, as often as not, he cooked his own meals. He was still coming up to his peak as a runner in his first years as a medical student, and when I asked him one day how he managed to find the time for training he said that it mostly consisted of his running the streets each day to the hospital and back. Simultaneously he was competing in the Olympics, the European, Empire, and British championships, and it was in this context that he, with the help of the two Christophers, Chataway and Brasher, planned and brought off, on the Iffley Road track at Oxford, the first Four Minute Mile – the sporting coup of the century. I have as much respect for the professional in sport as anyone, and prize many friendships among those who have made their living playing cricket and golf. It is the idiotic modern denigration of the man who competes for the sheer love of doing so that makes me see red. Could there be a better vindication of the amateur spirit than the career of Roger Bannister?

I was invited into one other pulpit, this time to talk cricket, but I declined it and walked up and down the aisle instead. This was, of all places, at Pentonville Prison where I went with Mr Lancelot Spicer, who for years used to organize Monday lectures there on a wide variety of subjects. It is a slightly daunting experience driving through the heavy, iron-studded gates, and watching the prisoners descending, one by one, down spiral iron staircases from the floor above. But they were a good audience, and there were intelligent questions. As someone said of a prison talk, 'You don't feel you're presuming on their time.'

I've been civilly received, too, at several Borstal establishments but (lifting the company somewhat) just about the best audience I remember was the English College – for Roman Catholic ordinands – in Rome. As it was Lent I expected a frugal dinner first, but it was a very good one with a carafe of wine for each man. It's rather dangerous, they explained, to drink the Rome water. They say that only the very best are selected for the English College, and naturally on this evidence I'm inclined to think so.

Old lags and young men training for the priesthood – surely there must be a special magic in a game which fascinates people so widely separated in the social order. Talking of good audiences I gave several winter talks in Scotland at the time of International rugger matches and was always surprised at the Scots' close knowledge of English cricket.

Two centenary occasions in Scotland come to mind. One was at Fettes two years ago, where the boys celebrated their hundredth anniversary with a sparkling win over a good MCC side. Judging by this performance, and from what one had heard from those who play against them, the standard of cricket in the Scottish schools has nothing to fear nowadays by comparison with the other side of the border.

There was also a great night at Ayr when Hunter Cosh, then captain of Scotland, invited me to propose the health of cricket at the Centenary Dinner of Ayr CC. This visit had a sequel of some consequence for I met a youngster called Michael Denness who was anxious to try his luck in English cricket. Accordingly he came down on the Arab tour the following summer, made a hundred on his first appearance on a Kentish ground against the Navy at Chatham and, though under Les Ames's scrutiny next day at Canterbury he hit his first ball for four and was out to the second, Kent's secretary-manager declared he had seen enough, and Mike became a Kentish cricketer forthwith. Now he has joined the noble roll of captains of Kent.

The Forty Club audience of some six or seven hundred at the annual dinner at the Hilton is as good a one as any. We are, by definition, senior cricketers, a club of 3,000 in all founded, of course, in an inspired moment by Henry Grierson. He, alas! died this year aged eighty, but the club with all its activities, and these dinners, will always be a memorial to a remarkable man.

I have done my share of talking at club dinners, like everyone else whose name, in whatever capacity, is well known in the game. Making a speech is not unlike playing an innings. You try equally hard on each occasion; sometimes every stroke finds the middle of the bat, sometimes you can only edge and miss. In that case the best policy is to get out quick – a thing which, as all diners-out know to their cost, most performers find difficult to do.

I should not end without a general word of thanks to all the thousands who over many years have taken the trouble to put pen to paper to me about cricket and rugger. A regular stream of letters at the height of the summer has sometimes been an embarrassment, though everyone has had at least an acknowledgment. But to know what lovers of cricket are thinking on current topics is naturally of much value to a cricket-writer. It gives one an idea, among other things, what folk want to read about and what they do not.

Here again one can't hope to please all the people all the time, and though the majority of the letters are either sympathetic or at least reasonable some odd ones add a spice to one's breakfast reading. I've often quoted this letter, addressed to the Editor of the *Daily Telegraph*, at club dinners, and it never fails to raise a laugh:

Dear Sir,   July 1956

Don't you think that the time has arrived for your cricket
correspondent to be quietly disposed of, stuffed, and placed
in the Long Room with the curved bats, the sparrow, and
the other freaks of the noble game?

Yours faithfully . . .

Note the date, and spare some sympathy for the poor fellow
who opens his paper in 1972 and sees to his chagrin that his
pet aversion hasn't been stuffed yet!

What sort of person is best suited to write about cricket?
Norman Birkett had something to say on this in his Introduction to the collection of my reports called *The Test Matches
of 1956*. He says:

Much has been written from time to time about the nature
of cricket writing. It is quite clear that first-class writers on
cricket need not necessarily be first-class cricketers. Mr E. V.
Lucas is in the highest class as a writer, but as a player it
was said of him by Mr Rupert Hart-Davis when publishing
that lovely little collection of his writings called *Cricket All
His Life* that 'he was perhaps more at ease in the pavilion
than at the crease'. Lucas thought that one of the finest
pieces of writing about any game was Hazlitt's famous
description of Cavanagh the fives player in *Table Talk* for
1821; and Mr Bernard Darwin called it 'the noblest description of playing a game that was ever written'; yet it is very
much to be doubted whether Hazlitt ever played fives at any
time in his life. I should myself incline to the view that
the cricket writer should love the game for itself, be
familiar with its long history, and that he should, if possible,
have played the game in the best company. This last qualification is particularly important when the cricket writer is
reporting the playing of matches, for it adds authority to
what is written, and makes comment and criticism of great
practical value. Mr Swanton can lay claim to these qualities,
but as the great Bacon said:

'A man can scarce allege his own merits with modesty,
much less extol them . . . But all these things are graceful
in a friend's mouth, which are blushing in a man's own.'

I can only add to these too generous words as regards myself
that one has always been conscious of the job as a privilege
as well as a responsibility. There's no doubt that games-
writers do have a considerable influence on the games they

write about, and commentators on the air, likewise either for better or for worse.

There is one movement in which I have been associated in print these last few years that can only be for the good, and it makes, I hope, an appropriate note to end on. *The Cricketer* under my editorial directorship and under the management of the old Somerset captain, B. G. Brocklehurst, has either initiated or helped to organize, and has given publicity to, a number of competitions, all designed to keep cricket of various kinds virile and flourishing. Mentioning them in order of seniority there is The Cricketer Cup for the old boys of thirty-two of the most illustrious schools, founded five years ago at the instigation of Antony Winlaw; the London Schools *Cricketer* Trophy for secondary and comprehensive schools.

There is The National Club Knock-Out for three hundred-odd of the top clubs in England, Scotland and Wales, of which Derrick Robins is the sponsor and moving spirit, I his vice-chairman. MCC generously allow the Final to be played at Lord's, where this year will also appear the finalists of the Haig National Village Championship. This, the joint brainchild of Ben Brocklehurst, the Chairman of the National Cricket Association, Aidan Crawley and M. B. Henderson, managing director of John Haig, has in its first year attracted nearly eight hundred villages, and so at one bound has become the biggest cricket competition in the world.

Also in its first year is the Esso Colts Trophy for Schools, another affair on a national scale run by The English Schools Cricket Association in conjunction with *The Cricketer*. The object here is to enlist the enthusiasm of the boys before they become bedevilled by 'A Levels'.

Talking of capturing the interest of the young, I should mention, too, the Anglo–West Indian tours instigated by the Sir Frank Worrell Memorial Fund. The West Indian boys have already made a highly successful visit to England under Wes Hall. This summer the England Young Cricketers, managed by Jack Ikin and Alan Duff, are touring the Caribbean.

These are all new developments attaching now to the traditional framework of cricket, and they are much to be welcomed. But there will still be room for the clubs and schools of varying stature for whom a friendly match, strenu-ously contested, is an end in itself. I am thinking especially of the wandering clubs, headed by such venerable ones as I Zingari and the Free Foresters, who with countless others have given such pleasure to so many for so long. The rich diversity of clubs and players has always been an important aspect of cricket's attraction.

The truest of all axioms about cricket is that the game is as good as those who play it. If one looks in certain directions this might be a disquieting thought in one or two respects just at the moment. But cast the eye elsewhere, and note the zest and humour with which cricket is contested by club cricketers and by the young, and you may conclude, as I do, that the game can face the future confidently enough. In the opinion of this sort of a cricket person it is still a game of unique fascination and appeal which continues to draw its recruits from the best.

Index

Longhurst, Henry, 18, 65, 111, 266, 269

Lord's, 28–9, 31, 48, 56, 57, 66, 76, 84, 87, 90, 92, 96, 99, 100, 102, 110, 136, 153, 154, 169, 173, 175, 181, 182, 187, 192, 196, 208, 211, 213, 217, 221, 236, 249, 260, 263, 287

Lord's Taverners, 94, 162

Loxton, S. J. E., 165, 193

Lucas, E. V., 286

Lyle, Capt R. C., 41

Lyttleton, Hon G. W., 17

Macartney, C. G., 142

McCabe, S. J., 60, 65, 70, 84, 102, 142

McCanlis, M. A., 38, 39

McCanlis, Capt W., 38

McCool, C. L., 166

McCormick, E. L., 103

McDonald, E. A., 30, 62

Macdonnell, A. G., 50

McGlew, D. J., 196

Machin, Dr M., 34

McKenzie, G. D., 201, 234

McKinlay, Major, 124

McLachlan, I. M., 238, 244, 246, 248

Maclaren, A. C., 72, 87

Maclean, R. A., 243

Macpherson, G. P. S., 38

Maidstone, 24, 137, 231

Mailey, A. A., 29, 31, 54, 67, 140, 142, 146

Malaysia, 248f.

Malvern, 25

Manchester Guardian, 45, 175. See also Guardian

Mann, F. G., 98, 110, 166, 167–8, 172, 180

Mann, F. T., 28, 167–8

Mant, G., 15

March, Earl of, 224

Marlar, R. G., 241

Marlar, Mrs Wendy, 241

Marriott, C. S., 86

Marshall, Howard, 12, 21, 43, 102, 261, 262

Martin, 'Bosser', 27

Martindale, E. A., 74

Mason, J. M., 248

Mathers, J., 139–40

Maxwell, C. R., 81

May, P. B. H., 176–8, 184, 188, 193, 194f., 201, 202, 215, 221, 242

MCC, 15, 17, 28, 29, 47, 53, 54, 66, 68f., 82, 86, 87, 91, 95, 96, 101, 155, 170, 181–2, 184, 193, 197, 205–6, 209, 216–17, 219f., 234–6

Mead, C. P., 24, 30

Meckliff, I., 193–4, 198, 211

Melbourne, 70, 71, 140, 141, 148, 150, 171, 176, 184, 185–6, 187, 193, 198–9, 206, 207, 214, 235, 236

Melbourne Herald, 149, 150

Melford, Michael, 213, 234

Melville, A., 85, 108–9, 152, 153

Menzies, Rt. Hon Sir Robert, 149, 214, 275, 276

Mercury, training ship, 191

Merry, Maj W. H., 128

MI5, 116

Middleton CC, 204

Middleton, Guy, 111

Milburn, Colin, 201, 222

Miller, K. R., 143, 165, 177, 184, 185, 186, 189, 239

Mill Hill School, 37

Millward, F., 127

Mitchell, B., 105

Moore, P. B. C., 250, 251

Moore, R. H., 85

Moore, Robert, 219

Morgan, Cliff, 271

Morgan, (Teddy), 43

Morkel, D. P. B., 81

Morning Advertiser, 239

Morning Post, 15, 47, 62, 69, 78

Morris, A. R., 143, 165

Mortimore, J. B., 194

Morton, J. B., 52

Mountbatten, Lady, 131–2

Muir, A. A., 91–2

Munt, H. R., 81

Murdoch, Sir Keith, 149

Murdoch, Rupert, 149

Murray, J. T., 222

298

A Fontana Selection

Famous Animal Books in Fontana

Joy Adamson
Pippa's Challenge *(Illus.)*
The Spotted Sphinx *(Illus.)*

Born Free *(Illus.)*
Living Free *(Illus.)*
Forever Free *(Illus.)*

Gerald Durrell
Birds, Beasts and Relatives
Fillets of Plaice

Rosy is My Relative
Two in the Bush

Jacquie Durrell
Beasts in My Bed *(Illus.)*

Bruce Kinloch
Sauce for the Mongoose *(Illus.)*

Mary Chipperfield
Lions on the Lawn *(Illus.)*

Buster Lloyd-Jones
The Animals Came in One by One
Come Into My World

Harry Wolhuter
Memories of a Game Ranger

Fontana Books

Fontana Books

Fontana is best known as one of the leading paperback publishers of popular fiction and non-fiction. It also includes an outstanding, and expanding, section of books on history, natural history, religion and social sciences.

Most of the fiction authors need no introduction. They include Agatha Christie, Hammond Innes, Alistair MacLean, Catherine Gaskin, Victoria Holt and Lucy Walker. Desmond Bagley and Maureen Peters are among the relative newcomers.

The non-fiction list features a superb collection of animal books by such favourites as Gerald Durrell and Joy Adamson.

All Fontana books are available at your bookshop or news-agent; or can be ordered direct. Just fill in the form below and list the titles you want.

_____

FONTANA BOOKS, Cash Sales Department, G.P.O. Box 29, Douglas, Isle of Man, British Isles. Please send purchase price, plus 8p per book. Customers outside the U.K. send purchase price, plus 10p per book. Cheque, postal or money order. No currency.

NAME (Block letters)
_____

ADDRESS
_____

_____

_____